Intellectual Freedom Issues
in School Libraries

INTELLECTUAL FREEDOM ISSUES IN SCHOOL LIBRARIES

April M. Dawkins, Editor

LIBRARIES
UNLIMITED®

An Imprint of ABC-CLIO, LLC

Santa Barbara, California • Denver, Colorado

Library of Congress Cataloging-in-Publication Data

Names: Dawkins, April M., editor.
Title: Intellectual freedom issues in school libraries / April M. Dawkins, editor.
Description: Santa Barbara, California : Libraries Unlimited, 2021. |
    Includes bibliographical references and index.
Identifiers: LCCN 2020014984 (print) | LCCN 2020014985 (ebook) |
    ISBN 9781440872365 (paperback) | ISBN 9781440872372 (ebook)
Subjects: LCSH: School libraries—Censorship—United States. |
    School libraries—United States—Administration. | Intellectual freedom—
    United States. | Freedom of information—United States.
Classification: LCC Z675.S3 I447 2020 (print) | LCC Z675.S3 (ebook) |
    DDC 025.1/9780973—dc23
LC record available at https://lccn.loc.gov/2020014984
LC ebook record available at https://lccn.loc.gov/2020014985

ISBN: 978-1-4408-7236-5 (paperback)
       978-1-4408-7237-2 (ebook)

25 24 23 22 21   1 2 3 4 5

This book is also available as an eBook.

Libraries Unlimited
An Imprint of ABC-CLIO, LLC

ABC-CLIO, LLC
147 Castilian Drive
Santa Barbara, California 93117
www.abc-clio.com

This book is printed on acid-free paper (∞)

Manufactured in the United States of America

The information provided in this book does not, and is not intended to, constitute legal advice; instead, all information, content, and materials are for general informational purposes only. Readers of this book should contact their attorney to obtain advice with respect to any particular legal matter. Only your individual attorney can provide assurances that the information contained herein—and your interpretation of it—is applicable or appropriate to your particular situation.

Contents

Introduction ix

PART I: INTELLECTUAL FREEDOM IN SCHOOL LIBRARIES

1—**What Is Intellectual Freedom?** 3
   Helen R. Adams

2—**Intellectual Freedom 101: Core Principles for
   School Librarians** 6
   Helen R. Adams

3—**The Choices That Count** 10
   Christine Eldred

4—**Fewer School Librarians: The Effect on Students'
   Intellectual Freedom** 13
   Helen R. Adams

**PART II: INTELLECTUAL FREEDOM ADVOCACY AND
   THE RIGHT TO READ**

5—**Intellectual Freedom Leadership: Standing Up for
   Your Students** 19
   Helen R. Adams

6—**Advocating for Intellectual Freedom with Principals
   and Teachers** 23
   Helen R. Adams

7—**Understanding Advocacy for Effective Action** 26
   Elizabeth Burns

8—**The Intellectual Freedom Calendar: Another Advocacy Plan
   for the School Library** 30
   Helen R. Adams

9—Banned Books and Celebrating Our Freedom to Read 34
Chad Heck

10—Reaching Out to Parents 36
Helen R. Adams

11—Library Books and Reading-Level Labels: Unfettered,
Guided, or Constrained Choice? 39
Maria Cahill

12—Computerized Reading Programs: Intellectual Freedom 41
Helen R. Adams

13—Protecting Students' Rights and Keeping Your Job 43
Helen R. Adams

PART III: POLICIES AND PROCEDURES

14—Coping with Mandated Restrictions on Intellectual
Freedom in K–12 Schools 47
Sara E. Wolf

15—The Materials Selection Policy: Defense against Censorship 53
Helen R. Adams

16—Ten Steps to Creating a Selection Policy That Matters 55
April M. Dawkins

17—Ten Steps to Creating Reconsideration Policies and
Procedures That Matter 58
April M. Dawkins

18—Collection Development Policies in Juvenile Detention
Center Libraries 62
Kristin Zeluff

19—The "Overdue" Blues: A Dilemma for School Librarians 66
Helen R. Adams

20—Unrestricted Checkout: The Time Has Come 69
Kathryn K. Brown

21—Policy Challenge: Consequences That Restrict Borrowing 73
Judi Moreillon

22—Policy Challenge: Leveling the Library Collection 76
Judi Moreillon

23—Policy Challenge: Closed for Conducting Inventory 79
Judi Moreillon

PART IV: HANDLING CHALLENGES

24—Managing Challenges to Library Resources 85
Dee Ann Venuto

25—The Problem of Self-Censorship 88
Rebecca Hill

26—Ex Post Facto Self-Censorship: When School Librarians
Choose to Censor 93
April M. Dawkins

27—Challenging Opportunities: Dealing with Book Challenges 97
Sabrina Carnesi

28—The Challenges of Challenges: Understanding and
Being Prepared 99
Gail K. Dickinson

29—The Challenges of Challenges: What to Do? 103
Gail K. Dickinson

30—Can a School Library Be Challenge-Proof? 107
Helen R. Adams

PART V: FILTERING, TECHNOLOGY, AND THE DIGITAL DIVIDE

31—Leadership: Filtering and Social Media 113
Judi Moreillon

32—Internet Filtering: Are We Making Any Progress? 116
Helen R. Adams

33—Equitable Access, the Digital Divide, and the
Participation Gap! 120
Patricia Franklin and Claire Gatrell Stephens

34—Bring Your Own Device (BYOD) and Equitable Access
to Technology 123
Helen R. Adams

35—Baby Steps: Preparing for a One-to-One Device Program 125
Monica Cabarcas

PART VI: STUDENT PRIVACY IN THE SCHOOL LIBRARY

36—Privacy: Legal Protections 133
Helen R. Adams

37—Practical Ideas: Protecting Students' Privacy in Your
School Library 136
Helen R. Adams

38—Protecting Your Students' Privacy: Resources for
School Librarians 139
Helen R. Adams

39—How Circulation Systems May Impact Student Privacy 142
Helen R. Adams

40—Retaining School Library Records 144
Helen R. Adams

41—The Age of the Patron and Privacy 146
Helen R. Adams

42—The Troubled Student and Privacy 148
Helen R. Adams

43—Confidentiality and Creating a Safe Information
Environment 150
Chad Heck

44—Privacy Solutions for Cloud Computing: What Does It Mean? 152
Annalisa Keuler

PART VII: ACCESS, EQUITY, AND DIVERSITY

45—Library Access on a Fixed Schedule 157
Ernie Cox

46—Using Assistive Technology to Meet Diverse Learner Needs 160
Stephanie Kurtts, Nicole Dobbins, and Natsuko Takemae

47—Online Accessibility Tools 164
Heather Moorefield-Lang

48—Google Accessibility for Your Library 166
Heather Moorefield-Lang

49—Deaf ≠ Silenced: Serving the Needs of the Deaf/ Hard-of-Hearing Students in School Libraries 168
Kimberly Gangwish

50—Serving Homeless Children in the School Library 172
Helen R. Adams

51—Literature as Mirrors, Windows, and Sliding Glass Doors 177
Lucy Santos Green and Michelle Maniaci Folk

52—Collection Development for Readers: Providing Windows and Mirrors 179
Mary Frances Zilonis and Chris Swerling

53—Building School Library Collections with Windows and Mirrors 181
Mary Frances Zilonis and Chris Swerling

54—Moving Diverse Books from Your Library Shelves and into the Hands of Readers 184
Mary Frances Zilonis and Chris Swerling

55—Serving Rainbow Families in School Libraries 186
Jamie Campbell Naidoo

56—Whose History Is It?: Diversity in Historical Fiction for Young Adults 191
April M. Dawkins

57—Progressive Collection Development = A Foundation for Differentiated Instruction 195
Judi Moreillon

Annotated Bibliography 199
Sources 203
About the Editor and Contributors 207
Index 211

Introduction

Intellectual freedom is a basic tenet of the library profession. However, as school librarians, we are often challenged to defend the rights of our students, sometimes even defending those rights with other adults in our own school buildings. My first true experience with censorship actually occurred early in my career as a high school librarian. I had just completed a display of new arrivals in the library when a member of the faculty wandered in during his planning period. I excitedly encouraged him to explore all of the new books that had just been added to the collection. After several minutes of perusing the new books, he brought one of them to me with the question, "Why on earth would you include this book in the library?" I was taken aback. I was totally unprepared for the question. The book was *Boy Meets Boy* by David Levithan. Luckily, I recovered quickly and was able to have a conversation with this teacher about why teenagers should have access to books that might not reflect his own personal beliefs. While he did not leave that day in agreement with me, I believe that our conversation was a pivotal moment in my own belief in the importance of protecting the rights of students to read.

When hearing the phrase "intellectual freedom," many often equate the phrase only with censorship and the banning of books. However, intellectual freedom has a much broader application in the school library world. The rights associated with intellectual freedom include not only the right to read, but also the right to free and equitable access to technology, the right to privacy in intellectual and personal pursuits, the right to access diverse content that reflects not just our own identities but provides insights into those different from ourselves. As school librarians, we are called upon to remove as many barriers to access to information as we possibly can.

As the editor of this book, I have selected articles from *School Library Connection*, and its predecessors, *School Library Monthly* and *Library Media Connection*, which highlight intellectual freedom issues that are faced by school librarians as they seek to protect the rights of students and guarantee them equal and free access to information. Each of the seven parts of this book addresses a different aspect of the intellectual freedom issues that arise in school libraries. While the book can be read from beginning to end, I hope that you will be able to pull information from the book as you find it useful in defending the intellectual freedom rights of your students. Each chapter has been reviewed, edited, and updated with the most recent information available.

Part I, Intellectual Freedom in School Libraries, introduces the topic of intellectual freedom and how school librarians impact the protection of the rights of students. It is a good starting point for school librarians who need to know the basics including the legal foundations of intellectual freedom rooted in the First Amendment to the Constitution. Although many school librarians associate intellectual freedom with the defense of reading and dealing with challenges, intellectual freedom actually has a broader application, expanding to include privacy and confidentiality, access, the right of personal choice, filtering, and diversity. Part I of this book sets the stage for the remainder of the volume.

Part II, Intellectual Freedom Advocacy and the Right to Read, examines the many ways school librarians can advocate for student access to the library and their right to read. Several articles in this section explore leadership and advocacy. Particularly helpful are articles about how to advocate with specific stakeholder groups including teachers, principals, and parents. Additionally, this section provides an introduction to Banned Books Week and a terrific section on advocating for intellectual freedom throughout the school year. Several articles also examine barriers to the right to read including labeling books with reading levels and the use of computerized reading programs such as Accelerated Reader.

School librarians can use Part III, Policies and Procedures, to develop or revise their selection and reconsideration policies as well as explore how other circulation policies may restrict access to information. The articles in this section provide practical tips on developing selection policies as well as acceptable use policies for computer and Internet usage. Additionally, articles explore relevant laws that impact the access of students such as the Children's Internet Protection Act (CIPA). Two of my own articles appear in this section providing tips for developing selection policies and reconsideration policies. Articles on circulation policies, overdues and fines, and providing access in juvenile detention centers provide information on current issues and trends in intellectual freedom news.

Part IV, Handling Challenges, explores challenges to materials in libraries. Dealing with attempts to censor materials or restrict access to content is a situation that many school librarians face with dread. This section of the volume can alleviate fear of the challenge process by providing guidance on how to be prepared for the time when a challenge might arise. School librarians can get practical tips for preparing for potential challenges and how to handle a challenge when one occurs. Two articles in this section explore how we as school librarians must work to overcome our own tendencies to self-censor during the selection process because of a fear of a potential challenge to potentially controversial content.

One area that is often overlooked when exploring intellectual freedom issues in school libraries is technology. Part V, Filtering, Technology, and the Digital Divide, provides insights into the digital divide, filtering, and exploring ways to create equitable access to technology through bring your own device (BYOD) and one-to-one computing programs. Several articles in this section examine filtering, its evolution as an intellectual freedom issue, and its impact on inclusion of social networking sites as learning tools.

Part VI, Student Privacy in the School Library, examines privacy issues in the school library providing an excellent overview of the legal issues involved in protecting the privacy of minors. One article examines the impact of the Family and Educational Rights and Privacy Act (FERPA) on access to school library records. School librarians can use articles from this section to help educate students about their own privacy rights, to develop library policies to protect student privacy, and explore how circulation systems and common procedures (such as overdue notices) impact student privacy. These articles will help guide school librarians when they are faced with sticky privacy questions like sharing patron checkout histories and contracting with technology providers.

The final section of the book deals with Access, Equity, and Diversity. While these topics may not seem like obvious intellectual freedom issues, access to information is fundamental to intellectual freedom and that access should be to the broadest possible information. This is why equity and diversity are key factors to consider. The articles in this section provide guidance about accessibility issues in school libraries, including the impact of fixed scheduling, accessibility and universal design, and using online accessibility tools. Several articles provide guidance to school librarians working with students experiencing homelessness. Finally, school librarians can learn more about serving all students by exploring several articles that provide insights into diversifying collections and serving students of diverse backgrounds and abilities.

In selecting these articles for this volume, my goal has been to gather information that will help new, experienced, and future school librarians as they advocate for the intellectual freedom rights of the students in their schools. In total, there are fifty-seven articles written by twenty-nine different authors. My role as editor has been to provide updates to content and references when necessary while respecting the integrity of the original author's voice and vision. I am indebted to the many authors who contributed their articles for original publication in *School Library Connection*, *School Library Monthly*, and *Library Media Connection*. A particular debt for this book is owed to Helen R. Adams who has written on intellectual freedom issues in school libraries on a regular basis for many years and is the author of more than twenty of the articles. She has provided guidance and support to many school librarians, including me, about intellectual freedom issues.

Part I

Intellectual Freedom in School Libraries

"[I]t's not just the books under fire now that worry me.

It is the books that will never be written.

The books that will never be read.

And all due to the fear of censorship.

As always, young readers will be the real losers."

—Judy Blume, Author

1

What Is Intellectual Freedom?

Helen R. Adams

According to the American Library Association (ALA), "Intellectual freedom is the right of every individual to both seek and receive information from all points of view without restriction" (Magi et al. 2015, 3). Intellectual freedom is one of the core beliefs of librarians and includes access to information, First Amendment liberties, and the right to privacy in using library facilities, resources, and services. School librarians take responsibility for promoting and maintaining students' intellectual freedom seriously. They are the schools' resident intellectual freedom experts—the people with the most knowledge about the strong link between students' free speech rights under the First Amendment and unrestricted patron use of the school library's print collection, electronic resources, and the Internet. Intellectual freedom is not a fuzzy concept but rather has its basis in the First Amendment. The First Amendment states that "Congress shall make no law respecting an establishment of religion, or prohibiting the free exercise thereof, or abridging the freedom of speech, or of the press, or the right of the people peaceably to assemble, and to petition the government for a redress of grievances" (U.S. Bill of Rights). In the First Amendment, freedom of speech refers to more than oral communication and has been interpreted as including a minor's right to read and receive information and ideas.

In addition to First Amendment protections, the concept of intellectual freedom has been strengthened through case law or "law based on judicial decision and precedent rather than on statutory law" (Answers.com). The lawsuit, *Counts v. Cedarville School District* (2003), is an example of a legal battle that resulted in case law. In this lawsuit, the school board voted to limit access to the Harry Potter books in the school library collection because it perceived that the books encouraged disobedience and included characters engaging in witchcraft and the occult. The board required students to have signed permission slips from their parents or guardians before checking out the books. The Court reversed the board's decision ruling that "the restrictions violated students' First Amendment right to read and receive information" (ALA Notable First Amendment Court Cases). As a result, the Harry Potter books were returned to unrestricted circulation in the school library. The American Library Association Office for Intellectual Freedom website has detailed information on other First Amendment-related court cases involving the right to read and minors' First Amendment rights (http://www.ala.org/advocacy /intfreedom/censorship/courtcases).

Knowing the legal basis for intellectual freedom and its definition are not enough. What does intellectual freedom really mean in a school library? The spirit of intellectual freedom is present when students may:

- exercise their First Amendment right to receive ideas and information without restriction,
- use resources freely without undue scrutiny,
- ask reference questions without being questioned as to why the information is needed,
- select books to read without being forced to select only those titles that match their reading levels,
- borrow materials without having their use of library resources divulged,
- request interlibrary loan services to obtain information not available within the local collection, and
- seek information using the Internet without filtering software blocking educationally useful websites.

Students' intellectual freedom is also greatly affected by the practice of school librarians. Intellectual freedom exists when school librarians:

- select materials based on their district's collection development policy and do not allow their own personal biases, beliefs, or fears to restrict material selection,
- encourage students to read books of interest to them and provide reader guidance,
- refrain from shelving controversial titles separately from the rest of the collection,
- defend student and staff access to information using the Internet by advocating for the least restrictive level of filtering,
- collaborate with teachers to instruct students about evaluation of information on websites and how to be responsible searchers,
- ensure materials, services, and facilities are accessible for students with special needs,
- treat those who question the appropriateness of library materials respectfully and assist with the reconsideration process,
- serve as an advisor to the principal during a challenge,
- provide information to the Reconsideration Committee about the challenged resource,
- protect the confidentiality of student library records,
- refrain from imposing economic barriers such as fines and lost/damaged book fees,
- inform the entire school community proactively about minors' rights under the law and the importance of having a wide range of materials on various topics with varied points of view represented in the collection, and
- demonstrate support for intellectual freedom in schools and school libraries daily.

The "Freedom to Read," a joint statement by the ALA and the Association of American Publishers proclaims, "The freedom to read is essential to our democracy" (Magi et al. 2015, 23). While school librarians may not consider themselves "defenders of democracy," they frequently act in that capacity when they protect minors' rights to read and receive information under the First Amendment and case law. Daily actions and advocacy by school librarians affect youthful patrons' intellectual freedom and have far-reaching implications in their lives. They can speak up, and speak out, for intellectual freedom!

REFERENCES

American Library Association Office for Intellectual Freedom. *Notable First Amendment Court Cases*. http://www.ala.org/advocacy/intfreedom/censorship/courtcases.

Answers.com. What Is the Difference between U.S. Case Law and English Common Law? Retrieved from https://www.answers.com/Q/What_is_the_difference_between_U .S.case_law_and_English_common_law.

Magi, Trina, Garnar, Martin, & Office for Intellectual Freedom. (2015). *Intellectual Freedom Manual*. 9th ed. Chicago: American Library Association.

U.S. Bill of Rights. The Bill of Rights: What Does It Say? Retrieved from https://www .archives.gov/founding-docs/bill-of-rights/what-does-it-say.

2

Intellectual Freedom 101: Core Principles for School Librarians

Helen R. Adams

The school year is well under way, and it's time to reflect on students' intellectual freedom and access to information. Are local filtering practices depriving your students of their First Amendment rights? Does your library have a formal materials selection policy? Are you prepared for any challenge to library resources? Review the following core intellectual freedom principles for school libraries, and examine the resources that can assist you in protecting students' right to read.

FUNDAMENTAL INTELLECTUAL FREEDOM PRINCIPLES

THE RIGHT TO READ

Students possess the right to read and receive information, regardless of format, based on their First Amendment free speech rights and court decisions including *Board of Education, Island Trees Union Free School District v. Pico* (1982).

Resources for more information:

- American Library Association. *Notable First Amendment Court Cases.* http://www.ala.org/advocacy/intfreedom/censorship/courtcases.
- Chmara, Theresa. (2015). The Law Regarding Minors' First Amendment Rights to Access Information. In T. Magi et al. (Eds.), *Intellectual Freedom Manual.* 9th ed. Chicago: American Library Association.

SELECTION OF LIBRARY MATERIALS

Every school should have a board-approved school library selection policy that forms the legal basis for selection and reconsideration of the school library collection. The policy provides guidance to a school librarian during selection of resources, explains to the community how and why specific materials are chosen, and offers a defense for questioned materials.

Resources for more information:

- American Library Association Office for Intellectual Freedom. *Selection & Reconsideration Policy Toolkit for Public, School, & Academic Libraries* (http://www.ala.org/tools/challengesupport/selectionpolicytoolkit).
- Kerby, M. (2019). *An Introduction to Collection Development for School Librarians.* 2nd ed. Chicago: American Library Association.
- Marcis, M. A. (2016). *The Collection Program in Schools: Concepts and Practices.* 6th ed. Santa Barbara, CA: Libraries Unlimited.

SELF-CENSORSHIP

Librarians must adhere to their professional ethics and avoid letting their fear of challenges, personal beliefs, values, or biases influence their selection decisions.
Resources for more information:

- American Library Association. (2008). Article VII. *Code of Ethics of the American Library Association.* Retrieved from http://www.ala.org/tools/ethics.
- Jacobson, Linda. (September 26, 2016). Unnatural Selection: More Librarians are Self-Censoring. *School Library Journal.* Retrieved from https://www.slj.com/?detailStory=unnatural-selection-more-librarians-self-censoring.

CHALLENGES AND CENSORSHIP

School librarians must resist all attempts to remove or restrict library materials that meet the materials selection policy selection criteria. Although citizens have the right to communicate concerns about school library materials to administrators, questioned materials should not be removed from the library's collection without due process represented by the library's reconsideration procedures.
Resources for more information:

- American Library Association. *Banned & Challenged Books.* Retrieved from http://www.ala.org/advocacy/bbooks.
- American Library Association. (2019). *Challenged Resources: An Interpretation of the Library Bill of Rights.* Retrieved from http://www.ala.org/advocacy/intfreedom/librarybill/interpretations/challenged-resources.

FILTERING

The desire to protect students, fear of parental complaints, and misinterpretation of the Children's Internet Protection Act (CIPA) result in overly restrictive filtering in many schools, causing the blocking of legitimate educational and constitutionally protected online content. School librarians should advocate that acceptable use policies include a process for students to access information when online resources are inaccurately blocked.
Resources for more information:

- American Association of School Librarians. *Banned Websites Awareness Day.* Retrieved from http://www.ala.org/aasl/advocacy/bwad.
- American Library Association. (2015). *Internet Filtering: An Interpretation of the Library Bill of Rights.* Retrieved from http://www.ala.org/advocacy/intfreedom/librarybill/interpretations/internet-filtering.
- Batch, K. R. (June 2014a). *Fencing Out Knowledge: Impacts of the Children's Internet Protection Act Ten Years Later.* Chicago: American Library Association Office for Intellectual Freedom. Retrieved from http://www.ala.org/aboutala/sites/ala.org.aboutala/files/content/oitp/publications/issuebriefs/cipa_report.pdf. (This is an extensive examination of the impact of filtering including in K–12 schools.)

- Batch, K. R. (June 2014b). *Fencing Out Knowledge: Revisiting the Children's Internet Protection Act 10 Years Later. Policy Brief No. 5*. Chicago: American Library Association, Office for Information Technology Policy, and the Office for Intellectual Freedom. Retrieved from http://www.ala.org /aboutala/sites/ala.org .aboutala/files/content/oitp/publications/issuebriefs/cipa_report.pdf.
- Chmara, T. (2009). Minors' First Amendment Rights: CIPA & School Libraries. *Knowledge Quest*, 39(1): 16–21. Retrieved from http://www.ala.org/aasl/sites /ala.org.aasl/files/content/aaslissues/bwad/KNOW_39_1_MinorsFirst_16-21 .pdf.

PRIVACY AND CONFIDENTIALITY

State privacy laws regarding library records and the Family Educational Rights and Privacy Act (FERPA) are difficult to interpret and may clash with minors' privacy rights supported by the ALA Code of Ethics. Students' privacy is safeguarded best by a board-approved privacy policy that details how their library records are protected and to whom and the circumstances under which they may be released.

Resources for more information:

- American Library Association. (1986). *Policy on the Confidentiality of Library Records*. Retrieved from http://www.ala.org/advocacy/intfreedom/statementspols /otherpolicies/policyconfidentiality.
- American Library Association. (2016). *Library Privacy Guidelines for Students in K–12 Schools*. Retrieved from http://www.ala.org/advocacy/privacy/guidelines /students.
- American Library Association. (2019). *Questions & Answers on Privacy and Confidentiality, Section IV, Minors' Privacy Rights*. Retrieved from http://www.ala.org /advocacy/intfreedom/privacyconfidentialityqa#Minors'%20Privacy%20Rights.

RESTRICTING ACCESS AND PERSONAL CHOICE

In schools using computerized reading management programs such as Accelerated Reader, spines of library books are labeled with "book levels," and students are frequently limited to selecting only those books that match their reading levels. School librarians should advocate for students' free choice of library materials.

Resources for more information:

- American Association of School Librarians. (2011). *Position Statement on Labeling Books with Reading Levels*. Retrieved from http://www.ala.org/aasl/advocacy /resources/statements/labeling
- American Library Association. (2014a). *Labeling and Rating Systems: An Interpretation of the Library Bill of Rights*. Retrieved from http://www.ala.org/advocacy /intfreedom/librarybill/interpretations/labelingrating.
- American Library Association. (2014b). *Restricted Access to Library Materials: An Interpretation of the Library Bill of Rights*. Retrieved from http://www.ala .org/advocacy/intfreedom/librarybill/interpretations/restrictedaccess.
- Dawkins, April M. (August 15, 2017). The Problem with Reading Levels. *Intellectual Freedom Blog*. Retrieved from https://www.oif.ala.org/oif/?p=10625.

STUDENTS WITH SPECIAL NEEDS

Federal and state laws and professional ethics require that individuals with disabilities be afforded educational opportunities offered to their peers. To fulfill their legal and ethical responsibilities, school librarians must provide programs, resources, and accessible facilities to meet the needs of disabled students and others with special needs (such as homeless students, English language learners, at-risk students, and gifted children).

Resources for more information:

- Adams, Helen R. IF Matters: Intellectual Freedom @ Your Library columns [homeless students]. *School Library Monthly.*
- American Library Association. (2018). *Services to Persons with Disabilities: An Interpretation of the Library Bill of Rights.* Retrieved from http://www.ala.org /advocacy/intfreedom/librarybill/interpretations/servicespeopledisabilities.

Every librarian must know the principles of intellectual freedom and strive to educate administrators, colleagues, students, parents, and the larger community about students' First Amendments rights and the connection between students' access to information and a vibrant democracy with informed citizens.

3

The Choices That Count

Christine Eldred

Librarians tend to consider intellectual freedom issues only during Banned Books Week or if a materials challenge arises. In the course of attending to all the daily demands in the library, intellectual freedom can sometimes feel intangible, theoretical, and academic. Fear or anxiety is sometimes associated with this topic, too, especially if a librarian connects it with conflict, worries about administrator support, or feels out of their comfort zone.

INTELLECTUAL FREEDOM ENGAGEMENT

Developing knowledge about intellectual freedom doesn't require a major time commitment, however, and there are different levels of engagement. Learning more about the policies and practices of intellectual freedom is not only a professional responsibility, it is a choice that supports student learning and can give librarians the ability to defend their resources, programs, and even their jobs in the face of controversy. These are the choices that count.

Librarians reading this article were probably introduced to the basic principles of intellectual freedom during their graduate or professional training. Librarians who want to go beyond their baseline knowledge and put those principles into action can consider the following three levels of engagement:

LEVEL 1: GATHER INFORMATION

▶ **Learn the local and school culture.** Intellectual freedom principles help guide librarians by providing fundamental ideas and values important to the profession. But every librarian works in a unique context; sensitivity and knowledge about context allows a librarian to use good judgment in applying those principles.

▶ **Become familiar with district policies on materials selection and reconsideration of materials.** It's critical to know current policies regarding the library and how to access them quickly.

▶ **Ask about past materials challenges and get a feel for the administrator's approach.** Explore what precedents may have been set in the past; people will probably look to previous experience as a guideline. Have library challenges been treated differently from classroom challenges? Is the principal prepared to discuss the topic or are they unclear about intellectual freedom issues?

▶ **Learn about local, state, and national resources.** Many state school library associations have an intellectual freedom committee or a district library coordinator who may maintain resources that provide information and support. National organizations such as the American Library Association, the Comic Book Legal Defense Fund, the National Coalition Against Censorship, and the National Council of Teachers of English have valuable online materials.

▶ **Become familiar with state law on library privacy.** Forty-eight states have laws specifically addressing library patron privacy and confidentiality. In schools, library records are also covered by the Family Educational Rights and Privacy Act (FERPA) and are considered educational records; thus, they require disclosure to parents or guardians upon request. Nevertheless, aspects of state library confidentiality law can impact some school library practices such as handling overdue notices (http://www.ala.org/advocacy/privacy/statelaws).

▶ **Synthesize information on policies, procedures, culture and past practices, resources, and state laws to put together the big picture.** After this research, a librarian should know:

- What the district policies are and how to access them.
- How state library laws impact school library practices.
- How past challenges (if any) have been handled in the school.
- The school administration's familiarity with intellectual freedom issues and policies.
- Local and state resources on intellectual freedom.

LEVEL 2: IMPLEMENT BEST PRACTICES

▶ **Use reliable sources for selection.** An important aspect of responding to materials challenges is providing a rationale for the selection of challenged items. Citing specific and reputable selection tools that support a challenged book or video helps demonstrate that materials selection is a professional and deliberate process, not simply a matter of personal choice by the librarian. Selection tools include professional reviews, guides to core subject materials, lists of recommended reading by library and educational organizations, and award winners.

▶ **Promote privacy.** Assess library practices that impact student privacy. Common areas of concern are notifying students of overdues, records of past patron checkouts, maintaining discretion with reference requests, and sharing student information with teachers and administrators.

▶ **Update selection policies and reconsideration procedures.** Policies should be renewed and updated periodically. Older policies may not promote current best practices or adequately address technology or multimedia materials, including images, video, websites, apps, graphic novels, manga, and eBooks.

▶ **Do a self-censorship check.** Everyone has biases, but it's a critical professional responsibility for librarians to question how their own personal biases may impact the intellectual freedom of others. An analysis of the collection allows a librarian to check that a range of viewpoints is presented and to identify topics, authors, or genres that may be missing or incomplete. Evidence of a balanced collection can be a helpful asset when faced with a materials challenge.

LEVEL 3: EDUCATE AND ADVOCATE

▶ **Take opportunities to educate within the school community.** Reach out proactively to the school administration, school board, and community. Look for chances to inform others about the materials selection process and why patron privacy is important.

▶ **Post a privacy notice.** Craft a brief statement informing patrons about the library's commitment to their privacy and use it as a springboard for discussion with students and staff.

▶ **Look for opportunities to talk with administrators and IT staff about web filtering.** Web filtering is required in schools, but educators can improve its limitations by seeking an open dialogue with IT staff and administrators. When students are denied access to educational content, that is perhaps the best time to demonstrate the impact of filtering and to discuss ways to fine-tune the filter.

▶ **Offer professional development to teachers.** Create a workshop or presentation for teacher colleagues on dealing with controversial materials and on the link between intellectual freedom in the library and academic freedom in the classroom.

▶ **Support colleagues on intellectual freedom issues.** Offer practical or moral support to librarians who are dealing with intellectual freedom controversies. Write letters of support in materials challenge cases, attend public hearings, and contribute to a community interest in free expression and free choice. Consider joining the state library association's intellectual freedom committee and help to promote access and privacy for all patrons.

4

Fewer School Librarians: The Effect on Students' Intellectual Freedom

Helen R. Adams

In recent years, school districts have been eliminating or reducing school librarian positions, and giving those remaining on the job more responsibilities in multiple schools. In some schools, library assistants and volunteers, who once worked under the direction of a school library professional, are now operating libraries.

A MAP WITH CONSEQUENCES

In March 2010, Shonda Brisco, assistant professor and curriculum materials librarian at Oklahoma State University, posted a Google map titled "A Nation without School Librarians" (http://tinyurl.com/253ehp3; Note: this requires a Google account to view). Red and blue flags on the map represent communities that have either cut certified school librarian positions (blue flag) or are requiring those professionals remaining to work in two or more school library programs (red flag). The map tells a story; and behind every flag, there are hundreds, sometimes thousands, of students with diminished access to the resources, instruction, and the services that school librarians provide. Elementary school library professional staffing is especially threatened. The graphical representation is disheartening to those who understand the positive impact school librarians have on student academic achievement as evidenced by state school library impact studies (https://www.lrs.org/data-tools/school-libraries/impact-studies/).

The map reveals that in spring 2010, the Fullerton Joint Union High School District (California) eliminated four teacher librarian positions, leaving two school library professionals to serve six high schools with assistance from one library technician per building (http://tinyurl.com/253ehp3). Local media reported, "In all, the district estimated it would save $440,000 annually by suspending four of its teacher librarian positions. But in doing so, these libraries lost their greatest resource, the person who makes all that the library has to offer come alive . . . these teacher librarians are the ones who offer cyber-safety lessons, teach

13

students how to cite reputable sources, how to integrate video with class assignments, and yeah, how to track down that Greek mythology book for an essay" (Cabrera 2010). Students at Troy High School notice the difference with one library user stating, "No one knows as much as Ms. Slim [teacher librarian Marie Slim] did. Students would come in and she'd help them with essays and projects. There's just no one to do that anymore" (Cabrera 2010).

In 2018, Deb Kachel and Keith Curry Lance studied National Center for Education Statistics data to examine the trends in school library staffing between 1999 and 2016. They found that:

> Between the 1999–2000 and 2015–16 school years, the National Center for Education Statistics (NCES) reports that the profession lost the equivalent of more than 10,000 full-time school librarian positions nationwide. That translates to a 19 percent drop in the workforce, from 53,659 to 43,367. The most rapid declines happened from 2009–10 to 2013–14. The decline slowed from then to 2014–15; but resumed larger losses in 2015–16, the latest data available. (Lance 2018)

Kachel and Lance identified several factors that might be contributing to the declining numbers including administrative turnover, replacement of school librarians with instructional coaches, and difficulty in finding and hiring qualified school librarians.

WHAT WILL HAPPEN IF . . . ?

The "Nation without School Librarians" map and the Kachel and Lance data are alarming to those who value students' intellectual freedom and the role school librarians have in protecting minors' First Amendment right to access information. According to the American Library Association, between 2014 and 2018, 1,283 challenges were reported to the ALA Office for Intellectual Freedom (http://www .ala.org/advocacy/bbooks/frequentlychallengedbooks/statistics). Intellectual freedom is fragile if it is not nurtured and defended vigorously.

What will happen to students' intellectual freedom if there is no school librarian to:

- ensure the existence of library policies related to materials selection and provide for reconsideration of a resource, circulation of resources, confidentiality of library records, interlibrary loan, and Internet use;
- model best practices in selection of library resources by resisting outside pressures to avoid selecting materials considered by some to be controversial;
- demonstrate leadership when there is a formal challenge to a library resource;
- educate administrators and teachers proactively about materials selection, reconsideration of library materials, and how to respond to a complaint about a library resource;
- protect the First Amendment right of children and young adults to receive information in a school library;
- speak out against restricting students' choice of library books based on computerized reading management programs title lists and assigned reading levels;
- advocate for the reduction of overly restrictive filtering that limits students' access to constitutionally protected information online;
- champion the rights of students with special needs and provide access to library resources and services for students with physical, cognitive, and learning disabilities;

- welcome and provide resources and support for English language learners;
- reflect on ways in which the library staff can support the learning needs of homeless children and young adults;
- create flexible solutions for children from low-income families to overcome economic barriers such as fines for overdue materials;
- maintain the confidentiality of students' library records;
- guard the privacy of students using library resources;
- teach students to recognize "Intellectual Freedom is every learner's right," a common belief within the AASL Standards Framework for Learners (2018); and
- build support for students' access to information with the principal, school staff, students, parents, and community members.

Former school librarian Ann Dutton Ewbank supplies one answer to the question of what will happen if there is no school library professional:

> In December 2005, I was the President-elect of the Arizona Library Association. Our state Superintendent of Instruction, Tom Horne, sent a letter to all Arizona K–12 principals warning them about "morally objectionable" materials in school libraries. The book in question was *The Perks of Being a Wallflower* by Stephen Chbosky. While Horne did not have authority to remove the book from school libraries, he strongly encouraged principals to review the book. The source of the complaint was the grandmother of a sixth grade student who had obtained the book from her K–6 school library. After some investigation, I discovered that the clerk who operated the library ordered the book because it was designated "4th grade reading level" in the Accelerated Reader program and therefore inappropriately selected the book for this elementary school population. (Ann Dutton Ewbank, e-mail to author, November 28, 2010)

Horne's remarks prompted the removal of the book from several middle school and high school libraries across Arizona that didn't want to invite controversy. This unfortunate situation may have been prevented if a certified school librarian with appropriate training and an understanding of the difference between "reading level" and "interest level" had been responsible for materials selection.

ACT FOR INTELLECTUAL FREEDOM

There's an app for protecting intellectual freedom in school libraries; it is a school librarian! Students will not learn about the principles of intellectual freedom unless a full-time school librarian is in place. If students' full access to library resources and patron privacy are to survive, remaining school librarians and professional associations must take action. The American Association of School Librarians provides a wide range of advocacy tools on its website. Ways to promote intellectual freedom throughout the school year can be found in Part II of this book in the article, "The Intellectual Freedom Calendar: Another Advocacy Plan for the School Library."

REFERENCES

American Library Association. *Frequently Challenged Books.* Retrieved from http://www.ala.org/advocacy/bbooks/frequentlychallengedbooks.

American Association of School Librarians. (2018). *AASL Standards Framework for Learners.* Retrieved from https://standards.aasl.org/wp-content/uploads/2017/11/AASL-Standards-Framework-for-Learners-pamphlet.pdf.

Brisco, S. *A Nation without School Librarians.* Retrieved from http://tinyurl.com/253ehp3.

Cabrera, Y. (October 18, 2010). Fullerton Teacher Librarian Is Last One Standing. *Orange County Register.* Retrieved from http://www.ocregister.com/articles /school-271735-teacher-students.html.

Kachel, D. E., & Lance, K. C. (April 2018). Changing Times: School Library Staffing Status. *Teacher Librarian.* Retrieved from http://teacherlibrarian.com/2018/04 /11/changing-times-school-librarian-staffing-status.

Lance, K. C. (March 16, 2018). School Librarian, Where Art Thou? *School Library Journal.* Retrieved from https://www.slj.com/?detailStory=school-librarian-art-thou.

Part II

Intellectual Freedom Advocacy and the Right to Read

On the challenge toward *The Land*: "Although there are those who wish to ban my books because I have used language that is painful, I have chosen to use the language that was spoken during the period, for I refuse to whitewash history. The language was painful and life was painful for many African Americans, including my family. I remember the pain."

—*Mildred D. Taylor, Author*

5

Intellectual Freedom Leadership: Standing Up for Your Students

Helen R. Adams

"Intellectual freedom is every learner's right" (Mardis 2017, 51). This bold statement is one of the guiding assumptions on which the new American Association of School Librarians' (AASL) standards are based. In addition to protecting and preserving the principles of intellectual freedom, school librarians must also cultivate in students and educators the inclination toward personal free expression and protecting the free expression of others (Mardis 2017, 51).

LEADERSHIP AND FEAR

Because intellectual freedom is fundamental to the profession, school librarians must provide leadership to protect and preserve this core value for students. Several years ago during a discussion in my graduate class, the group was talking about a situation in which a principal directed a librarian to remove a book from the library after a parent complaint. Edith, a practicing elementary librarian, said, "I'll do what the principal tells me. I have three kids, and I need this job!" The statement was startling in its contrast to the comments of other class members. Edith was demonstrating fear, not leadership. Fear that, by reminding her principal about following the district's reconsideration policy, her job could be in jeopardy.

In contrast, consider how Gwen, a middle school librarian, handled her principal's directive to cancel a gaming magazine subscription and remove all issues from the library based solely on one parent's oral complaint. Proactively, Gwen made an appointment with the principal and reviewed selection policy criteria, considering arguments that would persuade the principal to follow the district's reconsideration process for informal oral complaints. During the meeting, Gwen respectfully explained why the magazine had been selected, how much students read and enjoyed the magazine, and the fact that "we can't just pull something every time someone has an issue with it" (Adams 2008, 129). Even though the principal was not fully satisfied, he agreed to follow the process by contacting the parent and explaining the school's policy not to take action without submission of a formal written request for reconsideration (Adams 2008, 130). Gwen showed leadership by employing a number of strategies, including drawing on her previously cultivated good relationship with the principal and their mutual respect. This combination created the successful outcome of continuing to provide students with access to a popular periodical.

STARTING A SMALL REVOLUTION

Melly and Marilyn are school librarians in a large district on the West Coast, and both were concerned about students' privacy and intellectual freedom. Melly experienced a shock when she was absent from school for a few days and returned to find that the library aide had posted a list of overdue books with students' names on the library door visible to everyone. Melly talked with the aide who felt posting the list was acceptable. She had no knowledge of state library records law, the Family Educational Rights and Privacy Act (FERPA), and the confidentiality of students' records. Student privacy was only one of Melly and Marilyn's intellectual freedom-related concerns. They were also aware that students in some schools in their district were required to choose library books based solely on their Independent Reading Level Assessment (IRLA) levels rather than on their personal interests (Suzanne [pseudonym], email to author, April 26, 2017).

Being strong advocates for students' intellectual freedom, the two librarians took their concerns to Suzanne, a district-level library staff member. As a result, the district formed a committee of librarians and aides that was given responsibility to create a professional development session for all library staff. The small group studied their state's library records law, FERPA, and American Library Association (ALA) intellectual freedom and privacy documents and created library privacy guidelines. They also added support for students' intellectual freedom—specifically stating that students were encouraged to select books based on their personal interests and were not restricted to IRLA reading levels (email to author, May 22, 2017).

All school librarians and aides attended the professional development offering. After the legal and ethical information about students' privacy was presented, those attending were asked to support the draft library guidelines. Not everyone did. Some middle school librarians who did not have aides were concerned that if they used student assistants to check out the library materials of peers, they would be breaking the law by allowing peers to view confidential student library records. The vote in favor of the guidelines was not unanimous, but the planning group did not give up. The draft guidelines were sent to the district's legal team, approved, and put into practice. Many librarians are thankful because it is now clear how to protect students' library records and support students' free choice of personal reading. The core planning group is continuing to work toward solutions for middle school librarians (email to author, October 23, 2017).

Although the process was not without its hurdles, those involved demonstrated leadership and began a small revolution. Suzanne summed it up: "This has been a learning experience for all involved, including me. It is often easier to just push tough issues under the rug and not correct them, but in this case, it was necessary to identify firm guidelines that all library staff in our school district could follow. The experience proved to be very empowering to those of us who worked hard to make sure the guidelines moved forward and were adopted by the district. In the end, the guidelines protect student library privacy and the rights of students to select books that fit their interests and needs, while helping library staff feel supported in their work" (email to author, December 1, 2017).

LEADERSHIP IN THE FACE OF RISK

Emily, an elementary librarian in a Southern coastal state, annually checked award-winning books to select titles for her library's collection. Knowing her district supported diversity in library collections, she found *This Day in June,* an elementary-level Stonewall Award winner and added it to her list. Because she surmised her principal might feel this book could be a risk for a reconsideration request, she checked if other elementary libraries in the area owned the book. Although finding none, she ordered the book. When *This Day in June* arrived, Emily sought the opinions of the principal and school counselor. After they had read the book, there was consensus that the book filled a need for students in the school. Proactively, Emily emailed other elementary librarians in the district sharing book reviews, rationale for adding the title to the collection, and offering to lend it through interlibrary loan (Emily [pseudonym], email to author, November 29, 2017).

When *George* received a Stonewall Award the following year, Emily followed the same process. Her new principal read *George,* noting she was not enthusiastic about the writing style and flagged one page she felt was provocative. While waiting for the school counselor to read *George,* Emily had another conversation with the principal, who acknowledged the high probability of students in the school needing this, although at the same time realizing there was a risk of a reconsideration request. Emily told the principal, "I really appreciate that you gave me your feedback but are leaving the decision to me. I'm planning to put it on the shelves, but I'm waiting for Tami [school counselor] to finish reading it" (email to author, November 29, 2017). When the school counselor enthusiastically endorsed the book, Emily added *George* to the collection.

Librarians in Emily's district had had a recent discussion about adding diverse books including LGBTQ titles, and a few other librarians named books they have in their collections. The district's library supervisor was supportive, noting the school library needs to represent *all* students. Referring to a current kindergarten student with two moms, Emily said, "I want to be sure she can find herself in our library and isn't always looking 'out the window' in the books she is reading" (email to author, December 2, 2017).

In a time when LGBTQ books are frequently challenged, Emily's leadership in adding *This Day in June* and *George* to her collection is creating opportunities for students to see themselves in the books as well as for others to learn about individuals who may be different from them. Emily is showing a path to the collection diversity to which the district has made a commitment. She articulated her vision, commenting, "If I can build a core elementary LGBTQ mini collection, elementary librarians in my local area may feel safer putting the books in their collections. There is power in numbers" (email to author, November 29, 2017).

CONCLUSION

Over time, every librarian faces intellectual freedom-related situations of varying types and must decide whether to stand firm on principle or step back. In December 2017, Kristin Pekoll, assistant director at the ALA Office for Intellectual Freedom, tracked and assisted with forty open book challenge cases around the country (Kristin Pekoll, phone call with author, December 14, 2017). Obviously, many librarians are actively defending their patrons' right to read. Leadership in intellectual freedom is not without risk—enduring an uncomfortable work atmosphere, experiencing personal verbal attacks during a heated formal book challenge, or making the decision that a situation is untenable and seeking another position. At times, school librarians must look at the big picture and make the difficult ethical and personal decision that one has done as much as possible at the time. Leadership in intellectual freedom comes back to our profession's shared belief that "Intellectual freedom [and privacy] is every learner's right" (Mardis 2017, 51). The school librarians spotlighted in this article have a passion for students' access to information and privacy and acted on their ethical convictions.

RESOURCES

- ALA. *Schools and Minors' Rights (intellectual freedom)*. http://www.ala.org/advocacy/intfreedom/minors.
- ALA. *Top Ten Challenged Books*. http://www.ala.org/advocacy/bbooks/NLW-Top10.
- American Library Association. *State Privacy Laws Regarding Library Records*. http://www.ala.org/advocacy/privacy/statelaws.
- American Library Association. (2019). *Privacy and Confidentiality Q&A*. http://www.ala.org/advocacy/intfreedom/privacyconfidentialityqa.
- U.S. Department of Education. *Family Educational Rights and Privacy Act (FERPA)*. https://www2.ed.gov/policy/gen/guid/fpco/ferpa/index.html.

REFERENCES

Adams, H. R. (2008). *Ensuring Intellectual Freedom and Access to Information in the School Library Media Program*. Santa Barbara, CA: Libraries Unlimited.

Mardis, M. A. (2017). On the horizon: New standards to dawn at AASL 2017. *Knowledge Quest, 46*(1), pp. 48–54. Retrieved from http://knowledgequest.aasl.org/wp-content/uploads/2017/09/KNOW_46_1_OntheHorizon_48-54.pdf.

6

Advocating for Intellectual Freedom with Principals and Teachers

Helen R. Adams

Intellectual freedom is "the right of every individual to both seek and receive information from all points of view without restriction" (Magi et al. 2015, 3). Unlike school librarians, it is rare for principals and teachers to learn about intellectual freedom in their education classes. Nor is it likely that they are taught about First Amendment court decisions that affirm minors' rights to receive ideas and information in school libraries. Therefore, if minors' intellectual freedom is to be protected, school librarians must take responsibility for educating administrators and teachers. The concept of "intellectual freedom" can be advocated by school librarians to other educators as providing "access" to a wide range of resources. Also, use of stories will make intellectual freedom principles more concrete to colleagues.

Prior to beginning an advocacy campaign, the school librarian should first check the status of intellectual freedom in schools—locally, statewide, and nationally. The following strategies for promoting intellectual freedom for students are recommended by the American Library Association (ALA):

- Seek up-to-date information on censorship, privacy, and other intellectual freedom issues in library professional literature and other media sources and through attendance at conferences and workshops.
- Subscribe to intellectual freedom-related electronic lists such as ALA's *Intellectual Freedom News* (http://ala.informz.net/ala/pages/oif_ifnews_signup).
- Become familiar with pro-First Amendment organizations and their advocacy efforts (National Council of Teachers of English, Comic Book Legal Defense Fund, The American Civil Liberties Union, National Coalition Against Censorship).

Next, the school librarian can develop an advocacy plan to promote intellectual freedom concepts. The American Association of School Librarians (AASL) has defined advocacy as the "On-going process of building partnerships so that others will act for and with you, turning passive support into educated action for the library media program." Although one resolute person can achieve a great deal, having administrators and teachers as allies can change a school's climate. AASL's online "Advocacy Toolkit" can be used to prepare a local plan for promoting intellectual freedom principles (AASL 2018).

As educational leaders, principals exert a great deal of influence; therefore, winning their support for students' intellectual freedom is critical. If the principal does not support a collection with materials reflecting a broad range of ideas on controversial issues, does not believe that students' library records should be confidential, or does not accept that minors have the right to research a variety of topics, it is difficult for the school librarian to ensure students' access to information and guard their intellectual freedom. To help administrators understand the importance of protecting students' information needs, school librarians can:

- Assist administrators in making the connection between intellectual freedom and "growing" future citizens. To ensure that today's students are educated for citizenship in a global society, students must be able to use resources on a wide range of subjects in print and electronic formats. Unrestricted access to information in the school library creates an academic atmosphere in which students learn how to evaluate competing ideas, a skill needed by all citizens.
- Meet with the principal to review the materials selection policy, how materials are selected, and district reconsideration procedures, clarifying any steps that are unclear.
- Initiate a discussion when issues such as the confidentiality of students' library records arise.

Teachers also need to be educated about intellectual freedom. They may not have a clear understanding of the difference between the broad administrative control that public school principals and boards of education have on the removal of curricular materials required in courses, and the narrow control that administrators and boards have when it comes to removing library resources intended for free inquiry by students (Doyle 2007, 182–186). To nurture teachers' development as supporters of students' rights, the library professional, using these strategies, can:

- Meet with new teaching staff to explain library policies related to materials selection, reconsideration, privacy of library records, interlibrary loan, and Internet use.
- Plan and work collaboratively with teachers and students on learning experiences incorporating First Amendment speech rights.
- Integrate a different facet of intellectual freedom into each staff development program.
- Select professional materials related to censorship and make them available to staff.

By reaching out to principals and teachers, the school librarian has the potential to create allies who will support minors' access to information when a challenge occurs. The advocacy process is not quick, and it requires more than celebrating Banned Books Week each September. The school librarian must model the principles of intellectual freedom in year-round, day-to-day actions. However, when advocacy is successful, it can change students' lives and impact their effectiveness as citizens.

REFERENCES

American Association of School Librarians. (February 2018). *AASL Advocacy Toolkit.* Retrieved from http://www.ala.org/aasl/sites/ala.org.aasl/files/content/aasl issues/toolkits/AASLAdvocacyToolkit_180209.pdf.

American Association of School Librarians. *What Is Advocacy?* Retrieved from http://www.ala.org/aasl/advocacy/definitions.

American Library Association, Office for Intellectual Freedom. *What Can I Do to Oppose Censorship?* Retrieved from http://www.ala.org/advocacy/intfreedom/censorship/faq#ifpoint16.

Doyle, R. P. (2007). *Banned Books: 2007 Resource Guide.* Chicago: American Library Association.

Magi, T., Garnar, M., & Office for Intellectual Freedom. (2015). *Intellectual Freedom Manual.* 9th ed. Chicago: American Library Association.

7

Understanding Advocacy for Effective Action

Elizabeth Burns

School librarians are asked to advocate for school libraries, their positions, and their library programs. It is expected that they have knowledge and understanding of advocacy and that activities library professionals have defined as advocacy will be undertaken. However, recent studies show school librarians have different perceptions of advocacy and although the word "advocacy" is widely used, rarely does it carry the same connotation across multiple audiences (Burns 2014; Ewbank 2011).

CLARITY NEEDED

The national professional library organizations, the American Library Association (ALA) and the American Association of School Librarians (AASL), create and maintain resources and toolkits to assist school librarians with advocacy implementation. Within these resources, AASL defines advocacy as the "on-going process of building partnerships so that others will act for and with you, turning passive support into educated action for the library program" (AASL 2007). But, definitions of Public Relations (PR) and marketing coexist under the definition of advocacy, leaving school librarians to discern for themselves what actions constitute advocacy and how blended the understanding of these concepts should be. This fractured, multi-tiered definition of advocacy leads to varied understandings among practicing school librarians and creates a lack of consistency in how school librarians interpret and engage in the practice of advocacy. If school librarians are going to advocate effectively, they must have a clear understanding of what advocacy means. Further, they must identify effective advocacy actions they can implement into their practice. To explore what school librarians know and believe about advocacy and how they engage in advocacy in their practice, a national sample of school librarians were asked to define advocacy and the activities they practice in their setting. Participants were 815 practicing, state-certified school librarians, representing seventeen states, who engaged in a conversation in which they described their understanding of advocacy activities. Findings offer insight into what school librarians understand about advocacy and the advocacy initiatives they implement in their practice.

WHAT DO SCHOOL LIBRARIANS DEFINE AS ADVOCACY?

The majority of survey respondents (68.61%) could identify the published AASL definition of advocacy. However, when providing a personal definition of advocacy, the school librarians' definitions did not demonstrate a comparable level of under-standing. Participants had difficulty articulating advocacy as a process designed to develop a stakeholder relationship with the intent of gaining support. The con-tent of their statements was more synonymous with definitions of public relations and marketing and was contradictory to the language used in AASL's definition of advocacy. Participant definitions focused heavily on program promotion and com-municating activities taking place in the library and the duties performed by the school librarian. This demonstrates a misalignment in understanding of advocacy.

HOW DO SCHOOL LIBRARIANS ENGAGE IN ADVOCACY?

Actions of advocacy are implemented with the intent to educate a stakeholder base and build program supporters. To explore advocacy activities congruent with the AASL advocacy definition, participants of the study were asked to identify activities from an established list in which they participate. The participants did not engage in most activities on a regular basis.

Only 28.79% have spoken at a school board or PTA meeting and 29.80% have conducted professional development for staff on school library advocacy. The sur-veyed school librarians are not regularly participating in activities that engage mem-bers of their school community and parents. They are not initiating activities that foster stakeholder relationships and build support for their library program. The only activity with above 50% participation was "organized meeting with adminis-trator to discuss library program" (65.82%). Because of this lack of advocacy activ-ity, they may not have an educated base of supporters when times of crisis arise.

Survey Respondents Responses of Advocacy Activity

Advocacy Activity	n	Total (%)
Organized meeting with administrator to discuss library program	391	65.82
Read/distributed literature or information on school library advocacy	294	49.49
Provided comments to decision makers through phone calls, faxes, emails, or letters	290	48.82
Committee/volunteer work in a library association or other group	254	42.76
Encouraged others to write/speak to decision makers about library issues	234	39.39
Conducted professional development for staff on library advocacy	177	29.80
Spoke at a School Board/PTA meeting	171	28.79
Sponsored an advocacy event for parents and/or community members to gain support for the library	133	22.39
Attended library legislative days/participated in a demonstration/other organized event to influence decision makers	94	15.82
Established an advocacy committee for school library	45	7.58
Not been involved in advocacy activities in last 3 years	43	7.24

WHAT IS SCHOOL LIBRARY ADVOCACY?

Results of this study show school librarians do not yet have a clear understanding and definition of advocacy. There is still work to be done to define the message of advocacy for the school library profession. Advocacy involves a deliberate and sustained effort to foster understanding of the school library program while influencing the attitudes of key stakeholders. To achieve this goal, relationships with stakeholders must be built and the mission and goals of the school library should be shared. This ensures that stakeholders will form an educated support network. These ideals form the basis of a school library advocacy definition.

GOING BEYOND PROGRAM PROMOTION

School librarians need clear guidelines on the activities and strategies that will align with the goals of advocacy put forth by such a definition. It is not enough to simply do a good job or have a good program. Focusing on the strong programs they create, school librarians must take opportunities to articulate the impact of their program to not only administrators and the teachers they work with, but to their larger school community and outside decision makers. A systemic, widely implemented advocacy plan is most successful in achieving advocacy goals.

Advocacy goes beyond the promotion of the school library program to a change of perception about the school library program and the role of the school librarian. This includes sharing with multiple stakeholders the unique role that a school librarian holds. The first step is educating each stakeholder group on the value that school library programs add to the school culture. If stakeholders and policymakers are to support a program, they need to understand the program's function and how it impacts the academic success of students.

Altering perceptions requires deliberate, consistent relationship-building efforts. Relationships must be built with local stakeholders, such as teachers and parent groups, so that these groups will in turn support the necessity of having a school library program. Building positive relationships with stakeholders within the school is a start in redefining the school library position. Teachers and parents will then become advocates willing to speak on behalf of the importance of the library for the success of students with other, outside stakeholders. School librarians with a successful, mature understanding of advocacy develop a plan to build effective relationships with multiple stakeholder groups both inside and outside the school community.

EFFECTIVE ADVOCACY ACTION

The first step to effective advocacy action is an articulated definition of what advocacy is for the school library program. With a clearer understanding of activities that constitute successful advocacy, school librarians will have a better sense of activities they can implement in their own practice. Establishing an advocacy plan and targeting varied stakeholder groups is essential for successful advocacy.

An advocacy message must be articulated to stakeholders in a way that demonstrates a positive effect on student achievement. One of the best ways to demonstrate school librarians' value is for them to articulate how they directly impact student learning. This can be achieved by showing the role the school library plays in the academic support and enhancement of students.

Successful advocacy is conducted when librarians advocate for students, not necessarily programs. Being able to demonstrate the program's worth to administration and decision makers is vital in helping these individuals understand it.

Using data on student achievement to substantiate claims and having a few facts ready to recite to stakeholders whenever there is an opportunity to discuss the library program is a good start. Librarians must be able to articulate the value of the educational impact they have on students and do so in a manner that is meaningful to their stakeholders. Parents and students must also be aware of the unique contribution school librarians make to the educational experience of students. School librarians must provide opportunities to articulate this message to these groups as well.

School librarians can stress the importance of their services by demonstrating they are indispensable resources. One way to achieve this is through the role of instructional partner and teacher. They must foster a relationship with other school personnel to demonstrate how their role facilitates student achievement. They can focus on the ways the role of the school librarian supports classroom curricula. The school librarian has expertise that only they can provide. This message should be conveyed through the advocacy message.

To facilitate stakeholder support, school librarians must be able to articulate the benefits of a strong school library program. This will ensure they are reaching multiple stakeholder groups to provide a perception of an essential library program led by an influential school librarian. The ultimate goal of advocacy is to gain support for exceptional school library programs that enhance student learning.

REFERENCES

American Association of School Librarians. *What Is Advocacy?* Retrieved from http://www.ala.org/aasl/advocacy/definitions.

Burns, E. (2014). Practitioner strategies for effective advocacy engagement in the USA. *Proceedings of IFLA WLIC Lyon, France*, pp. 16–22.

Ewbank, A. (July 2011). School librarians' advocacy for the profession: Results of a U.S. national survey. *School Libraries Worldwide, 17*(2), pp. 41–58.

8

The Intellectual Freedom Calendar: Another Advocacy Plan for the School Library

Helen R. Adams

When school begins, many school librarians look forward to celebrating Banned Books Week in September. It's certainly a good starting point, but advocating for intellectual freedom should not be confined to that single week. Ways to celebrate intellectual freedom throughout the entire school year are suggested in a month-by-month calendar in this chapter. Ideas and resources are included to highlight intellectual freedom and educate administrators, teachers, and other school staff, students, and parents about students' First Amendment right to use library resources and the confidentiality of students' library records.

AUGUST

Get the year off to a good start by focusing on the principal, the educational leader of the school who sets the tone. Make an appointment with the principal to review the materials selection policy and reconsideration procedures, and to describe the areas of the collection on which you will focus selections this school year. A principal who is knowledgeable about the selection of library resources and the reconsideration process will not easily yield to a demand to remove an "inappropriate" book or other resources from the school library without following the district's reconsideration process.

Arrange with the principal for an opportunity to speak to teachers about how library materials are selected, to solicit suggestions for library materials, and to review reconsideration procedures. Ensure transparency in materials selection by posting the materials selection policy and reconsideration procedures on the library's website.

SEPTEMBER

Train library staff, volunteers, and student assistants to keep student library records confidential. Discuss students' privacy when using the library and library record confidentiality with the principal, and schedule an after-school privacy information session for teachers. Model protecting the confidentiality of student library records when students, teachers, or the principal asks who has a library resource checked out.

Celebrate Banned Books Week the last week in September. Provide teachers with information for downloading the yearly promotional materials from the Banned Books Week website. Share the Association for Library Services to Children (ALSC) brochure, "Kids, Know Your Rights," with students. The American Library Association (ALA) website includes ideas for activities and displays. Where there is administrative resistance to the phrase "banned books," refocus the topic as promoting the "right to read." Create a display using the Freedom to Read Foundation's tag line "Free People Read Freely."

OCTOBER

Focus on parents! Establish regular communication with parents and community members through a "library column" in the school newsletter, on the library blog, or through the school library's social media channels. Provide information on such topics as checkout policies, online library resources accessible remotely by students at home, new books added to the collection, and upcoming special events such as a book fair.

Sponsor a library open house during parent/teacher conferences. Create bookmarks with the library's website address and information about grade-appropriate online resources students can access at home. Demonstrate the resources, and emphasize that the library provides information on many topics from varying points of view to teach students to critically evaluate information and reach their own conclusions.

NOVEMBER

If overly restrictive filtering is limiting access to educationally useful websites for instruction and student research, share concerns with the principal. Describe the educationally appropriate websites that are blocked by filters and inaccessible to faculty and students and suggest establishing a faculty committee to study the issue and make recommendations.

Request five minutes during faculty meetings to introduce a topic related to intellectual freedom. For example, highlight library resources and services to support students with physical, cognitive, and learning disabilities, or make a case for not restricting students' library reading choices to only those books on Accelerated Reader or other reading management program lists.

DECEMBER

Help students understand the First Amendment and their right to freedom of speech and expression. Collaborate with social studies teachers to observe the Bill of Rights Day on December 15, the date the first ten amendments to the U.S. Constitution were ratified. Make the connection between democracy and the need for well-informed citizens and have access to information from many perspectives.

Check out resources at the National Archives, the Library of Congress, and the National Constitution Center with its interactive "Bill of Rights Game".

Using holiday treats, lure teachers and the principal to peruse new books. Discuss additional needs of staff to support their curricula.

JANUARY

Get better acquainted with families by initiating a book club for parents. Introduce some of the best new contemporary children's and YA literature and candidly discuss the portrayal of youth, family, and societal issues. Emphasize how students learn to question and think more critically through their encounters with new ideas in books.

FEBRUARY

Post the *Library Bill of Rights* (LBOR) and the *Code of Ethics of the ALA* in the library, and be prepared for questions and "teachable moment" conversations with students, faculty, and the principal!

MARCH

Share "Minors and Online Activity: An Interpretation of the *Library Bill of Rights*" with the principal and offer to introduce faculty to selected online tools aimed at increasing students' technology literacy skills and personal expression online. Showcase the creations during spring parent/teacher conferences and gain support for the use of technology for instruction.

APRIL

April is School Library Month. Use the resources on the AASL website to plan activities. Tie the theme to intellectual freedom by sponsoring a contest for students to tell their stories of why the school library is important to them and how it supports their learning as "citizens in training." Share ideas and events with colleagues by posting them on the AASL *Knowledge Quest* blog, the school library social media pages, Instagram, or Twitter.

MAY

Spotlight students' right to privacy during ALA's Choose Privacy Week held annually during the first week of May or at another time during the school year. Visit ALA's Choose Privacy Every Day website to find privacy news and resources.

JUNE

Extend students' reading choices and information access during the summer. Team with the public library youth services librarian(s) to initiate a public library card signup for students and help kick off the summer reading program for children and teens.

Schedule a final meeting with the principal to report on library program accomplishments, including advocacy for intellectual freedom and privacy, and confer about program goals for next year.

ENCOURAGING THOUGHTS

School librarians are a major force in protecting intellectual freedom in their libraries and having allies who support students' access to information can make the school climate friendly to intellectual freedom. It may take years, but progress in educating about students' First Amendment and privacy rights in school libraries can be made one teacher, principal, parent, and student at a time.

9

Banned Books and Celebrating Our Freedom to Read

Chad Heck

Every year, during the last week of September, librarians, booksellers, and intellectual freedom advocates around the globe celebrate our freedom to read. As librarians, we have a responsibility from our Code of Ethics to "uphold the principles of intellectual freedom and resist all efforts to censor library resources" (American Library Association). As teachers, we have an obligation to teach our students about the importance of intellectual freedom and free speech. Banned Books Week, held during September each year, is the perfect opportunity to educate our students and teachers alike.

Books are considered challenged if there has been an effort to remove access to that book. A book is banned if that effort has been successful. During Banned Books Week, we celebrate our access to these banned and challenged books. One way to celebrate is to make students aware of materials in your library that have been challenged. Every year, the American Library Association (ALA) puts out a list of the ten most challenged books in libraries around the United States. That list is a great place to start to find materials to share with your students. For an even greater list, every few years, the ALA publishes a much larger guide by Robert P. Doyle entitled *Banned Books: Defending Our Freedom to Read.*

It is important to engage with students about banned and challenged books. Start with questions like, "Do you think that other people should be able to tell you what you can and cannot read?" Inevitably, a student or group of students will agree that teachers, librarians, or school administrators should be able to limit access to students. Discussion about controversial ideas is a fundamental principle of intellectual freedom. Having students openly discussing a controversial issue like library censorship is exactly what intellectual freedom is about. The librarian can then moderate a discussion between students about choosing materials that are right for them or having other people making those decisions for them.

Looking down the list of frequently banned or challenged materials, it becomes very apparent that books on sex, sexuality, or gender identity frequent the list. For high school students, after discussing with them about making book decisions for themselves, it is an interesting activity to flip the script on them. Ask the students about a book for younger grade students. One such book might be the classic book, *And Tango Makes Three* by Justin Richardson and Peter Parnell, illustrated by Henry Cole. High school students may not always be used to a picture book read aloud in the library—they love it. Reading about how Roy and Silo are different from the other penguins, and how they form a family by hatching an egg with penguin chick Tango, sends the message that families come in different configurations. Of course, in an intellectual freedom-rich environment, there will be differing opinions among high school students about whether or not this book is appropriate in the primary school library that may be attended by their younger siblings.

Students having a voice on this issue continues to grow and foster a spirit of intellectual freedom. The librarian should lay down some ground rules about respect and serve as the moderator. Sometimes, if one side of the issue is underrepresented, it is appropriate for the librarian to help that side form questions to give to the other side. Discussion can get quite spirited! When wrapping up the discussion, leave students with a thought such as: "While most believe that teachers, librarians, or administrators should not make decisions about what they read for them, is it okay for you to make that decision for younger students?" and "When there are some families in this school that look like Tango's family, is it okay for people to say that books about their families are inappropriate in the library?" The goal is not to change minds, rather to get the student to think about their positions.

Banned Books Week is a special time in libraries. It is a time to educate. It is a time to reflect and think. Most of all, it is a time to celebrate our freedom to read.

REFERENCE

American Library Association. *Code of Ethics*. Retrieved from http://www.ala.org/tools /ethics.

10

Reaching Out to Parents

Helen R. Adams

Cheryl, a K–12 librarian in the Midwest, recounts the following "parent story:" "Last May at the end of my second year in the library, our superintendent received a call from an unhappy parent. Her eighth grade daughter brought home a book that she did not approve of—in her words it was 'pornographic.' She was disgusted and wanted to know how this book ended up in a school library. She wanted to know how many other middle school kids had been allowed to read this 'trash.' Additionally, the parent wanted a committee, including her, to select all library books" (Online Post, October 1, 2010).

OTHER "STICKY" SITUATIONS

Parents can be supportive allies for school librarians, but they can also cause complications, as Cheryl learned. The concerns of some parents over specific library titles can lead them to ask the school librarian to take actions that clash with the *Library Bill of Rights* and the ALA *Code of Ethics*. For example, parents may request that their child(ren) not be allowed to check out books on such topics as Halloween, vampires, or sex education. Unfortunately, it may be nearly impossible for school library professionals to monitor what individual students are checking out. Automated circulation systems can "flag" a student's circulation record, but some libraries allow student self-checkout, creating the potential for a student to borrow books on the family's prohibited topics list. One solution that upholds intellectual freedom principles is to ask the parents to speak with their child(ren) about guidelines for personal reading choices that meet family values. The school librarian can emphasize that enforcement of family reading parameters is a matter between the parent and child, not the school librarian and student.

Another potential conflict can occur if a parent requests that an "inappropriate" book be removed from the collection. Some parents want only to be heard and have their viewpoints acknowledged, although others are serious about removing or restricting the book to protect all children. If the concern is not resolved informally, the school librarian should explain the reconsideration process to the complainant, who then has the option to challenge the book formally following district policy.

Given situations such as those described, how can a school librarian become a positive partner with parents to create lifelong readers and encourage the use of the school library?

PARENTAL RIGHTS AND COMMON GROUND

Parents are legally and morally responsible for caring for and educating their children including overseeing their child(ren)'s reading. "Access to Library Resources and Services for Minors: An Interpretation of the Library Bill of Rights" confirms this right and explains the relationships among the parent, child, and school librarian:

> . . . We affirm the responsibility and the right of all parents and guardians to guide their own children's use of the library and its resources and services. Libraries and their governing bodies cannot assume the role of parents or the functions of parental authority in the private relationship between parent and child. Libraries and their governing bodies shall ensure that only parents and guardians have the right and the responsibility to determine their children's—and only their children's—access to library resources. Parents and guardians who do not want their children to have access to specific library services, materials, or facilities should so advise their own children. Libraries and library governing bodies should not use rating systems to inhibit a minor's access to materials. (http://www.ala.org/advocacy/intfreedom/librarybill/interpretations/minors)

According to "Access to Resources and Services in the School Library: An Interpretation of the Library Bill of Rights," it is the responsibility of a school librarian to create and manage a program that ". . . serves as a point of voluntary access to information and ideas and as a learning laboratory for students as they acquire critical thinking and problem-solving skills needed in a pluralistic society" (http://www.ala.org/advocacy/intfreedom/librarybill/interpretations/accessresources). Additionally, the school librarian selects ". . . materials that support the intellectual growth, personal development, individual interests, and recreational needs of students" (http://www.ala.org/advocacy/intfreedom/librarybill/interpretations/accessresources). With clearly defined roles and responsibilities, parents and the school librarian can be good partners because each wants students to be successful.

PUTTING OUT THE WELCOME MAT

Parental interest in their children's development can be used proactively to educate them about quality children and young adults' literature, as well as minors' use of a school library. Discussions between the librarian and parents can foster the concept of giving students personal choice in what they read, connecting "choice" to exploring new ideas and diverse viewpoints as well as developing literacy skills.

The school librarian can employ these strategies to reach out and engage parents:

- Post the district's materials selection policy on the library's webpage.
- Initiate a parent reading group that meets regularly to learn about new books that interest children and young adults, trends in children's and adolescent literature, ideas for helping children select books commensurate with their social, emotional, and cognitive development, and skills for discussing books with their children (Adams 2008, 72).

- Create a school newsletter column aimed at parents with suggested titles in various genres and tips for sharing the books with children, preteens, and teens (Adams 2008, 72).
- Organize a "Back to School" program for parents and students featuring an author, break-out sessions for book sharing discussion, and a book fair (Adams 2008, 72).
- Present a "show and tell" new titles booktalk for parents at a parent/teacher organization meeting. Describe how materials are selected using the district's material selection policy (Adams 2008, 72).
- Develop a parent collection and add books encouraging parents to develop lifelong readers . . . (Adams 2008, 72).
- Open the library for family browsing and checkout during parent-teacher conferences (Adams 2008, 213).

During discussions with parents about what students are reading, the school librarian walks a fine line between promoting children and young adults' self-selection in reading choices while at the same time acknowledging parental rights to guide their offspring's reading. The school librarian must also be cognizant that grandparents are raising many children, and these older adults may find it difficult to accept the "edgier" books. Reaffirming the parent's (or grandparent's) right to guide their child's reading may allay personal concerns over individual titles and begin to build the trust and respect necessary for a positive partnership.

REFERENCES

Adams, H. R. (2008). *Ensuring Intellectual Freedom and Access to Information in the School Library Media Program*. Santa Barbara, CA: Libraries Unlimited.

American Library Association. *Access to Library Resources and Services for Minors: An Interpretation of the Library Bill of Rights*. Retrieved from http://www.ala.org /advocacy/intfreedom/librarybill/interpretations/minors.

American Library Association. *Access to Resources and Services in the School: An Interpretation of the Library Bill of Rights*. Retrieved from http://www.ala.org/advocacy /intfreedom/librarybill/interpretations/accessresources.

11

Library Books and Reading-Level Labels: Unfettered, Guided, or Constrained Choice?

Maria Cahill

For our November 2017 question of the month, we asked school librarians to select the statement that most closely indicated their position on labeling books with reading levels. The majority of the 229 participants who responded harbor beliefs aligned with the AASL (2011) position statement on labeling books by reading level and do not support the practice. School librarians explained their philosophies as follows:

> I believe that labeling books by reading level is among the most troubling and offensive practices in education, whether or not it's in a classroom or a library. Besides the fact that it can stigmatize a child who has a reading disability, it flies in the face of the research that states that freedom to choose books is one of the cornerstones of developing independent readers.
>
> Ugh—labeling books!!! Let kids read whatever they want to read. If they can't read it, they can look at the pictures or just feel important with a "big" book. We'll catch them with a better choice the next go round. Teach them to love the library first and see it as a place to get the things they want!

Another small percentage of the respondents do not label books, but that is more due to contextual factors than philosophical beliefs.

> I write reading levels on the inside cover and/or spine. We do not currently do AR [Accelerated Reader] but I want to be prepared if we ever go back to it.

More than one-sixth of the school librarians who participated in the survey expressed a rift between their beliefs and their practices: these librarians do not support labeling books, yet this is not the battle they choose to fight with other stakeholders.

> I have the smallest colored dot on the spine near the bottom to be the most subtle. I did not choose AR [Accelerated Reader] testing for our school, but our principal wanted it.

Nearly 10% of those responding to the survey indicated that they choose to label books by reading level because they believe doing so supports children in making informed choices that will eventually help them become proficient readers.

> Though I do label books with broad AR [Accelerated Reader] color codes, I also place an importance on showing students that the number only means how hard the words are to decode and not about whether the story is complicated and might need a more mature reader . . . [F]or students who do need help narrowing down a target comprehension level, the guide is there.
> . . . We are about the business of helping children learn to read. We do not put them in a life raft and set them adrift in the ocean of available reading material. We guide and help them.

As is expected, given the nuanced nature of school libraries, a significant number of school librarians selected "Other." Many of these respondents indicated that they do not label the outsides of the book but that they do write a level on the inside and/or indicate the reading level in the MARC record.

School librarians currently engaging in book labeling practices might want to consider revisiting the AASL (2011) position statement on labeling books by reading level and pay close attention to the following: "Student browsing behaviors can be profoundly altered with the addition of external reading level labels."

REFERENCE

American Association of School Librarians. (2011). *Position Statement on Labeling Books with Reading Levels.* Retrieved from http://www.ala.org/aasl/advocacy/resources /statements/labeling.

12

Computerized Reading Programs: Intellectual Freedom

Helen R. Adams

Some school librarians are concerned about the possible consequences that computerized reading programs, such as Accelerated Reader (AR), may have on students' selection of reading materials and their privacy. Although depending on how a program is implemented, here's a disquieting story from an elementary librarian:

> As the 5th graders enter the library, the teacher announces, "Find an AR book that is on your reading level." While the class browses, one student, whispers to me, "Can you help me find a book?" Jim is required to read AR books near his AR-tested 3rd grade reading level. Because the spines of the books are labeled with reading levels, Jim is embarrassed and avoids browsing with his peers, most of whom are reading titles many grade levels above his. Jim comes to me each week, and I know what he might want—a short chapter book that would be of interest to a middle grade boy reading "below" his AR tested reading level, one that doesn't scream "picture book." I discreetly lead him to a book suitable for his reading assignment. (Margaret, email message to author, June 9, 2011)

CHOICE VERSUS READING LEVELS AND POINTS

Even though there are thousands of books in the collection, Jim's choice is limited. For his class assignment, he may select only a title within his reading level range and for which an AR test is available. After Jim completes the book, he will take a test to earn "points." The "points" translate into classroom rewards such as a pizza party and also affect individual student grades. Jim doesn't want to be excluded from a class treat, nor does he want a poor grade.

The restriction of choosing a book within his reading level combined with the lure of earning "points" changes Jim's search from finding an appealing read to a hunt for a book with the greatest number of points, even if the book does not engage his interest. Although the library's collection supports classroom instruction, teachers should ensure that program assignment guidelines allow students to seek books that pique their intellectual curiosity and correlate with their social and emotional levels. From Margaret's perspective, "AR advocates say that labels on library books will offer students reading success. But I see some kids feeling singled out and cautious about browsing with much of the fun gone" (Margaret, email message to author, June 9, 2011). Additionally, reading levels do not always correlate to a student's emotional or social levels.

HOW LABELING AFFECTS STUDENT PRIVACY

Traditionally, library books are labeled on the spine for subject organization and easier location. Adding the reading level of the book on its spine allows others to view the numbers and, thus, threatens student privacy. Only the student, the child's parents, the teacher, and the librarian should know the student's reading capabilities. Jim's reluctance to have his peers know his reading level is understandable. Knowledge of a child's reading level can cause classmates to tease or ridicule a child who reads less skillfully. School librarians, therefore, have ethical and legal responsibilities to protect a student's privacy related to library materials.

UNINTENDED CONSEQUENCES

In addition to restricting choice and privacy issues, some librarians are being urged to arrange library collections according to reading levels. This nonstandard shelving practice makes it difficult for library staff and students to find individual titles. Additionally, students using a public library may be confused about how to find a book, since those collections are not "leveled." Maintaining the confidentiality of a child's reading level is even more difficult in a leveled collection.

SEEKING A SOLUTION

Is there an answer for school librarians? They can consider these steps:

- Resist placing reading level labels on book spines and "leveling" the library,
- Advocate for district policies that take into account privacy concerns, and
- Educate the principal and teachers about students' First Amendment right to freely choose library materials.

Whatever the individual school librarian's stand may be on this issue, there should still be reflection on how implementation of a computerized reading program impacts students' intellectual freedom.

RESOURCES

- American Association of School Librarians. *AASL Position Statement on Labeling Books by Reading Levels.* Retrieved from http://www.ala.org/aasl /advocacy/resources/statements/labeling.
- American Library Association. *Questions and Answers on Labeling and Ratings Systems.* Retrieved from http://www.ala.org/advocacy/intfreedom /labelingratingqa.
- American Library Association. *Restricted Access to Library Materials: An Interpretation of the Library Bill of Rights.* Retrieved from http://www.ala .org/advocacy/intfreedom/librarybill/interpretations/restrictedaccess.

13

Protecting Students' Rights and Keeping Your Job

Helen R. Adams

How do you reply to a fellow school librarian who states, "If my principal tells me to remove a book from the shelves, I'm going to do it. I need this job." Or, when discussing book selection, a librarian in a neighboring district comments, "I'll never buy those titles. There would be complaints, and my principal already thinks libraries can be run by aides." It is understandable that school librarians are feeling threatened as school districts across the United States cut library positions and replace certificated librarians with assistants. Will standing up for students' intellectual freedom put a school librarian's job at additional risk?

FINDING THE BALANCE

In today's economy, there are no guarantees for any position. Championing students' access to information reflecting diverse points of view, speaking against overly aggressive filtering practices, defending students' privacy when using library materials, advocating for students with special needs, and resisting censorship raises the visibility of the school librarian and may make some administrators uneasy, especially when scrutiny of schools is high. Does this mean that school librarians should step back from advocacy of minors' rights in school libraries? No, it is just the opposite; it is important to continue to consciously integrate the tenets of the ALA *Code of Ethics* and the *Library Bill of Rights* into daily practice. How can a school librarian find the balance between protecting students' First Amendment right to access information and risking job loss? Two common sense strategies strengthen the librarian's position: establishing a positive relationship with the principal and building a network of intellectual freedom supporters.

TARGET THE PRINCIPAL

The principal has huge responsibilities and will appreciate a library professional who takes time for regular communications about current library issues. Be proactive from your first day on the job. As a starting point, go through the district's selection policy with the principal—describe how selection is accomplished, outline areas of the collection that need strengthening, and explain your plan for the upcoming year. Annually review the reconsideration process together before an oral complaint or challenge occurs. Over time, teach the principal about students' First Amendment rights to read and research topics in the school library and how students' evaluation of unbiased information contributes to their education as "citizens in training." These actions and others will create a positive, collaborative relationship with the principal.

BUILDING AN INTELLECTUAL FREEDOM NETWORK

Think strategically about creating a network of allies who oppose censorship and support the intellectual freedom principles and policies on which effective school library programs are based. Potential supporters who can help protect minors' intellectual freedom include:

- Faculty: Be visible in your school, and make it a priority to communicate information about the library's services, resources, and policies to teachers, especially new staff. Create an open selection process by inviting teachers to recommend library materials for their curricular areas. Those who participate are likely to be supportive if concerns about library resources arise.
- Students: Young adults can also be part of the intellectual freedom network that protects their right to read and receive information in a school library. They can be vocal and effective voices when a popular book is threatened with removal.
- The Community: Reach out to parents, extended families, and community members through the library's website, a library newsletter, and special events such as Internet safety programs and book fairs. Give presentations to local groups, and solicit volunteers to work in the library. Make certain the community is aware of the school's selection policy, and help families understand the importance of students having choices in their library selections.
- Public Librarians: Build a collegial relationship with youth services staff by planning jointly sponsored activities such as a public library card signup campaign. Public library staff can provide a sounding board and professional support in difficult times.

FINAL THOUGHTS

Despite a school librarian's best efforts, a principal may, for example, remove a book without following policy, causing intellectual freedom principles and minors' rights to be compromised. In those instances, you must be content knowing that you have done all that is possible. Realizing that there will be other advocacy opportunities and challenges ahead, regroup and continue to work with the principal and library allies.

ESSENTIAL DOCUMENTS

- *Access to Resources & Services in the School Library: An Interpretation of the Library Bill of Rights*: http://www.ala.org/advocacy/intfreedom/librarybill /interpretations/accessresources.
- *ALA Code of Ethics*: http://www.ala.org/tools/ethics.
- *Library Bill of Rights*: http://www.ala.org/advocacy/intfreedom/librarybill.

Part III

Policies and Procedures

"To build up a library is to create a life.
It's never just a random collection of books."

—Carlos María Domínguez, Author

14

Coping with Mandated Restrictions on Intellectual Freedom in K–12 Schools

Sara E. Wolf

INTRODUCTION

Within the K–12 school arena, the two main constituencies having primary concern regarding intellectual freedom are the teachers and students. School librarians serve in a unique position within schools, in that they support both teachers and students in the pursuit of information access in schools. The American Library Association (ALA) has published several statements pertaining to intellectual freedom that are used as support in situations involving the restriction of information access to students. They can be briefly described as stating that all individuals have the right to free access to information without regard to "origin, age, background, or views" (ALA 1996, para. 5). This right is seen as part and parcel of the freedoms of speech and expression granted to U.S. citizens by the Constitution.

This sounds as if students and teachers have access to any information they would like to have in order to prepare lessons and learn lessons. Wouldn't that be nice? One would assume that access to information would be an essential part of our educational system. The reality is, however, that there are laws and policies in effect that can restrict what information is available to students and teachers in K–12 schools. Selection policies, acceptable use policies, circulation policies, as well as federal laws and acts, all place restrictions of some sort on the access to information by students and teachers. How can the ideal of free and open access to information be achieved in an environment governed by policies and laws? The school librarian has a challenge in merging these two responsibilities.

SELECTION POLICIES

Selection policies guide school librarians in the acquisition of materials. Ideally, the selection policy addresses materials in a variety of formats, but many selection policies focus primarily on print resources or resources that are available through online databases such as Alabama's Virtual Library. A cursory examination of selection policies available online shows that few policies explicitly address the selection of websites (e.g., to be included as links on the school website). Multimedia resources may be addressed, but typically in language that implies the multimedia is computer software packages. Online games, informational sites, or video links are seldom addressed. A well-written selection policy will also include provisions for the handling of challenged materials.

Most selection policies examined contain language that specifically addresses intellectual freedom. In some form or fashion, most of them state that in cases of challenged materials, the principle of intellectual freedom will be defended (rather than the specific item that has been challenged). Therefore, the question becomes, how does a policy that supports the concept of intellectual freedom restrict the intellectual freedom of students or teachers?

Methods of Restriction

Selection policies may restrict intellectual freedom by failing to address the fact that information formats will change and develop over time. Policies that use format-restrictive or vague language leave the policy open to interpretation that might conflict with the principle of intellectual freedom. Most selection policies are written using language that is intended to be as inclusive, in terms of format, as possible. But, as with many policies, they are sometimes developed and then not revisited for a number of years. Technological advances are such that a reevaluation or revision of these policies is important in order to maintain currency of language.

Methods of Support

Selection policies also support the intellectual freedom of students and teachers. When sections communicate the intent to support the American Library Association's *Library Bill of Rights* (http://www.ala.org/advocacy/intfreedom/librarybill) and the intent to select materials that range in viewpoint and format, selection policies provide the basis for the exploration of a variety of ideas and topics by both students and teachers. Specifically, statements such as:

- Provide materials that will enrich and support the curriculum, taking into consideration the varied interests, abilities, learning needs, learning styles, and maturity levels of the students served.
- Provide materials for teachers and students that will encourage growth in knowledge, and that will help to develop literary, cultural and aesthetic appreciation, and ethical standards (Hawaii State Department of Education, Policies and Procedures Section).
- Provide explicit support for the inquiry into topics that may not expressly fall under the direct instruction within a particular school's curriculum.

Yet, this language also acknowledges the responsibility of information seekers to carry out information requests within ethical standards.

Coping in the School Library

School librarians can help combat the restrictions of selection policies, as well as ensure that the policy will remain supportive of intellectual freedom, by examining them for current language. Policies that require revision should undergo that process according to school and district procedures. Language that acknowledges the shifting formats of information should be included, so as multimedia becomes more ubiquitous in the form of audio clips, podcasts, video clips, and other information sources, the policy does not have to be subject to as frequent of a revision cycle.

Second, school librarians can regularly review selection policies in place for currency in relation to the current school environment in which they work. A regular revision may not be needed, but a regular review will help identify areas that can be updated before an issue occurs.

Two well-written selection policies are available from the Hawaii Department of Education (http://boe.hawaii.gov/policies/Board%20Policies/Hawaii%20State%20 Public%20Library%20System%20Collection%20Development%20Policy.pdf) and the Central Fulton School District (PA) board of education (see sections 109 and 109.1: https://go.boarddocs.com/pa/cful/Board.nsf/Public?open&id=policies#).

ACCEPTABLE USE POLICIES

Acceptable use policies govern how students, teachers, and staff will use computing resources in schools. Typically, an acceptable use policy will spell out that resources should be used to support instructional activities directly or possibly indirectly related to the school curriculum, and any consequences for violating the policy. Well-written acceptable use policies provide explicit guidelines regarding the use of network resources as well as the expected behavior of network users. They spell out not only consequences for misuse but also a method or procedure to follow for the modifications of network use permission (e.g., the method for having a particular website unblocked by the school Internet filter).

Methods of Restriction

Acceptable use policies can restrict intellectual freedom when parents elect not to sign them, thus disallowing access to Internet materials to their child or children. Some acceptable use policies include language that acknowledges the fact that sometimes information on the Internet can be offensive, and that while the teacher and other school officials do everything to prevent students from seeing that information, sometimes students will (by accident) come across offensive material. For the parent who is especially wary of this type of accident occurring, not signing the policy, thereby ensuring their child will not be permitted to access the Internet effectively, removes intellectual and physical access to information for that child. As information is made available in electronic form, more students will be required to use effective information-seeking skills in order to make evaluative decisions regarding authority, currency, and applicability of online information. Preventing students from accessing information in this format may effectively bar students from participating in required school-based activities, or even being able to demonstrate mastery of certain instructional objectives.

Also consider that while many acceptable use policies contain language that says access to network resources is a privilege not a right, it would be hard to say the same about access to textbooks during the regular school day. When instructional materials are presented in an online format, restricting access to the Internet effectively prevents students from having access to the planned instruction.

Coping in the School Library

When a school librarian has to mediate the information-seeking behavior of a student who does not have permission to access the Internet, she may need to be creative in this endeavor. A conversation with the parent to help alleviate concerns would likely be in order. A modified plan of access for that child to complete required class activities might need to be developed.

Two well-written acceptable use policies are available from the Kentucky Department of Education (https://education.ky.gov/districts/tech/pages/acceptable-use -districts.aspx) and the Bedford County school district in Virginia (https://bedford .sharpschool.net/departments/tech/aup_student).

CIRCULATION POLICIES

Circulation policies define the scope of borrowing privileges for members of the school community. Aspects such as length of borrowing period, number of items permitted, and the consequences for overdue or lost items are described in a well-written circulation policy.

Methods of Restriction

Circulation policies may restrict the information freedom of students, especially when they include language that limits students of certain ages or grades (normally the younger students) to only a certain section of the library, or restricts students in their borrowing outside of a school-adopted reading incentive program. It is tempting to place limits on student borrowing practices in cases where the library collection is limited due to budget constraints, outdated items, or unexpected increases in school enrollment.

Coping in the School Library

This is why it is important that circulation policies be developed by school librarians in such a way that students have open access to information within the school library as well as information accessed from the school library. Sometimes, teachers will impose a circulation policy on students that restricts items students are able to borrow or access.

In these situations, it is incumbent on the school librarian to negotiate with the student and teacher an alternative to allow for the freedom to access information for personal interest as well as to meet the instructional needs in the classroom.

By far, written policies of all varieties that have been vetted by school boards and other governing agencies address the need for free and open access to information for students. Most policies use inclusive language that does not discriminate on the basis of grade or age, race, culture, or other characteristic. Most policies provide clear guidelines for acceptable and unacceptable behaviors and practices and clearly delineate the consequences for violating the policy. Most school-based policies support intellectual freedom for the students and teachers in that building.

FEDERAL LAWS AND ACTS

However, most school policies also make statements that can be interpreted broadly as, "we intend to follow federal and state laws," or "we intend not to violate federal or state laws." But what do those federal laws actually say? What restrictions do they impose on schools and school districts regarding information access to students?

According to the Federal Communications Commission (FCC 2017), the Children's Internet Protection Act (CIPA) requires that schools receiving E-rate funding have and enforce policies for the monitoring of online activities by minors, but does not require the tracking of Internet use by minors. Those two requirements seem contradictory, don't they? Also, CIPA addresses the access to pictures and other harmful-to-minors material that students may access in schools. Such material should be blocked or there should be policies and procedures in place to ensure that this material is unavailable. But, the question remains, "who determines whether material is harmful or not?" Is the moniker of "harmful" one that can be applied in a standard manner across and between different communities? Or, does it vary by location, district, state, or region?

Methods of Restriction

CIPA, a controversial federal law, can restrict intellectual freedom by placing restrictions on the access of information by students. Broad and vague language can seem contradictory and thus be either narrowly interpreted or incorrectly interpreted by well-meaning K–12 district-level administrators and school principals.

While CIPA does include language that allows for the disabling of filters for "bona fide research or other lawful purposes" (FCC 2017, sec. "What CIPA Requires," para. 4) by adults, it does not mention the same provision for the research purposes of students. The implication of this omission is that the research needs of adults are somehow more worthy than the research needs of students.

Younger students may or may not have provocative research interests, but as they progress through the K–12 curriculum, their interests will change as will their research needs. The topics that high school students discuss may fall under those that would be blocked by some filters in place in many schools. CIPA does not have language to allow for the filters to be unblocked in these situations.

Coping in the School Library

One of the best ways a school librarian can cope with CIPA in the school library is to establish a relationship with the proper authority in the school or district who is able to disable the school filter. Better yet, *become* that person of authority in the building. This way, students who have legitimate research interests or questions and teachers who are conducting personal research in the creation of curriculum-related materials will not have to wait an undue amount of time in order to have potential sites unblocked (if, indeed, they are blocked). Also, by being the person who can unblock filtered websites, the school librarian creates an atmosphere where the pursuit of information is primary and one where students and teachers have a reliable source of assistance during information-seeking activities.

POLICIES AND INTELLECTUAL FREEDOM

In general, school-based policies intend to support the intellectual freedom of the students and teachers who are required to abide by them. In order to ensure that these policies uphold the principles of intellectual freedom, a school librarian should:

- Have a plan for regular review and revision (if necessary) of each policy.
- Be a part of the team that develops policies that are implemented at the district level (if appropriate).

- Work with administrators, teachers, students, and parents to ensure that all parties understand the policies.
- Demonstrate a commitment to intellectual freedom through daily activities and guidance provided to students and teachers.
- Be an advocate for students and teachers who have information needs that may be negatively impacted by the overly restrictive enforcement of policies or laws.

REFERENCES

American Library Association. (2019). *Library Bill of Rights*. Retrieved from http://www
.ala.org/advocacy/intfreedom/librarybill.
Federal Communications Commission (FCC). (2017). *Children's Internet Protection Act
(CIPA)*. Retrieved from https://www.fcc.gov/consumers/guides/childrens-internet
-protection-act.
Hawaii State Department of Education. *School Libraries*. Retrieved from http://www
.hawaiipublicschools.org/BeyondTheClassroom/LibraryServices/Pages/home
.aspx.

15

The Materials Selection Policy: Defense against Censorship

Helen R. Adams

Picture this scenario. Your principal leaves a note in your mailbox directing you to take library resource off the shelf because a parent has complained about it. You suffer heart-in-the-throat panic and then stop to think. Remembering the *Code of Ethics*, you realize removing the resource is not the right thing to do. Isn't there a policy to follow in case of a complaint? After a frantic search, you find it in your library policy manual and, thankfully, read through the passages describing the process for reconsidering materials. Initially, the procedures call for trying to resolve the parent's concern informally. No further action should occur unless a formal, written request for reconsideration of the resource is submitted by the complaining party. Other words in the policy stand out, "The challenged material will not be removed from circulation during the reconsideration process." You determine that speaking to the principal as quickly as possible is your next step.

Using this scenario as a starting point, ask yourself:

- Does your school have an officially approved materials selection policy that includes reconsideration procedures?
- Can you locate a copy easily?
- Are you well informed about the various parts of the policy?
- Is the policy current or more than five years old?
- Are the reconsideration procedures detailed enough to offer guidance to you, the principal, and the reconsideration committee during a challenge?
- Is your principal knowledgeable about the policy and what to do when a complaint is voiced?

These are not irrelevant questions since a materials selection policy is a working document, and a challenge could occur in your school library at any time.

A formally approved materials selection policy with review procedures is the legal basis for selection and reconsideration of all instructional materials used within a school including school library resources. Some states, including Wisconsin and Arkansas, require public schools to have materials selection policies and procedures for reconsideration approved by their governing boards. In addition to providing guidance to the school librarian, the selection policy gives an explanation to the broad school community as to why certain materials are chosen and others are not.

A materials selection policy contains criteria for selection of all types of materials for the collection from books to DVDs to eBooks to computer software to electronic databases. It provides guidance on the selection of potentially controversial resources. It communicates the school's support for intellectual freedom by endorsing professional association documents such as the American Library Association (ALA) *Library Bill of Rights* and the *Freedom to Read*, a joint statement of the ALA and the Association of American Publishers. The policy opposes censorship in any form referring to students' rights to receive information under the First Amendment. Significantly, it also includes the process through which materials will be reviewed by a reconsideration committee if a formal written complaint is received.

The selection policy contains the seeds for defense in case of a challenge. When selection criteria are consciously considered while identifying resources to be purchased, those same criteria can be used to justify the acquisition if a formal challenge is filed. Being able to demonstrate how the challenged resource meets approved selection criteria is a powerful argument for retention of the resource. Additionally, drawing on the policy's statements of support for intellectual freedom, the reconsideration committee must consider how the withdrawal of the challenged title would affect the First Amendment rights of students to access information or read freely.

A policy, however, is only as effective as the people in charge. If school personnel follow policy, a book or other library resource will not be removed from the collection without due process. But, if the principal is afraid of challenges and gives in to pressure to remove an item from the collection without following the reconsideration process, the policy is useless. School administrators or board of education members who do not follow written policy may leave themselves open to legal action.

If your school does not have an approved selection policy, take immediate action by discussing this situation with the principal. A school without a selection policy is vulnerable to complaints about library resources with no guidance on how to proceed and little legal basis for protecting students' First Amendment rights.

Because policies do not have an infinite shelf life, every school or district should develop a schedule for the systematic review of all school library policies to ensure currency. A three-year policy review cycle would be a useful time span. In three years, resources in new formats may be available requiring some modification in selection criteria, selection tools may change, or acquisitions procedures may be altered.

There are several resources that may be useful to you in developing or revising a materials selection policy including:

- American Library Association, Office for Intellectual Freedom. *Selection & Reconsideration Policy Toolkit for Public, School, & Academic Libraries.* Retrieved from http://www.ala.org/tools/challengesupport/selectionpolicy toolkit.
- Marcis, M. A. (2016). *The Collection Program in Schools: Concepts and Practices.* 6th ed. Santa Barbara, CA: Libraries Unlimited.

16

Ten Steps to Creating a Selection Policy That Matters

April M. Dawkins

Have you ever gotten a surprise package of books in your library that included a note saying, "For your collection"? At first, you're excited that someone sent you free books, but upon closer examination you begin to question if it would be a good idea to add the donation to the collection at all. Just as you ask your students to examine sources of information they want to include in their research projects, you should be asking questions about donations, especially if they are unsolicited ones.

This year in North Carolina, many middle and high school librarians posted to the school library association listserv questioning a book that appeared to have been sent by the Department of Public Instruction. Upon investigation, it turned out that a former governor had donated a book about his time as governor. Once additional information was shared about the book, an interesting discussion ensued over whether the book should be added to library collections. Several questions were raised: Would it provide a balanced perspective? Would we need to find other selections to provide balance? Do we have policies in our libraries about gifts and donations and how they are to be handled?

The final question is perhaps the most important: Do we have selection policies that help guide us in our decision-making? If we do, how closely do we follow these policies, and are there gaps, like a lack of a gift or donation policy, that make our lives more difficult? Policies are important because they help us make sure we are providing access to good information for our students. And, access is a fundamental component of who we are as librarians. The new *National Standards for School Librarians* includes intellectual freedom as a common belief and a right for every learner:

> Learners have the freedom to speak and hear what others have to say, rather than allowing others to control their access to ideas and information; the school librarian's responsibility is to develop these dispositions in learners, educators, and all other members of the learning community. (https://standards.aasl.org/beliefs/)

55

At the core of intellectual freedom is the idea that school libraries and school librarians must provide access to ideas and information for our students. This is why policies matter. Selection policies are essential to providing access.

Several years ago, I was asked to join a group of librarians from public, academic, and school libraries to work on updating the American Library Association's *Workbook for Selection Policy Writing*. The workbook was created in 1998. I think all of us involved were aware of the need for an update. There were two big issues: It reflected a view of libraries that was almost entirely print or text-based, and it was designed as a guide for writing policies for school libraries only. The new *Selection & Reconsideration Policy Toolkit for Public, School, and Academic Libraries* is now available online at the American Library Association website (http://www.ala.org/tools/challengesupport/selectionpolicytoolkit).

It is a wonderful resource including sample text for each type of library, which can be adapted for each library's unique characteristics. So, take this new resource as an opportunity to either update your existing policy or write a new one! Before you begin, you first should determine exactly which materials are being governed by this policy. Is it only for library materials? Or do other instructional materials or even classroom collections fall under its guidelines as well. Here are some areas you should include and some questions you should consider during your policy-writing/revising process.

Does your policy include your library's mission?

You always want to include your mission. It can be used to justify your purchases and your decisions to retain materials in the collection if they are called into question.

Is there a section with a statement or explanation of the purpose of the policy and the school library's role in supporting intellectual freedom?

This is a great section that explains why selection is so important and why intellectual freedom and unfettered access to materials are an essential right of all students. Here is an opportunity to explain the difference between selection and censorship. This is your chance to promote the *Library Bill of Rights.*

Who is ultimately responsible for the selection of materials for the library?

If you are revising your district's selection policy, you'll want to make sure the section on responsibility clearly states the importance of your role as the professional expert in selection.

What are the procedures, including the use of reviewing sources, that will be followed in selecting materials?

You'll want to review any processes involved in selecting materials. Is there a role for student, parent, faculty, and staff input? Unfortunately, I've seen policies and procedures where the students are never even mentioned! Student access and input should be front and center in your policy. Another area of concern is the review and vetting of materials to determine if they should be added to the collection. Try to avoid including a list of acceptable reviewing sources or a minimum number of positive reviews. While sometimes helpful, this can also serve as a barrier for materials reflecting diverse cultures and viewpoints that might not be reviewed in traditional trade publications. If you want to include a list, make sure it is broad and suggested (not required) and that it includes nontraditional sources for review such as blogs.

Does your policy reflect more than just a print collection and provide guidance for nonprint materials, databases, and digital curation?

We aren't just collecting print books any more. Your policy should reflect that and be flexible enough to allow for new formats as they arise.

How are potentially controversial materials selected?

It's important to acknowledge in your policy that materials may sometimes cover sensitive or controversial topics and that you have procedures for selecting them. You want to make sure these materials are not automatically excluded from consideration.

How are gifts and donations handled?

It's wonderful to receive a donation or a gift, but it's important that you have clearly outlined in your policy that those gifts and donations will go through the same selection procedures as other materials. You want to make it clear that being donated doesn't mean an item will be automatically added to the collection or kept forever. You don't want to end up with someone's entire *National Geographic* magazine collection from 1900 onward!

What are the procedures for maintaining the collection and removing outdated, worn, or inaccurate items?

Weeding . . . it can be controversial, but it's necessary. This is one topic that those outside of the library really don't understand: Why are school librarians throwing away books?! Use this opportunity to explain why it's important to maintain the collection and remove materials. You should also explain why most of those materials should not be passed on to classrooms.

Is there information that outlines the policy and procedures for reconsideration of materials?

Provide a general overview about removing materials from the collection, including the need for a formal procedure and review process. The reconsideration procedures themselves will need to have special review. They are typically in a separate section at the end of the selection policy itself.

Is there a timeline or guidance provided for revising the policy itself?

All policies should include a date of adoption and guidelines for revising the policy. If this is a district level policy, does your district allow individual school-level policies? If not, is the district policy broad enough to be applicable to all types of schools in your district?

As you are revising or writing your policy, keep in mind that its purpose is to provide access to quality resources and information for students. Are there procedures or guidelines in your policy that might be barriers to student access? Explore other school and district selection policies to see how these issues are being handled. And, be sure to take advantage of the new Toolkit for sample language and additional items to consider.

17

Ten Steps to Creating Reconsideration Policies and Procedures That Matter

April M. Dawkins

What you have been dreading since library school has happened. Your principal emailed to let you know that a parent had requested a book be removed from the library because it was "inappropriate for any student to read." And you panic. How do you stand up for every student's right to read and keep your job? How do you avoid becoming defensive in the face of someone questioning your morality and professionalism? There really is only one way to prepare—with policies and procedures that support you in times of crisis, so you don't have to panic.

In 2018, I wrote "Ten Steps to Creating a Selection Policy That Matters." Step 9's question was:

Is there information that outlines the policy and procedures for reconsideration of materials?

Provide a general overview about removing materials from the collection, including the need for a formal procedure and review process. The reconsideration procedures themselves will need to have special review. They are typically in a separate section at the end of the selection policy itself (Dawkins 2018).

Now, here are ten steps to creating reconsideration policies and procedures that matter. These are the questions you should think about as you and your district either create or revisit your procedures. And always remember that you should not attempt to revise policies or procedures during a challenge.

Do the reconsideration procedures include guiding principles while undergoing a challenge?

Your policies and procedures should include statements about diversity of content, formats, and ideas, the right to access information, and the freedom to read. Inclusion of the *Library Bill of Rights* and the *Freedom to Read* Statement of the American Library Association (ALA) is a great idea. These guiding principles might be included in the selection policy or as part of the reconsideration procedures. For a good outline of what to include, take a look at the *Selection & Reconsideration Toolkit for Public, School, and Academic Libraries* (http://www.ala.org/tools/challengesupport/selectionpolicy toolkit).

Do your procedures include information on how to handle an informal/oral complaint versus a formal/written complaint?

A parent, teacher, or administrator may voice a concern about an item in the library collection without wishing to go through the formal process for reconsideration. You should be prepared to discuss informal concerns with parents, patrons, teachers, administrators—well, anyone who might say they are uncomfortable with an item in your collection. The policies and procedures for reconsideration should be shared during this conversation. However, an honest, open, and respectful conversation will often lead to resolution of the complaint without a formal reconsideration process taking place. But, be sure that your policy explicitly states that an item cannot be removed without a formal request for reconsideration being submitted and a complete process being undertaken.

Is there information about the timeline to be followed?

You really don't want things to drag on forever. Therefore, your procedures should include a timeline for response to a complaint, committee proceedings, and final determination. Keep the timeline reasonable and remember that committee members will need to obtain and read the challenged material in its entirety prior to discussion. Your procedures might also include a clause that stipulates challenged materials cannot be challenged again within a certain time frame (maybe five years).

Is there information about who to contact in your school, district, as well as external resources for support?

The procedures should include who within your school and district should receive copies of the request for reconsideration and who is ultimately in charge of the reconsideration process. It's also helpful to keep school district public relations or media contacts in the loop about potential challenges and outcomes from reconsideration proceedings so that they may field any press questions. Information about challenges and reconsidered materials is subject to Freedom of Information Act (FOIA) requests. Therefore, it's important to determine where information about challenges is housed in your district. Additionally, you will want to know about the resources available to you through your state library, your state school library organization, and ALA's Office for Intellectual Freedom.

Is there information included about who has the standing to challenge content in the library or as part of the curriculum?

Within the policy, you'll want to include who can actually challenge materials that are part of the curriculum or in the library collection. Some of this may be determined by state law. However, when your district can make the determination, you'll want to weigh the costs and benefits of either limiting who has standing to challenge or keeping it pretty open. Some districts allow any citizen to file a request for reconsideration. Other districts limit this by allowing only parents of children within the district to request reconsideration of materials.

Is there a clear, easy-to-complete reconsideration form? Does the reconsideration form include the following information: What is being challenged and why? What is the outcome the complainant wishes from the reconsideration process?

Make sure you have a publicly accessible reconsideration form that can be completed and submitted. The form should include contact information for the complainant, information about the item for which reconsideration is being requested, and why the request is being made. The form should include clear directions about where the form should be submitted and the timeline for an initial response to the request. Be sure to include a question asking what the complainant wants to happen to the material, but I don't suggest including a list of options for this. Leave that up to the committee to decide.

Does the policy explain how challenged materials are to be handled while the challenge is being considered?

The policy should include a statement that challenged materials will remain in use and available until the conclusion of the reconsideration process. Limiting access during the process is an infringement on student intellectual and academic freedom.

Does the policy explain composition of the reconsideration committee and procedures the committee should follow at both the school and district level?

The policy should outline basic membership of the reconsideration committee for both the school and district levels. Typically, the committee is comprised of the school librarian, the principal or other administrative representative, teacher representatives, and even student representatives (particularly in upper grades). Additionally, the policy should explain what the committee should do to reconsider the material in question: reading it, discussion, voting, and so on.

Does the policy outline the role of the school librarian during the reconsideration committee proceedings, and what is the role of the complainant?

Often, the policy will designate the school librarian as the chair of the school-level reconsideration committee. You'll want to know that ahead of time. As the school librarian, you are often the main spokesperson for intellectual freedom and the students' right to read. This should be the cornerstone of your role in the committee proceedings. Additionally, the procedures should clearly state if this is a public or private committee meeting and if the complainant has the opportunity to either submit a statement, attend the meeting, or participate in the proceedings in any way other than the initial written request for reconsideration.

Do the policy and procedures provide guidelines for notification of the complainant after a decision is made?

It's always good to have a plan about how to notify the person who made the challenge. It's even better to have sample letters ready to go. You won't need to panic or worry about being eloquent if you already have an outline of what to include at the very least. Your procedures should also determine from whom that letter should come. Should it be the chair of the reconsideration committee, which might be you as the librarian, or your principal?

Final things to consider

Policies are only as good as those who follow them. Plan to meet with your school's administration at the start of each school year to review important policies. Each fall, I met with my principal to talk about three things: the place of the library in the overall school budget; copyright and fair use and teacher use of video materials; and a review of the selection policy and reconsideration process.

It's important that you and your administration are on the same page when handling challenges to instructional materials both in the classroom and in the library. Many of the school library discussion forums include stories of principals arbitrarily removing materials from school libraries because of parent complaints. However, this is what gets administrators and school districts into hot water. When officials subvert their own policies and procedures, they open themselves up to litigation. Follow the process, and they are unlikely to face a lawsuit about infringing on students' First Amendment rights to access information.

Additionally, make sure that your school (or school district's) selection and reconsideration policies are publicly available on your school and district websites. The public needs to know how and why you are selecting content and the importance of protecting student access to information. Often just understanding the difference between parents' rights to make decisions about their own child as opposed to inhibiting access for all children is all it will take to prevent a challenge.

For more information, explore these resources about collection development and selection policy writing:

- *Selection & Reconsideration Policy Toolkit for Public, School, and Academic Libraries* from ALA's Office for Intellectual Freedom (http://www.ala.org /tools/challengesupport/selectionpolicytoolkit).
- Kerby, M. (2019). *An Introduction to Collection Development for School Librarians*. 2nd ed. Chicago: AASL.
- Mardis, M. A. (2016). *The Collection Program in Schools: Concepts and Practices*. 6th ed. Santa Barbara, CA: Libraries Unlimited.

REFERENCES

Dawkins, A. M. (October 2018). Ten steps to creating a selection policy that matters. *School Library Connection.*

Office for Intellectual Freedom. (2018). *Selection & Reconsideration Policy Toolkit for Public, School, and Academic Libraries.* Chicago: American Library Association. Retrieved from http://www.ala.org/tools/challengesupport/selectionpolicytoolkit.

18

Collection Development Policies in Juvenile Detention Center Libraries

Kristin Zeluff

INTRODUCTION

Looking for literature about collection development policies for juvenile detention facility libraries is discouraging. Very little exists to support librarians in developing and maintaining collections for incarcerated youth, and the guidelines that do exist are dramatically out of date. This makes an already difficult task harder than it has to be and leaves detention center collections vulnerable to censorship based on the personal stances of facility personnel.

While policies that support a collection for juvenile offenders may not at first glance be useful to the majority of librarians, the meticulous care and attention to detail necessary to support librarianship in this most challenging of librarian roles could help *all* librarians protect their collections in an increasingly litigious society. There is some irony, then, in the fact that a survey revealed that "the vast majority of services to [juvenile detention centers] operate without a written service agreement, collection policy, or materials reconsideration procedure" (Jones 2004, 16).

In March 2011, Amy Cheney of the Alameda County Library created a wiki for library personnel who serve incarcerated youth, to initiate a "nationwide discussion [among] all school, public, academic, and special librarians who provide or support the provision of library services to incarcerated youth" (paragraph 1). The wiki and the discussion are critical. So few materials exist that support librarianship in general for this population, and even fewer for collection development in particular. Juvenile detention centers (JDCs) with libraries are rare, and information about those libraries is elusive.

WHERE "WHAT IS" AND "WHAT SHOULD BE" MEET

Published standards for collection development policies to serve incarcerated youth do exist. In 1999, the Association of Specialized and Cooperative Library

Agencies (ASCLA) published *Library Standards for Juvenile Correctional Facilities*. Although twenty years old, these standards remain a strong blueprint for issues to consider when writing a collection development policy. *Library Services to the Incarcerated* by Clark and MacCreaigh (2006) contains solid practical advice in the chapter on Collection Development. The following list is a synthesis of the criteria listed in these two sources.

At a minimum, a collection development policy for a JDC library should discuss:

- A "community profile" of the facility's population and a method for regularly assessing reading interests and abilities of the wards
- Intellectual freedom statements
- Availability and extent of interlibrary loan services
- Clear statement of responsibility for collection development decisions
- Subjects/titles that will be excluded from the collection because of facility regulations
- Formats that will be purchased (DVDs, CDs, computer software, etc.), including stance on hardcover books or magazines with staples
- Whether or not any other nonbook materials will be purchased, such as board games or puzzles
- Qualitative criteria to guide material selections, including suggestions for professional review sources
- Any special needs populations that require materials, such as hearing or visually impaired wards or non-English speaking wards
- Materials to support the curriculum or any other program of the parent facility
- Whether or not legal material will be made part of the collection
- Specific requirements for the reference collection, keeping in mind the extremely limited (or nonexistent) Internet access in most JDC libraries
- Procedure for processing gifts and donations
- Procedure for handling challenged materials, including whether or not the challenged item will remain in the collection, and whether or not the item can be individually restricted
- Methodology for considering collection suggestions from nonlibrary staff and wards of the facility
- Criteria for maintenance of the collection, including when items shall be weeded, discarded, replaced, or repaired
- A schedule for reexamination and/or revision of the collection development policy

RESTRICTIONS ON THE JDC LIBRARY COLLECTION: NECESSARY CENSORSHIP

Logic dictates that some restrictions beyond what you would expect in a regular school library are necessary, both for the safety of the facility staff and of the juveniles themselves. A carefully considered list of criteria published in an approved collection development policy would protect the library staff and the wards of the facilities from the arbitrary and idiosyncratic censoring that can occur when there are no clearly established guidelines for what is acceptable and what is over the line. The literature is awash with anecdotes about censoring free-for-alls (Clark & Mac-Creaigh 2006; Gilman 2008; Guerra 2010; Jones 2004; Madenski 2001). Without a formal policy, the answer to the question "Who determines restrictions?" becomes "Whoever protests the loudest."

A JDC librarian can use precise criteria for material selection to defend contested items and group some items by age appropriateness. These activities are not unlike those of a librarian in a different type of library, but the difference is in who has the final say about the items in the collection and who can view them. "On the outside, parents have the right to decide what their children will read. Inside the facility, however, the detention staff acts *in loco parentis*, and librarians must agree to limitations that would normally cause them to cringe" (Gilman 2008, 65).

CHALLENGES TO LIBRARY MATERIALS: THE ART OF COMPROMISE

A significant portion of a collection development policy examined for this chapter discusses dealing with challenged materials. Given the rampantly inconsistent censorship by facility officials reported in the literature, this is not surprising.

The policy (marked as "In Progress") does not yet provide detailed procedures, but includes statements that indicate a cooperative stance with the officers of the parent facility and places the focus on individual wards, not the group as a whole. "Some materials [in the collection] may be considered counterproductive to individual student treatment goals. Cooperation will be given to any counselor or JIO wishing to restrict materials which, in their opinion, do not support the treatment plan for the individual. This does not support removal of the material from the collection. Other students have a right to free access to the material in question" (Cheney 2011, 3).

I could not locate an "official standard" protocol for this potentially incendiary situation. An explicitly described protocol combined with the cooperative statements in the examined policy might yield the most effective method for dealing with the inevitable challenges to materials, in a respectful, equitable, and ethical way.

GIVING READERS THE BOOKS THEY WANT TO READ

How does the JDC librarian figure out what her readers are going to want to read? *Connecting with Reluctant Teen Readers: Tips, Titles and Tools* by Jones, Hartman, and Taylor focuses on methods of assessing challenging teens and establishing rapport. It offers up the single most important phrase evident in all the consulted literature regarding the use of lists and the selection of titles: "There is no magic bullet" (Jones, Hartman, & Taylor 2006, 75).

Many potentially useful lists such as the Young Adult Library Services Associations "Quick Picks for Reluctant Young Adult Readers" can be overwhelming if the population to be served is not clearly defined. The Jones et al. text and other sources agree that one or two standardized lists will not adequately inform the librarian as to the interests and needs of their particular brand of "troubled teen" or "reluctant reader" (Clark & MacCreaigh 2006; Guerra 2010; Jones, Hartman, & Taylor 2006).

The JDC librarian's primary focus then must be on thoroughly understanding the population of the parent facility. Clark and MacCreaigh offer excellent suggestions for community needs assessment, tailored to suit the needs of a correctional facility environment. The Jones et al. text includes a chapter called "What Kinds of Books Will Work?" that correlates different genres of books with different kinds of readers, and analyzes popular trends in (reasonably) current literature that provide inspiration from every angle. Use of community needs assessment techniques is essential in determining each JDC population's multiple areas of interest, which must in turn inform the selection process.

CONCLUSION AND FUTURE DIRECTIONS

The scarcity of resources to assist JDC librarians in collection development leaves this field of inquiry wide open to researchers looking to make an impact on a dramatically underserved population. Grassroots movements such as the lockdown wiki indicate the strong need and eagerness to collaborate in professionals that serve incarcerated youth. In the short term, publication of the collection development policies of libraries serving JDCs would be very useful to those facilities struggling to create them from scratch. In the long term, revisions of the *Library Standards for Juvenile Correctional Facilities* are certainly in order (ASCLA). Updating and extending these standards under the auspices of the American Library Association would centralize the information for librarians who cannot locate much information in the professional literature.

Librarianship to the JDC population is not for the faint of heart. Into such a challenging and yet potentially rewarding arena, no librarian should go unarmed—meticulously crafted collection development policies are the critical foundation to successful service to incarcerated youth.

REFERENCES

American Library Association. *Prison Libraries LibGuide.* Retrieved from http://libguides.ala.org/PrisonLibraries.

Anderson, S. (2005). *Extreme Teens: Library Service to Nontraditional Young Adults.* Westport, CT: Libraries Unlimited.

Association of Specialized and Cooperative Library Agencies (ASCLA). (1999). *Library Standards for Juvenile Correctional Facilities.* Chicago: ASCLA, ALA.

Cheney, A. (2011). Alameda County Library Write to Read Juvenile Hall Literacy Book Selection Policy. *Library Services to Incarcerated Youth.* [No longer available].

Clark, S., & MacCreaigh, E. (2006). *Library Services to the Incarcerated: Applying the Public Library Model in Correctional Facility Libraries.* Westport, CT: Libraries Unlimited.

Gilman, I. (January/February 2008). Beyond books: Restorative librarianship in juvenile detention centers. *Public Libraries, 47*(1), pp. 59–66.

Guerra, Stephanie. (Fall 2010). Reaching out to at-risk teens: Building literacy with incarcerated youth. *PNLA Quarterly, 75*(1), pp. 50–60.

Jones, P., Hartman, M. L., & Taylor, P. (2006). *Connecting with Reluctant Teen Readers.* New York: Neal-Schuman.

Jones, P. (Fall 2004). Reaching out to young adults in jail. *Young Adult Library Services, 3*(1), pp. 16–19.

Madenski, M. (July 2001). Books behind bars: Working in a teen correctional facility. *School Library Journal, 47*(7), pp. 40–42.

19

The "Overdue" Blues: A Dilemma for School Librarians

Helen R. Adams

Overdue and lost library materials are no joke. At the end of each school year, school library e-lists frequently have questions about handling missing library resources. *School Library Journal* reported the return of two books to a high school library after fifty-one years. With the book, the anonymous borrower included a $1,000 money order stating, "At 0.02 cents per day it works out at $745.00 for 51 years. I've sent along a few more dollars in case the rates changed" (Staino 2009). Although the news report is amusing, the problem of overdue materials is serious for school library professionals.

THE "OVERDUE" SCENARIOS

Here's the usual situation. A student checks out a book from the school library and fails to return it on time. The school librarian notifies the student, but the item is not brought back. The item may become weeks or even months overdue. In another scenario, the overdue item is returned, but the fines are not paid. In yet another variation, the student gives back a library resource in a damaged condition or loses the item and does not reimburse the school. In these circumstances, what are the consequences to students with overdue materials and unpaid library fines or replacement fees? Should students with fiscal obligations be allowed to check out more library materials?

School library professionals have a fiduciary responsibility to ensure that the users of the collection return or pay for the replacement of library resources damaged or lost. Before cutting off borrowing privileges, however, school librarians should consider these points. Students have a First Amendment right to receive information in school libraries. School librarians are ethically and legally responsible to provide access to library resources to all students. "Economic Barriers to Information: An Interpretation of the Library Bill of Rights" cautions school librarians, "Libraries should examine policies and procedures, particularly those involving fines, fees, or other user charges, and actively move toward eliminating any that may create potential barriers to access or academic achievement" (http://www.ala .org/advocacy/intfreedom/librarybill/interpretations/economicbarriers). Marcia, a school librarian in the Midwest, says, "I consider WHY kids have overdue books. I am particularly sensitive to those kids who may have two or three 'homes' such as those who live in split households or those who are homeless and 'stay' with other family members" (WEMTA IFSIG list 2009).

CHECK THE LIBRARY'S POLICY

Most library policies are clear. Overdue books? Borrowing privileges for students are limited or cancelled until the materials are returned. Have a lost or damaged book? A replacement fee is charged with options such as payment of a uniform amount based on format (paperback or hardcover book, DVD) or restitution of the partial or full replacement cost. Some policies allow students to bring a suitable substitute for the lost or damaged item. Many libraries charge fines, although others do not because of potential economic inequities. To induce students to take care of library responsibilities, schools may deny attendance at special school events, like dances, or withhold report cards. In some districts, failure to clear a library record before the end of school or before transferring means the next school is notified of the student's outstanding library obligation. Of all the policy implications, the most damaging is barring students from checking out library resources. This is especially true for economically disadvantaged students who are unable to reimburse the district, may have little or no access to a public library, and may also lack suitable reading materials at home. For these students, stringent policies can mean years of not being able to borrow library resources.

STRATEGIES FOR CLEARING LIBRARY OBLIGATIONS

Students should be held accountable in some way for lost, damaged, or overdue books, but there are many ways to teach the lesson of responsibility. Library policies should be sufficiently flexible to take into account individual student personal and economic circumstances and to ensure that students have full access to library resources. As a first step, discuss with the student the concept of responsibility and the desire to keep the door open to borrowing the library's resources. Marcia uses this approach. "For chronic book losers, we have them check out books but keep them in school. If there is financial hardship and the books are truly gone for good, I'll have students 'work' for me in the library. They actually enjoy it, and it gives me one-on-one time with a student who might really need it" (WEMTA IFSIG list 2009).

Other ideas to consider:

- Allow students to "pay off" their fines by reading—each page equal to a penny.
- Set up an "installment" plan for students to pay for a lost or damaged item.
- Create an "honor collection" where students with no other borrowing privileges may take a book and return it with no official circulation record. Obtain the extra books through book fairs, or buy gently used books at rummage sales.
- Help families of English language learner (ELL) students understand library use. "Prepare a short translated note explaining when library books must be returned. Include a bar code, a spine sticker, and library stamp on the letter to help parents identify library materials, which must be returned in

a timely manner, as opposed to . . . [classroom] materials. If [library] books are overdue, send home a printout from your catalogue that contains the book cover . . . Visuals can get better results than a translated note simply listing the name of the overdue book" (Jules 2009).

As school librarians struggle with retrieving missing library resources, they should consider the human side of the situation. Not every child or young adult has a stable home life or a good example of adult responsibility in their personal lives. Students may be homeless—forced to move due to home foreclosures or evicted because the family is behind on rent payments. Other families have seasonal employment and move several times in a single school year. Students are minors, not adults, and although there are students who are irresponsible or are trying to work the system, school librarians should not lose sight of the students who are struggling. Librarians can be proactive and look for creative alternative ways to ensure access to library materials for all students.

REFERENCES

American Library Association. *Economic Barriers to Information Access: An Interpretation of the Library Bill of Rights.* Retrieved from http://www.ala.org/advocacy/intfreedom/librarybill/interpretations/economicbarriers.

Jules, J. (2009). *10 ways to support ELLs in the school library.* Retrieved from http://www.colorincolorado.org/article/33008.

Staino, R. (November 16, 2009). High school library books returned 51 years late with $1,000 check. *School Library Journal.* [No longer accessible].

WEMTA IFSIG list. (November 17, 2009, 8:57 a.m.). *Marcia.* "Subject: circulation, overdue policies and intellectual freedom."

20

Unrestricted Checkout:
The Time Has Come

Kathryn K. Brown

WHAT'S THE ISSUE?

In our politically charged culture, people have strong opinions on everything from the environment to health care. I have recently found myself in the middle of a debate about the benefits of unrestricted checkout in my elementary school library.

I believe that the time has come to let children check out the number of books they want. My only requirements are that they must be able to carry them ("No, you may not ask your teacher to carry some for you, and no fair bringing a wagon!"), and if the student has an overdue book, they are restricted to one book until the overdue is resolved. In an ideal world, I would not impose that last restriction either, but one does have a budget, and children are learning organization and responsibility skills.

Other members of our faculty are concerned that unrestricted checkout is depleting our library of resources, that students aren't reading the books they check out, that they are irresponsible and don't return them, and that the books don't fit in their desks or backpacks.

AASL'S POSITION AND SOME RESEARCH

In its *Position Statement on the School Librarian's Role in Reading*, the American Association of School Librarians (AASL) states, "School libraries provide students, staff, and families with open, non-restricted access to a varied high quality collection of reading materials in multiple formats that reflect academic needs and personal interests" (2010). In *The Power of Reading: Insights from the Research*, 2nd edition (2004), Stephen D. Krashen writes that reading and having access to good books are critical to achievement in reading, writing, and spelling. Research

69

has shown that students who are given the opportunity for free voluntary reading (FVR), show dramatic improvement in test scores over time. FVR improves vocabulary development, grammar test performance, writing, and oral/aural language ability (Krashen 2004, 3). Students who are speakers of English as a second language dramatically improve fluency and comprehension when they have access to quality books (Krashen 2004, 149).

Assigned reading also has its place in reading instruction. It challenges students intellectually and exposes them to books they might not choose on their own, thereby expanding their free-reading horizons. These are powerful arguments for surrounding children with books.

Krashen's research also shows that students in poverty have access to fewer books than students who are more affluent. Not only are there fewer book stores and libraries in poor neighborhoods, there are fewer books in classroom collections and school libraries. In a California study by LeMoine, Brandlin, O'Brian, and McQuillan (1997), researchers found that

> . . . students in high-achieving schools in affluent areas are able to visit the school library more frequently, both independently and as a class, and are more likely to be allowed to take books home. Seven out of the fifteen low-achieving schools they studied did not allow children to take books home. (Krashen 2004, 72)

Affluent children have more books at home and more ways to get the books they want. Low-income students are more dependent on the school for their books (Krashen 2004, 68–73).

Our challenge is to provide books that are rich in content and variety, reflecting the curriculum and the diverse needs of our students (AASL 2010), and to make sure that children have the opportunity to read. We need to take every advantage of every tool in our arsenal to get them to read.

THE POWER OF CHOICE

Children have strong opinions about what they like to read. When I was a brand-new librarian, I assumed (incorrectly) that children would prefer picture books, as I always took my own children to the picture book section when we visited the public library. I was surprised to discover that many students prefer non-fiction books, which was reinforced when I began really paying attention to what my kids were bringing home from their visits to the school library (army books, cat books, dinosaur books). If no books are of interest to students, or if they are not allowed to check out the books they want to borrow, reading becomes an exercise in frustration, and the library is a place to waste time.

Just like adults, children like books that are attractive and in good condition. If shelves are overcrowded, children become overwhelmed and can't find the "good" books they want. This is why weeding is a critical activity for the librarian. Allowing unrestricted checkout also reduces overcrowding on shelves. The more books students check out, the easier it is to find the books they want!

CELEBRATING EMPTY SHELVES

The best collection, the tidiest shelves, and the most inviting library will do no one any good if books sit on the shelves. Library books are to be used. In the process, some books will be damaged and some will be lost. If the loss rate is too low, it indicates that the collection is not being used. Anne E. Ruefle, in the article "Rules or Reading" (2011), shared a story about a woman whose three daughters dreaded library day because they might forget their library books, in which case the children would not be allowed to check out another book and would be reprimanded by the librarian. In other libraries, children check out books but are afraid to take them out of their backpacks for fear of forgetting them. Every September, during our library orientation, I ask students, "What is the *most* important thing to do with your library book?" The answers include taking care of them, returning them, not tearing the pages, not letting little brothers or sisters read them, not writing in them, and not letting the dog chew them. Rarely does a child get the right answer: "The most important thing to do with your library book is to *read* it!" Have we become so rule driven that reading is an afterthought? If the time ever came that the shelves were empty, that would be cause for celebration! Can you imagine a library that is so intriguing and inviting that children can't wait to check out whatever book is available? When students are first given the opportunity to have unlimited checkout, they check out more books than they can possibly read (and in some cases, carry). If they have unrestricted access, however, they quickly learn that when they finish the books they have, they can return and get more. They learn to self-limit their selections. When a student is told that she can get three books, she feels that she (a) *must* get three books and (b) must select absolutely perfect books because she can only get three. Thus, limiting checkout creates anxiety and tension in the library as students are rushed because it is time to go and they haven't yet found the exact number of exactly the right books.

ADDRESSING CONCERNS

A teacher shared with me that assessing independent reading is very difficult if a child abandons books without finishing them. What an opportunity to collaborate with her to come up with solutions to this problem! I suggest that if students are allowed to check out as many books as they like, they will take more risk in their reading. If I can only get two books, I'd probably make sure they are books I already know I will like. If I can take more, I might be more willing to try a science fiction title (not my personal favorite), knowing that if I hate it, I still have something else to read. As the librarian, I can work with the teacher to ensure that each student has one book for her to evaluate the student's reading and several other books to explore.

Children check out books for reasons that have nothing to do with reading them. Is there really anything wrong with just looking at the pictures? That is how I read magazines. Some children just want to look cool or grown up. I still remember the first "grown up" book I read. I was in fourth grade, and I read Laura Ingalls Wilder's *Little House in the Big Woods.* To my young mind it was a grown-up book because it was thick. Many children have someone at home happy to read aloud to them, if there is something to be read. My children allowed me to read all seven Harry Potter books to them, even though my son was a senior in high school the summer we read the last one.

WHAT STUDENTS DESERVE

Our students deserve unrestricted access to a collection of high-quality, high interest books. As teachers, our goal is to get students to read. As students, their goal is to find something interesting that will entertain them and please us. Overall, their goals are the same as anyone else's: to find happiness, to be treated with respect, and to be valued as individuals. If we restrict checkout, we are violating at least one of those goals. We are telling them we don't trust them to return their books. We are telling them we don't care what *they* like—that we as educators know what is best for them; and so we are not valuing them as individuals. We are teaching them that reading is a chore that is controlled by us. That is in no one's best interest.

While a collection of print resources is the most obvious measure of a library, the library of the 21st century is not hampered by walls. There is a wealth of useful databases for students and professionals. Electronic books and programs such as TumbleBooks and myON books provide books to be read online. No collection of print resources can meet everyone's needs, and that is the beauty of electronic resources.

Our students need to read, and they need to be able to get the books they want when they want or need them. A flexible schedule is another way to provide unrestricted access to the library. If a student finishes a book on Tuesday, it does him no good to have to wait until Wednesday to check out another. On the other hand, if he checked out a book on Tuesday, why does he need to come to the library on Wednesday? Students need the books when they need them, not necessarily on their assigned library day. I have seen classes come to the library where half of the students leave without books because they already have something to read. What a waste of instructional time!

The AASL *Standards Framework for Learners* includes six shared foundations: inquire, include, collaborate, curate, explore, and engage. Learners use skills, resources, and tools to inquire, think critically, and gain knowledge; to draw conclusions, make informed decisions, apply knowledge to new situations, and create new knowledge; to share knowledge and participate ethically and productively as members of our democratic society; and to pursue personal and aesthetic growth. Unrestricted checkout for students assists them to use their skills of locating information to answer the questions they are curious about. They gather new knowledge by taking risks with their reading. They learn to share their knowledge as they discuss the books they are reading, and learn to participate by being responsible book users. Most of all, unrestricted checkout allows students to grow as individuals, as they read about topics of interest to them.

Limiting access to books might have been important fifty years ago, but that time has passed. It is time to allow our students free use of our school libraries. After all, aren't the libraries for them?

REFERENCES

American Association of School Librarians. (2010). *Position Statement on the School Librarian's Role in Reading*. Retrieved from http://www.ala.org/aasl/advocacy/resources/statements/reading-role.

American Association of School Librarians. (2018). *AASL Standards Framework for Learners*. Retrieved from https://standards.aasl.org/wp-content/uploads/2017/11/AASL-Standards-Framework-for-Learners-pamphlet.pdf.

Krashen, S. D. (2004). *The Power of Reading: Insights from the Research, 2nd Edition*. Portsmouth, NH: Heinemann.

Ruefle, A. E. (May/June 2011). Rules or reading? *Library Media Connection, 29*(6), pp. 34–35.

21

Policy Challenge: Consequences That Restrict Borrowing

Judi Moreillon

School librarians often struggle with logical consequences when students, faculty, or families are delinquent in returning materials, return them in worse condition than when they were checked out, or fail to return them at all. With limited budgets, school library programs can ill afford consistently large losses—losses which, unfortunately, tend to be the most recently purchased and most popular titles. While library collections do need to be preserved, library users should also be encouraged to develop excellent lifelong library borrowing habits. How, then, can librarians factor accountability into the mix and still preserve library resources?

School library policies are set for borrowing time limits so that materials can be kept in circulation, and library patrons have the opportunity to read, listen, or view a particular item. Are library due dates for print books and hard-copy media out of sync with sources of electronic media that students access? Can library users even keep an eBook past its due date? Few school librarians consider fines a revenue source so why are they assessed? Does today's online movie viewing involve due dates and late fees? Just as practices for searches have been influenced by Google, maybe library lending policies should be reviewed in light of Hulu!

STUDENTS' PERCEPTIONS OF RESTRICTED BORROWING

"Of all the policy implications, the most damaging is barring students from checking out library resources. This is especially true for economically disadvantaged students who are unable to reimburse the district, may have little or no access to a public library, and may also lack suitable reading materials at home" (Adams 2010, 48–49). A child or teen's personal or family circumstances may make it particularly difficult to practice good library borrowing habits. Many children spend various days of the week, weekends, or weeks of the month with one or the other parent. Late or lost library materials may be a consequence of shuttling back and forth between two families. Some children are living in difficult family situations; others are homeless. In these stressful circumstances, a library book may be low on a list of competing priorities.

TEACHERS' PERCEPTIONS OF RESTRICTED BORROWING

Do classroom teachers expect to adhere to strict due dates or pay fines for late or lost materials? While providing teachers with a list of their overdue items is common, few school libraries charge teachers fines. Many classroom teachers also use public libraries and can easily renew those materials online. Can teachers renew school library materials as easily? While the point of due dates is equitable access, sharing resources can be especially challenging in schools and districts when standardized schedules may require classroom teachers to use the same or similar resources at the same time. How the library handles the distribution of resources and supports interlibrary loan (usually from outside the district or from the public library) matters to classroom teachers. How, then, can the library best accommodate a standardized curriculum?

PRINCIPALS' PERCEPTIONS OF RESTRICTED BORROWING

Resources = money. Particularly in tight budget times, administrators pay attention to how precious monies are spent. Principals who see the annual library material loss figure as a percentage of the annual budget may be motivated to help faculty implement reasonable accountability measures. In years where there is no budget for materials, losses are especially painful and have long-term consequences to collection development. Enlisting the principal's support for developing an effective policy is critical.

PARENTS' PERCEPTIONS OF RESTRICTED BORROWING

Parents need to be informed about their shared responsibility for their children's and their family's school library material borrowing. If families have not used the resources and services of the public library before their children enter formal schooling, taking financial responsibility for replacing damaged or lost library materials can be an obligation some families do not want to assume and cannot afford. This may be a barrier for families who could most benefit from access to school library materials. Some parents who are public library users may be surprised if their students cannot renew their books online. Some may be upset by fines assessed and consequences such as withholding yearbooks or privileges. Having clear, publicly accessible policies and communicating them are important to maintaining positive relationships in the learning community.

ENCOURAGING RESPONSIBLE BORROWING HABITS

What about rewarding positive behaviors rather than focusing on undesirable ones? Instead of librarians and teachers announcing the list of overdues, what about giving students who return books on time a raffle ticket to enter a drawing? Why not give away books or other literacy materials to library users who have returned resources on time and in good condition during a specific time period? This can be done by class, grade level, or whole school and on weekly, monthly, or quarterly intervals depending on the need to reinforce good borrowing practices. Exemplary library users can be spotlighted during class visits, library lessons, or on the school library website.

Policies must be flexible to take personal circumstances into consideration. Grace periods, volunteering in the library to pay off fines, installment plans with continued checkout for on-time payments, and amnesty days or weeks may be appropriate for some or all of the students. Simply put, "Some critics contend charging fines is unethical, especially in public or school libraries, and the meager results are not worth the harmful public relations fines incur" (Mitchell & Smith 2005, 47). Codeveloping late, damaged, and lost book policies that do not inhibit library use is important for principals and faculty to consider. No school library budget, however, can long afford to lose materials. Still, if the goal is to get books into kids' hands, then there are risks involved. Policies should reflect the maximum benefit for learners with calculated risks for the collection.

REFERENCES

Adams, H. R. (May 2010). The "overdue" blues: A dilemma for school librarians. *School Library Monthly, 26*(9), pp. 48–49.

Mitchell, W. B., & Smith, F. W. (January 2005). Using rewards to minimize overdue book rates. *Journal of Access Services, 3*(1), pp. 47–52.

22

Policy Challenge: Leveling the Library Collection

Judi Moreillon

Many 21st-century school librarians have been wrestling with alternate ways to organize the library. Some have "dumped Dewey" in favor of a Barnes & Noble bookstore model by creating their own subject organizations. Others are replacing the beloved library term "nonfiction" with "information" books when labeling the topical titles in their collections. In light of these new approaches, library organization is a timely topic.

One of the long-debated controversies in school library organization is labeling books according to reading or Lexile levels. On the surface, this system may appear to be helpful because it could make it easier for young or striving readers to find "just right" books at their proficient reading levels. It could also help students and teachers in states that have adopted the Common Core State Standards (CCSS) find the most challenging texts for the English Language Arts CCSS requirement. Since many school librarians are former classroom teachers, labeling the library collection in this way may seem like a logical solution.

But is it? Why is this practice so controversial?

Some teachers and administrators may not truly understand the issues inherent in leveling reading materials by Lexile levels. Leveling is based on readability in terms of word frequency and sentence length. Lexile levels may not, in fact, reflect the complexity of accessing meaning in a text. For example, *The Book Thief* by Markus Zusak is a 730 Lexile book, a level that can be used to describe books in the fifth- or sixth-grade range. Initially written for adults, this sophisticated book about the Holocaust and narrated by Death would be far beyond the comprehension level of most upper elementary and middle school students.

In response to the pressures to level books that many school librarians face from their administrators and faculty, the American Association of School Librarians (AASL) has published a *Position Statement on Labeling Books with Reading Levels* (2011). In the position statement, AASL identifies the ways in which labeling runs contrary to core values of librarianship.

STUDENTS' PERCEPTIONS OF THE LABELED LIBRARY

When the spines on the books in the library are labeled, students may feel or may even have been told that they are only allowed to check out and read books at their 90% or higher accuracy reading level. When limited to particular titles based on reading level or whether or not there is a standardized test to accompany a title, readers, unfortunately, may not feel or be free to browse and explore. "A minor's right to access resources freely and without restriction has long been and continues to be the position of the American Library Association and the American Association of School Librarians" (AASL 2011).

Students' privacy is also jeopardized by being limited to titles with specific labels based on reading level. When a student's proficiency level is indicated on a book's spine, peers and other students' parents have access to confidential information. This loss of privacy should be of concern to librarians who hold confidentiality as a core value.

TEACHERS' AND ADMINISTRATORS' PERCEPTIONS OF THE LABELED LIBRARY

When the library is labeled, classroom teachers and administrators may perceive the library as a warehouse of resources that mirror the classrooms' use of literacy resources for reading instruction. If reading instruction is focused on decoding and is tightly constrained by a learner's proficient reading level, then some may assume that the library collection should be organized in this fashion as well. Does that mean that school librarians should be using the library's resources to teach decoding skills, which are effectively taught to individual students and monitored on an individual basis, rather than for coteaching reading comprehension strategies that benefit all learners?

PARENTS' PERCEPTIONS OF THE LABELED LIBRARY

Like teachers and administrators, parents can believe that leveling library books is the answer to their child's striving to become a more proficient reader. Parents can become competitive about their child's progress and may carefully monitor leveled book selections. But is there more to learning to be an effective, efficient, and motivated reader than the Lexile level of a book?

ENCOURAGING EXPLORATION, CAPITALIZING ON MOTIVATION, AND READING FOR DIFFERENT PURPOSES

Everyone reading this chapter has, no doubt, had the experience of coming upon a book or other resource through browsing. If readers are limited to a particular reading level, will they have that same joyful experience of serendipity? Should the library be a place of freedom where learners can be assured of opportunities to explore?

"The level of difficulty or complexity of a text is not the only factor in choosing texts; interest and motivation also matter" (NCTE 2012, 16). The role of motivation in reading cannot be underestimated. All readers, including those who are striving, should have had the experience of reading text that is above their proficient reading level. This can happen when readers are passionate about something for which they have no background knowledge or adequate vocabulary. Reading images or graphics in a text in which the print is too difficult for them to comprehend can further stimulate readers' curiosity or help them build the necessary background and prepare them to tackle the entire text.

Everyone has read books significantly below their reading proficiency level as well. Reading easy texts or rereading texts doesn't necessarily present cognitive challenges, but it can give readers meaning and the satisfaction that comes from the familiar. Sometimes, the easier text is just what readers need to maintain their confidence or reignite their enjoyment.

The diverse purposes for reading are significant as well. For example, when flying in an airplane at 36,000 feet in turbulent air, readers will get more out of a page-turner than attempting to read a research article on nuclear physics (particularly if they are not nuclear physicists). The same importance of purpose also applies to children and youth.

"Instruction across the school year needs to involve students in the reading of texts at a variety of levels" (IRA 2012, 2) and so does independent reading. The CCSS call for instruction with challenging texts with which readers will struggle in terms of fluency and comprehension. This instructional approach requires that educators scaffold these learning experiences through modeling with think-alouds and monitoring students' guided and independent practice. This is the type of support school librarians can provide 21st-century learners while still maintaining the core library principles of confidentiality and students' rights to the freedom to read.

REFERENCES

American Association of School Librarians (AASL). (2011). *Position Statement on Labeling Books with Reading Levels*. Retrieved from http://www.ala.org/aasl/advocacy/resources/statements/labeling.

Common Core State Standards Initiative (CCSS). (2019). *English Language Arts Standards*. Retrieved from http://www.corestandards.org/ELA-Literacy.

International Reading Association (IRA). (2012). *Literacy Implementation Guidance for the ELA Common Core State Standards*. Retrieved from https://literacyworldwide.org/docs/default-source/where-we-stand/ela-common-core-state-standards-guidance.pdf?sfvrsn=b1a4af8e_8.

National Council of Teachers of English. (September 2012). Reading instruction for all students: A policy research brief. *Council Chronicle, 22*(1), pp. 15–18.

23

Policy Challenge: Closed for Conducting Inventory

Judi Moreillon

ANYTIME INVENTORY

Traditionally, school librarians have conducted inventory as the school year winds to a close. In what seems like the long-ago past, librarians used a shelf list to account for every item in the collection. Inventory, using this method, required many days to complete. Thankfully, technology has made this formerly tediously task relatively fast and efficient.

What was once thought of as an exclusively end-of-the-year odious task can now be accomplished at any time during the school year. With lists generated by circulation software and with barcode scanners in hand, school librarians, library assistants, and volunteers can easily determine which titles are missing from the collection. The inventory crew can restore shelf order as they scan and pull books that need repair or replacements. The librarian can then review the reports for collection development purposes. There is no longer a compelling need to close the library for inventory and no need to conduct it at the end of the academic year.

WHY KNOW ALL THE "STUFF"?

Yes! It is important to know the "stuff" of the library collection. Making sure that items are organized and labeled in such a way that they can be located by students, library student aides, classroom teachers, principals, parents, and the librarian is important. But, while location is essential, it is only the beginning of the collection story.

Providing resources to ignite students' engagement in learning and enjoyment of reading is central to the mission of the school library. With a deep knowledge of the "stuff," it is possible to identify current, relevant, and exciting resources to integrate into the classroom curriculum. It is also possible to recommend resources to students, colleagues, and families for independent reading and research.

THE PHYSICAL AND VIRTUAL STUFF

Knowing the library stuff can be a great way to support students' learning and teachers' teaching, and it also helps librarians be prepared for classroom-library collaboration. For decades, inventory in school libraries was a matter of assessing just the physical stuff. The hardcover and paperback books, magazines, DVDs, kits, and equipment managed through the library seemed like the natural place to begin. Equipment may now include eReaders, digital cameras and recorders, netbooks, laptops, and other hardware as well. Making sure equipment is accessible and in good repair is ongoing work throughout the school year and should not be confined to the end of the year.

Today, the growing digital resources should garner as much attention as the physical stuff in library collections. What about the online resources? How about the links on the online pathfinder? Are all the links on the library website in working order? Is there outdated information linked to the library online collection? What areas in the digital collection need more attention? These questions must concern school librarians when 21st-century learners and educators spend more and more time engaged with online resources.

It is possible to include the school community in the online inventory process. Involving student library aides in checking the links to electronic resources is one way to increase their knowledge of what is available. In the process, librarians can solicit students' feedback as well as gather suggestions for what the library web presence and digital collection may lack. Connecting with classroom teachers and revisiting co-created Internet pathfinders is a great way to remind colleagues of future opportunities for continued collaborative work. Asking if they have identified additional resources for that unit of study can jump start curriculum conversations and result in renewed instructional partnerships.

INVENTORY: TIMING IS EVERYTHING

The best time to do inventory is during down times when services to library stakeholders will be minimally impacted. These down times may be teacher workdays, before or after school, or short intervals between classes during the day. "The library should never be closed to conduct inventory since resources can still be circulated while inventory is in process" (Purcell & Bradley 2011, 37). Inventory should not compromise access. The library should be kept open and engaged in teaching and learning.

What are other opportunities for the library program at the end of the school year? With summer fast approaching, students and teachers can become restless. When spring testing season is over, many educators schedule research projects in the last month or two of school. Then, when most large projects have all been turned in, what kinds of creative learning experiences can the librarian co-plan and co-teach during the final weeks of the academic year?

Many classroom teachers "let their hair down" a bit as the long break approaches. Feeling the summer breeze, they may be more willing to engage students in individual or small group inquiry projects. They may be more open to co-designing open-ended learning experiences or taking risks to give students opportunities to experiment with the latest technology tools. The weather is better, too. Taking students out into the community to explore real-world, real-time people, places, and problems becomes more doable. The end of the school year can provide breathing room needed to access creative reserves for the benefit of student learning and improved teaching practices.

In his book *The Atlas of New Librarianship*, R. David Lankes argues:

. . . it is time for a new librarianship, one centered on learning and knowledge, not on books and materials, where the community is the collection, and we spend much more time in connection development instead of collection development. (2012, 9)

Wise librarians know that keeping the library open and engaged with the learning community from the first bell until the last bell of the school year sends a positive message regarding the library program. Being open reinforces the central role of the librarian and the library in the academic program of the school. It is important to continue to make connections with colleagues, curriculum, students, administrators, and families right down to the day the custodians lock the doors to begin their summer clean up!

REFERENCES

Lankes, R. D. (2010). *The Atlas of New Librarianship.* Boston: The MIT Press.
Purcell, M., & Bradley, A. (November 2011). Inventory for the school library: Do you know your stuff? *School Library Monthly, 28*(2), pp. 37–38.

Part IV

Handling Challenges

"Banning books gives us silence when we need speech.

It closes our ears when we need to listen.

It makes us blind when we need sight."

—*Stephen Chbosky, Author and Director*

24

Managing Challenges to Library Resources

Dee Ann Venuto

THE PRINCIPLE OF INTELLECTUAL FREEDOM

The *Code of Ethics* of the American Library Association (ALA) states that librarians are to "uphold the principles of intellectual freedom and resist all efforts to censor library resources" (Magi 2015, 17). Thus, our profession is one with ethical principles and a responsibility to uphold the constitutional rights of citizens, including those students we serve. Classes taken in graduate schools often quickly gloss over the concepts and realities of supporting patrons' rights to intellectual freedom, and few programs offer entire courses on the topic. Additionally, these "principles can be discussed in the abstract with useful results, but their concrete expression often generates controversy" (Broderick 1977, 505).

Obviously, a challenge to materials in the library can be a difficult and stressful experience. Personal and professional relationships are potentially altered, significant time can be spent on managing the situation, and employment consequences to budgets or staffing can occur. Librarians who encounter challenges often experience a range of difficult emotions, such as fear, self-doubt, and anger, making it easy to understand why some librarians may simply choose to sacrifice a resource instead of fight. However, there is no greater mission of the library and librarian (Hill 2010, 12).

Without question, handling challenges requires thought, planning, and skill. Thankfully, policies, procedures, and resources exist to guide decisions, providing librarians direction and comfort if a challenge occurs. In short, the principle of upholding intellectual freedom is one reason librarianship is considered a profession, and librarians play an important role in protecting patrons' rights to access information. It is a unique and honorable responsibility not easily assumed.

THE SELECTION POLICY

Challenges can occur regardless of how careful and thorough the process of collection development is, and it is best to prepare before one occurs. The ALA interpretation of the *Library Bill of Rights* declares as a matter of firm principle that it is the responsibility of every library to have a clearly defined materials selection policy that reflects the *Library Bill of Rights* and that is approved by the appropriate governing authority. This policy serves as the basis for navigating a challenge, guiding decisions, and implementing procedures.

First and foremost, it is wise to be familiar with the Materials Selection Policy of the school or district. If none exists, the procedures for developing library collections are often grouped with those governing curricular materials selection. While this type of policy outlines procedures for selection and complaints regarding class-room content, it is better to collaborate with the administration to develop a policy that particularly adheres to libraries. Choice of library materials is very different from curricula, which dictate content rather than providing voluntary access.

Definite components, such as the library objectives for acquiring materials and procedures for handling challenges, should be included within the policy. Detailed language, such as the following example, should be used to explain the processes:

> . . . the school library's role is to make available to faculty and students a collection of materials that will enrich and support the curriculum, meet the educational needs of the students and faculty, and support the intellectual growth, personal development, individual interests, and recreational needs of students. (ALA 2010, 377)

Other parts of the policy outline who is responsible for selection, the criteria, and review sources. A statement on intellectual freedom, its importance to librari-anship, and an affirmation of the *Library Bill of Rights* should also be included. Additionally, procedures and a form such as the "Request for Removal (or Recon-sideration) of Library Materials" to handle complaints should be included. Actions and personnel should be clearly outlined: the job titles and responsibilities of com-mittee members who review the challenge, how the meeting will be conducted, and who can legitimately submit a challenge. Typically, anonymous submissions and those of political organizations or citizens living outside the sending district are not honored. Inclusion of specific steps for reviewing the challenged material is also necessary and helpful. For example, most policies require that the material be analyzed in its entirety, not just by excerpts, and that the complainant state the challenge's purpose, including a recommendation to the committee of whether the material be removed, restricted, or labeled.

The policy dictates the committee reviewing the challenge does so in the context of the selection policy criteria for purchase, which includes gathering reviews of the material in question from professional, valid sources; meeting to discuss the material; and ultimately making a recommendation with a rationale to the govern-ing body. Sample selection policies are abundant on the web, and quality guide-lines for handling challenges are detailed on the ALA Office for Intellectual Freedom website under "Challenge Support."

HANDLING CHALLENGES

Most librarians receive complaints about materials at some point in time. It is important to remain calm, providing a professional, respectful, and transparent response and to realize community members have a First Amendment right to share concerns. Adopted policies allow requests to remove library materials to be dealt with in a courteous manner with established, consistent procedures. Often sharing with the individual or group the purpose of libraries and the procedures for requesting removal of materials can avoid further action. However, the Request for Reconsideration of Library Materials will sometimes be submitted, and a review committee will make a decision. Occasionally, challenges are highly organized and result in media involvement, fostering public debate about the role of libraries and librarians. These situations pose questions regarding press/media coverage and soliciting public support. Parents and students can be our best advocates in these cases, especially if the library has established itself as an integral part of the school culture. In some cases, it is essential for the administration and librarian to seek legal counsel from the school solicitor or lawyers of professional associations.

Contacting the Office for Intellectual Freedom (OIF) at ALA or a state affiliate is of extreme value and highly recommended. The individuals working on this level take significant time offering supportive professional and personal advice through one-on-one conversations as a challenge progresses. ALA and its state associations, the American Civil Liberties Union (ACLU) and the National Coalition Against Censorship, offer letters of support and talking points.

It is important to realize challenges do not have to be faced alone and the services of our professional organizations are provided without cost to both members and nonmembers. Regardless of the circumstances of a challenge, a professional responsibility exists to report these challenges to state and national organizations. ALA provides an online form for privately reporting a challenge, so that they can keep accurate records regarding censorship. All communications with ALA and other professional organizations are held in complete confidence and disclosed publicly only with the consent of the librarian.

Before a challenge, it is paramount to establish or review the established selection policy and discuss with administrators the response to anticipated challenges. Preparing for questions regarding the library collection is the best defense to promoting free access to information in a democratic society. It is important to know, however, that if a challenge does occur, there are procedures in place and quality resources to support and guide decisions.

REFERENCES

American Library Association Office for Intellectual Freedom. (2010). Preparing for and Responding to Challenges. In *Intellectual Freedom Manual*, pp. 375–85. 8th ed. Chicago: American Library Association.
Broderick, D. (October 1977). Son of speaker. *American Libraries*, pp. 502–5.
Hill, R. (November 2010). The problem of self-censorship. *School Library Monthly, 27*(2), pp. 9–12.
Magi, T. (Ed.). (2015). Code of Ethics of the American Library Association. In Magi, T., Garnar, M., & Office of Intellectual Freedom, *Intellectual Freedom Manual*, pp. 17–18. 9th ed. Chicago: American Library Association.

25

The Problem of Self-Censorship

Rebecca Hill

You're nervous. The book in question is edgy, maybe controversial. Someone might complain so you have to decide. Does it stay or does it go? Do you put it on a restricted shelf or require parental consent? This is a crossroads that many school librarians face. When the pressure to self-censor happens, do you let fear determine what you do with the book?

WHEN NO CHALLENGE EXISTS

Self-censorship, not to be confused with actual censorship, is the most complicated but least understood form of censorship. In most cases of actual censorship, objections to a book are based on offensive language, sexual content, or unsuitability by age, and a complaint is filed to suppress the book. Often an internal review is undertaken, and a court case may ensue. Most often, parents file a complaint, but religious or political advocacy groups may also institute a complaint. Between 1990 and 2009, the American Library Association's Office of Intellectual Freedom recorded 10,415 cases of actual censorship on the record, 7,230 of which occurred in the school or school library (American Library Association *Infographics*). In all cases, someone or a group actively attempted to control or prevent access to a particular type of content. While it is easier to calculate the number of actual censorship cases, it is more difficult to quantify the number of self-censorship cases that occur. Why? Because no actual challenge exists.

What distinguishes self-censorship from actual censorship is a librarian's fear that something might happen. Second-guessing is the motivating force behind surreptitious acts like removing or misplacing a book or even restricting its access. Because of this, the librarian might act preemptively without going through the normal review process. According to Joan E. Bertin, executive director of the National Coalition against Censorship:

> Self-censorship is the kind of thing that you cannot measure and for that reason may be an even more widespread problem . . . By definition we don't hear about self-censorship. Librarians know the sensitivities of their communities, who the 'troublemakers' are

and how they operate, and I'm sure they act with that knowledge. It's certainly true of art museums, where directors and curators openly admit that there are some things 'we just don't show here.' I've heard enough from librarians to know that the same process is at work. (Joan E. Bertin, telephone interview with author, May 21, 2010)

CHALLENGES

For nineteen years, Dee Ann Venuto has been a school librarian, but only recently she experienced her first formal challenge. A group of individuals representing the 912 Project's county chapter visited her school board and asked for the removal of three titles based on social, political, and sexual content in the books. Not only did they ask to remove the books, they also wanted to know who purchased the books and how they were purchased. These demands put Venuto smack dab in the middle of a censorship challenge for the first time in her library career. This is a perfect example, Bertin says, of the type of inquiries that can result in the "intense anxiety over the personal position that they [librarians] are put in" (Bertin, May 21, 2010). At Venuto's school, the controversy resulted in one of the books being removed from the library while the other two were eventually returned to the shelves. Whether or not it has hurt her career in any way is still in question, says Venuto (Dee Ann Venuto, email interview with author, May 20, 2010). Even though many people have been supportive, she believes that with the large amount of press attention in this case, more people will pay more attention to the school library and her role as a school librarian "Given the sensitivity of the situation, people are choosing sides, and some members of the Board are none too happy with me. Some people seem hesitant to talk with me about this in both the community and in school. [. . .] At present, I know that this challenge has negatively affected my level of job and life satisfaction" (Venuto, May 20, 2010).

Given the public nature of Venuto's ordeal, other librarians could view this negative experience as a reason to self-censor in the event of a complaint or even a threat of a complaint. Librarians are put in a difficult position when censors claim "a kind of moral high ground, by framing their challenge in terms of protecting children (Bertin, May 21, 2010). Furthermore, according to Bertin:

When someone says they only want to protect kids, it sounds like a good idea . . . Librarians are understandably wary of looking like they're not protecting kids. But it depends on what you mean by protecting kids. Some people want to protect kids by keeping them from reading certain things, while those opposing censorship think that reading is essential to protect kids from ignorance and confusion. (Bertin, May 21, 2010)

As a result, people arguing for intellectual freedom are always on the defensive looking for a moral ground that is often, as Bertin says, pretty hard to get back. This perception alone may be all that it takes for a librarian to self-censor a controversial book. In fact, in a 2009 *School Library Journal* survey, the survey found that 70% of the school librarians interviewed said that they would not purchase a book based on a possible reaction from parents (Whelan 2009). In 2016, *School Library Journal* updated its data with its Controversial Books Survey. This survey found that even more school librarians were reporting that they engaged in self-censorship with 90% of elementary and middle school librarians and 75% of high school librarians deciding not to purchase materials because of the controversial nature of their subject matter (Jacobson 2016).

LONG-TERM COST

Unfortunately, many librarians may not immediately understand or realize the long-term cost of self-censoring. Author Chris Crutcher, no stranger to censorship challenges himself, has seen the tremendous cost of these challenges to teachers and librarians. "As much as the censors tell us their overriding religious philosophy is a loving one," Crutcher said, "they go after the teachers and librarians like cold-blooded politicians. Personal attacks and thinly veiled bullying become the order of the day" (Chris Crutcher, email interview with author, May 14, 2010).

But even Crutcher acknowledges that, although he understands why they do it, "it seems to me it erodes a little bit of their souls" (Crutcher, May 14, 2010). "So what happens," Dee Ann Venuto asks, "if we cleanse our collections and have nothing that interests or pertains to today's young adults? How will we encourage the use of libraries?" (Venuto, May 20, 2010).

VARIATIONS OF SELF-CENSORSHIP

Self-censorship can come in many seemingly innocuous forms like book labeling, parental control requirements, and restricted rooms and shelves. Even though they are not the actual banning of a book, Bertin believes that "these are all forms of subtly entrenching the ideas that lead to censorship" (Bertin, May 21, 2010). One of the first cases to deal with the restricted shelving issue was a 2002 case involving the Harry Potter series. Parents of a Cedarville Elementary School in Arkansas filed a lawsuit seeking to overturn a school board decision to place the Harry Potter books on a restricted borrowing list that required written parental protection (American Library Association *Notable First Amendment Court Cases*).

In this case, the parents argued that placing the book in restricted shelving requiring parental consent basically stigmatized the books and their readers. The court ruled in favor of the parents, saying that a requirement for parental permission was tantamount to the implication that the child was "evil" just for wanting to read Harry Potter (Pat Scales, telephone interview with author, May 21, 2010). Although Dee Ann Venuto has never had to seek parental consent for books, she says that this concept was addressed during a review committee meeting. "I believe students would hesitate to request certain materials if they had to seek parent permission and/or the library staff for access. [. . .] In fact, unless certain sensitive topics are addressed for student research assignments, it is my experience that students will not ask for help when seeking information on certain topics such as sexuality or abuse" (Venuto, May 20, 2010).

Labels stating that a book is for "mature readers" or stating a specific reading level like those in Lexile or Accelerated Reading programs may appear to be innocent, but this type of labeling opens the doors to censorship if schools and their librarians use these programs as their sole selection tools. In most cases, the problem arises and evolves into a censorship complaint when students are assigned a reading level and then read above or beyond their maturity level. Some of the more volatile censorship cases have come from books when the reading and maturity level do not match up, says Pat Scales, school librarian and columnist for *School Library Journal*.

In an elementary school in Arizona, we had a huge issue there when *Perks of Being a Wallflower* was found in an elementary school when it really wasn't appropriate for an elementary school reading level. We need to have open access, but you must engage with the students about books to ascertain their maturity level. Unfortunately educators that grade-level books are often not even reading the books. That road has led us down that dark path of censorship. You cannot use these computerized reading programs as selection tools. (Scales, May 20, 2010)

DECREASING THE RISKS OF SILENT CENSORSHIP

While no one can predict when and if a censorship challenge or complaint will arise, the risk of a challenge can be minimized and, at the same time, the likelihood of self-censorship can be decreased by being adequately prepared. As most librarians can attest, the most valuable tactic is a thorough selection policy and process. For Dee Ann Venuto, having these policies in place and an avid knowledge of them was invaluable. "Our school has a board policy concerning the media center, which includes statements on how and why materials are selected and another concerning complaints regarding instructional materials. [. . .] These documents, a Reconsideration Request Form that I had on file, and a large binder of resources I gathered were the basis for managing the challenge" (Venuto, May 20, 2010).

In addition, a thorough selection process that relies on professional review sources and a strong readers advisory approach to book selection is critical and will increase the comfort level about books available in the library. To keep parents in the loop, Pat Scales created the Communicating through Literature program where parents read and discussed the books that their teens were reading. A crucial aspect of this program was simply asking kids first what books they wanted their parents to read and then Scales asked the parents to read these books. She found that when parents read and discussed these books, they were less likely to object to the books' content. Through blogging and social networking, communicating through literature with parents becomes even more convenient and can provide ongoing feedback.

Scales believes that programs like these work because we are engaging the kids and their parents. "People don't think to engage the kids. They are afraid to engage the kids" (Scales, May 20, 2010). But, Scales believes, it is important to remember that a child and an adult could read the same book, and yet have different perceptions of the content, "You bring your own life experience to a book" (Scales, May 20, 2010). This, Scales believes, is one reason why censorship challenges arise. "In a challenge, we are imposing on children our adult view of things" (Scales, May 20, 2010).

Another way of engaging kids who read is to solicit their personal stories about reading not only banned books, but controversial books. These firsthand accounts can be valuable in defending the selection of a book or even in the event of a challenge. Collecting and using these accounts may also confirm the value of the book to parents, school boards, and others who might raise an objection to a particular book. Further, sharing these stories on an ongoing basis with the school administration can also demonstrate just how valuable these reading experiences are to students. Pat Scales was the chair of her school district's Materials Review Committee when a challenge to a book in a school in her district arose. "I went to the class that had been studying the challenged book, and asked them to share their own stories about the book and what it meant to them. [. . .] I took those stories to the committee and we retained that book. Sometimes, you just have to let the kids tell their stories" (Scales, May 20, 2010).

Just as Venuto did, librarians who want to be prepared in the event of a challenge do well to identify those national organizations like the National Coalition Against Censorship who can lend valuable support not only in the event of a challenge, but to develop policies and procedures that will help avoid a challenge. Most national organizations like the American Library Association Office for Intellectual Freedom or the National School Board Association have sample policies and procedures online that can assist in preparation for and against a censorship challenge. Further, they can assist school librarians in developing a defense against a challenge and help them keep in touch with others who have been through similar situations. Because they are in the position to offer this type of guidance, Dee Ann Venuto strongly encourages librarians to seek their assistance. For her, "the American Library Association and National Coalition Against Censorship were invaluable, both professional and personally. [. . .] The people working for these organizations are truly dedicated and supportive advocates" (Venuto, May 20, 2010). Most importantly, knowing that professional support and resources are available increases the comfort level while also ensuring adequate preparation.

CHALLENGE OF THE CHALLENGE

Everyone knows just how difficult a book challenge can be to a school, the school librarian, teachers, and even the school district as a whole. The amount of time taken in a challenge can be astronomical. Personal and professional relationships are affected. Librarians who go through a censorship challenge experience a plethora of emotions ranging from fear to shame to anger to apprehension. So it is not hard to see why many librarians would rather just "lose" the book rather than enter into a fight. Ultimately, though, no librarian needs to be told there is a greater mission of the library. "Librarians often have to be brave," said Joan Bertin. "They have to be willing to be misunderstood, be criticized, and sometimes even face employment consequences" (Bertin, May 21, 2010). According to Bertin, they have to avoid that little devil sitting on their shoulder who warns when something could cause possible trouble. But by being prepared, utilizing their policies and procedures, engaging their readers and parents on an ongoing basis, and then reaching out for help when they need it, they will be able to put those kinds of thoughts and fears aside and continue living, as Chris Crutcher says, "where ideas and readers meet" (Crutcher, May 14, 2010).

REFERENCES

American Library Association. *Infographics.* Retrieved from http://www.ala.org/advocacy/bbooks/frequentlychallengedbooks/statistics.

American Library Association. *Notable First Amendment Court Cases.* Retrieved from http://www.ala.org/advocacy/intfreedom/censorship/courtcases.

Jacobson, L. (September 26, 2016). Unnatural selection: More school librarians are self-censoring. *School Library Journal.* Retrieved from https://www.slj.com/?detailStory=unnatural-selection-more-librarians-self-censoring.

Scales, P. *Does Censorship Matter?* Retrieved from http://www.randomhouse.com/highschool/RHI_magazine/pdf3/RHI08.pdf.

Whelan, D. L. (February 2009). A dirty little secret. *School Library Journal, 55*(2), pp. 27–30.

26

Ex Post Facto Self-Censorship: When School Librarians Choose to Censor

April M. Dawkins

Vocabulary matters. When we, as school librarians, discuss intellectual freedom, the discussion primarily centers on the issue of selection versus self-censorship. The earliest discussions of the issue of self-censorship came from a 1953 article by Lester Asheim in the *Wilson Library Bulletin*. In it, he discussed the idea that when librarians are involved in creating library collections, they are going through a process of selection as no single collection can contain everything that is published. As a result, librarians must be careful to select but not censor.

One of the issues when discussing self-censorship is the narrow definition in the research literature of the terms censorship and self-censorship. Self-censorship is defined as the decision by a librarian to exclude material in a collection prior to purchase due to either external or internal factors. Ken Dillon and Claire Louise Williams refer to self-censorship as "a secret practice [that is] the least obvious but arguably most powerful and pervasive form of censorship which is informal, private, and originates with the decision maker" (1994, 11). Censorship occurs when material is removed from a collection after purchase and usually refers to external forces, such as requests from parents or members of the school community.

During the course of conducting forty-nine interviews with school librarians in North and South Carolina for my dissertation, I asked each librarian to tell me about a time when someone questioned an item in their collection. I really expected them to talk about their experience in going through a challenge for materials or how they were able to convince a person to drop the challenge. However, the interviews revealed that many librarians were choosing to remove materials from their own school library collections. I wasn't prepared for this, and I didn't have the vocabulary to describe it. The behaviors didn't fit with self-censoring behaviors (censoring prior to purchase) or censorship (attempts to remove materials by outside forces). So, I gave the phenomenon a name and a definition: They were engaging in ex post facto self-censorship, which I defined as the decision by a school librarian to remove materials after purchase from their own collection without going through a reconsideration process.

Specifically, what behaviors might be characterized as ex post facto self-censorship? I found five in particular through my interviews: weeding, redacting, transferring, labeling, and restricting. Weeding is something that all school librarians do and which has a legitimate and important function in collection development. It allows librarians to remove items from the collection for a variety of reasons including wear and tear, outdated content, and lack of circulation. However, the term weeding becomes ex post facto self-censorship when used to describe the decision to remove content from the collection because the librarian had a concern that the content might be objectionable and as a result might face a challenge. This "weeding" might occur immediately after purchase when the librarian has an opportunity to more closely examine the material in question, or it might happen at a later time when the questionable content is brought to the librarian's attention by students or faculty. Instead of choosing to go through a formal reconsideration of the material with review by a committee, the librarian chooses to "weed" the material.

Redacting is another form of ex post facto self-censorship. This refers to the decision by school librarians to mark out objectionable language or images from materials in their collections. It could mean using a black marker or even using scissors to remove pictures. The choice to redact becomes a decision to censor certain terms or images that might be deemed age inappropriate. However, this decision subverts the basic idea that we should judge a book as a whole.

Transferring was an alternative to weeding for some of the elementary and middle school librarians I interviewed. Rather than face a challenge on material that might be considered age inappropriate, they chose to transfer the item to a school that served older children. Therefore, they could avoid a challenge based on mature content.

Middle school librarians, in particular, engaged in either labeling or restricting access to content. Some librarians chose to stick a "YA" (young adult) label on some materials. While "YA" labels are somewhat neutral, they may serve as a barrier to access for some students, especially if the "YA" books are then placed on separate shelves away from other materials.

Finally, restricting access was another way the librarians chose to avoid challenges. Restrictions can not only take the form of separate shelving, but they can also take the form of removing items from the circulating collection and placing them in the professional development section of the library. This way, the items in question have not really been removed from circulation; however, in reality they are no longer readily accessible to all students. Additionally, some librarians required permission forms for students to check out YA materials if they were not in a certain grade.

What all of these forms of ex post facto self-censorship have in common is the decision by a school librarian to effectively remove an item from circulation in order to avoid a challenge. And often, the decision to engage in this type of self-censorship occurred even without someone (student, staff, or parent) actually questioning the content. Rather, it was the fear of facing a challenge that often motivated the decision. In almost every instance where an interviewee discussed this, it was with full awareness of the presence of a reconsideration policy or procedures that were in place.

Sometimes, it really is necessary to remove an item from your collection after purchase. An item may not have been what you expected based on its description, and you might not have had an opportunity to examine it fully prior to purchase.

However, following reconsideration procedures even in those cases sets the precedent that all decisions to remove materials from the collection must follow the policy that is in place. If you choose not to follow the policy in some instances, it becomes much more difficult to insist on using the formal reconsideration process when you have a challenge.

So, why do some librarians subvert the process? Facing a challenge is both stressful and time consuming. But when we have policies and procedures in place, we need to use them. I believe that one reason librarians choose to subvert the process is because we feel unprepared to become the vocal defender of our own collections. To avoid this, we must set ourselves up for success when faced with a challenge. There are some specific steps that every school librarian can follow:

1. Know your selection and reconsideration policies and procedures. Review them on a regular basis to determine if they need updating.
2. Make sure your school's administrators are aware of the policies and procedures.
3. Discuss the *Library Bill of Rights* with your administration and talk about how to handle oral versus formal complaints or challenges.
4. Have a standing committee in place in your school that provides support in collection development and might also serve as the reconsideration committee.
5. Gather outside support from ALA's Office for Intellectual Freedom (OIF), your state association's intellectual freedom committee, and from within your district.

What do you do if your school or district does not have a selection and reconsideration policy? Write one! The OIF has developed an updated "Selection & Reconsideration Policy Toolkit for Public, School, and Academic Libraries." Many library and information science textbooks have guidelines for writing selection policies. You don't have to start from scratch. Find one that you like, and work from that foundation.

In my career as a school librarian, I found that the key component in avoiding a challenge was not to avoid it by censoring. Instead, I chose to engage my school community in discussions about intellectual freedom, access, and the best educational practices. When a parent or faculty member asked, "Why is this book in the school library?" I always responded by discussing the *Library Bill of Rights* and meeting the needs of all of my students. Parents in particular responded positively when I thanked them for their involvement in their child's reading life and discussed with them how to handle material with which they might be uncomfortable. These conversations became the most critical factor in defending the right to read.

RESOURCES FOR FURTHER INFORMATION

- ALA's Office for Intellectual Freedom—http://www.ala.org/offices/oif
- ALA's Office for Intellectual Freedom Resources for School Libraries—http://www.ala.org/advocacy/intfreedom
- ALA's Questions and Answers on Labeling and Rating Systems—http://www.ala.org/advocacy/intfreedom/librarybill/interpretations/qa-labeling
- Interpretations of the Library Bill of Rights—http://www.ala.org/advocacy/intfreedom/librarybill/interpretations

REFERENCES

Adams, H. (2008) *Ensuring Intellectual Freedom and Access to Information in the School Library Media Program.* Santa Barbara, CA: Libraries Unlimited.

Asheim, L. (1953). Not censorship but selection. *Wilson Library Bulletin, 28,* pp. 63–67.

Dillon, K., & Williams, C. L. (Nov.–Dec. 1994). Censorship, children, and school libraries in Australia: Issues of concern. *Emergency Librarian, 22*(2), pp. 8–14.

Mardis, M. A. (2016). *The Collection Program in Schools: Concepts and Practices.* 6th ed. Santa Barbara, CA: Libraries Unlimited.

27

Challenging Opportunities: Dealing with Book Challenges

Sabrina Carnesi

It is the librarian's duty to ensure that all users have equal access to library books. When a librarian is faced with a parent, teacher, or another member of the community who feels a particular library book is inappropriate for a patron to read, the librarian and staff should be able to knowledgeably follow through with a set of clear procedural measures that ensures the successful handling of the complaint.

PREVENTIVE MEASURES ARE THE FIRST STEPS TO TAKE

To be fair and to protect everyone's intellectual freedom, these first steps taken in a complaint should always be preventive ones similar to the following:

1. Use the links on your state and national organizations' websites to help familiarize and/or reacquaint yourself with the concepts of intellectual freedom, censorship, and the First Amendment.
2. Use ALA's Challenge Support website (http://www.ala.org/tools/challenge support) to familiarize yourself with additional challenge terminology for expression of concern, oral complaint, written complaint, and public attack.
3. Create/review/update your selection policy.
4. Create/review/update your procedure for handling complaints.

SEQUENTIAL STEPS FOR AN ACTIVE CHALLENGE

If preventive measures do not prevail and your library becomes involved in an active challenge, here are a few sequential steps to follow:

1. Form a school committee of at least (a) the librarian, (b) the principal, (c) a classroom teacher, and (d) a parent.

2. Make certain all committee members are aware of their responsibility to read the entire book.
3. Create a list as to why this book falls under your selection policy. Make sure you always have a list of your selection policy present at all meetings regarding the challenge. The National Council of Teachers of English (NCTE) has two CDs for the rationale of over 200 books and additional support on how to generate rationales (www.ncte.org/action/anti-censorship /rationales).
4. Get support from colleagues: ALA, NCTE, PLA, and your state organization. Talk to others who have successfully faced challenges. Discuss your situation with your school staff and your library supervisor.
5. Gather up support for the book. Did it receive rewards? Is it on a standard bibliography list? Is it on any Best Book lists? Is it or has it ever been a required read or been suggested as additional reading for a class in your school district? Have students write supportive statements, especially students who can relate to the issues with which the book deals. Collect respected reviews from professional journals.
6. Take into consideration the situation from which the complaint arose. Did the student choose to read this book or was it required reading? Was the entire book read by the student? Did the challenger read the entire book? Is the challenger bringing attention to the book challenge via the media or community groups and organizations?
7. Make sure to report the challenge to your state organization, ALA, and NCTE.

School librarians, in particular, have additional responsibilities to uphold when faced with a challenge. In a school library, the emphasis for First Amendment rights goes beyond intellectual freedom to include academic freedom. Academic freedom guarantees a teacher's right to select academic materials that provide a broad enough selection of resources to provide opportunities for the student to develop a critical perspective on a given subject or idea. A school library shelf that is reflective of only one viewpoint does not support opportunities for this development to take place. With clear and defined guidelines such as this, the personal element in settling a complaint is minimized and the decision for inclusion becomes student-centered, which is the basic purpose behind the selection of materials for a school library overall.

28

The Challenges of Challenges: Understanding and Being Prepared

Gail K. Dickinson

One of my favorite quotes from John Dewey is "What the best and wisest parent wants for his own child; that should the community want for all of its children. Any other ideal for our schools is narrow and unlovely; acted upon, it destroys our democracy" (1905). I use that quote often when talking about school library budgeting because that is the time that the members of the school board have the responsibility to act as the best and wisest parents. What they want for their own children they should also want, expect, and demand for all of the children in the school district. It's their job.

When talking about intellectual freedom, however, that quote loses some of its altruistic flavor. The best and wisest parents now become parents who want all copies of Harry Potter removed from the school or see any mention of homosexuality as promoting an immoral lifestyle. Those parents (most likely a she) may earnestly believe that they are the best and wisest parents and as Dewey suggests—they earnestly want for every child in the school exactly what they want for their own children. Others, however, see their actions as narrow and unloving, and even as destroying democracy—exactly the opposite of Dewey's intent.

When a challenge gets difficult, it's hard to believe that people challenge instructional materials because they care. It's even harder to remember that educators want the general public, legislators, taxpayers, and parents to care about education. If we made a list of things that parents fear for their children, it would be a long one. If we made another list of the general life stressors on parents (e.g., financial, job, world affairs, etc.), it also would be a long one. Looking through the lens of stress we all share as adults and at the fears that all parents share about their children, we can understand challenges a bit better. The challenger may think, as a parent, I can't stop the war or improve the economy, but maybe I can take this one book out of my child's hand, and maybe even take a stand for all of the children in the school. I can't create a dike to dam the flood of popular music or popular culture, but maybe I can raise my thumb to stop just this one drop of unclean water from hitting my child.

School librarians and administrators have the same lens of stress that all adults have, along with the additional stresses of jobs in the education arena. It may help school personnel to continually strive to understand the concern of the challenger, but the challenge still creates a great deal of stress. Tempers flare, and regardless of the responsible efforts to manage budget, the choices made for well-selected collections, headlines trumpet with accusations that claim smut has been deliberately placed in the hands of children.

School librarians are the information resource experts in the school. They are the only ones trained to use the selection principles and criteria. Each school librarian's role in the challenged materials process is to act as informed counsel for the district in the matter of selection, to gather data about the resource, and most importantly, to defend the use of established policy and procedures.

HOW IT GOT THERE IN THE FIRST PLACE

In general, school librarians don't do a very good job of explaining the profession to others. Therefore, one of the most important areas of the job, the selection of materials, is often misunderstood. If the school librarians asked even the closest colleagues how materials are selected, they may reply that materials are purchased because it is perceived that people need them, or it is what the school librarian likes, or it is what is on sale—as if the process involves watching sale ads at discount stores for selections to add to the reference collection. This lack of shared knowledge about selection comes back to haunt school librarians when there are challenges to instructional materials.

Parents, fellow teachers, and maybe even administrators need to be informed that school board policies govern the selection of instructional materials, and that responsibility to purchase these materials is delegated through the superintendent to the teaching faculty. In the case of library materials, the person responsible is the school librarian. The selection policy, however, applies to all instructional materials in the school whether they are part of the library collection or housed as instructional materials in classrooms. The selection policy applies to materials in all formats and covers materials used in instruction whether purchased through taxpayer funds or through gifts to the school.

Even though school librarians are the only ones trained in selection processes, the hallowed principles of selection, such as accuracy, authority, literary merit, appropriateness, reputation of author, and relevance to curriculum, all apply equally. The selection principles are the reason that school librarians are involved in challenges to instructional materials, whether the challenge is in the classroom or the school library. School librarians are the information resource experts in the school.

The same procedure applies even if the resource was purchased by a predecessor long forgotten, should have been weeded, or was from the awards list in the past year. School librarians know the interests and information needs of their community within and without the school. They also select materials by reading reviews from authoritative sources written by those trained in selection, by consulting awards and recommended lists, and by seeking suggestions from teachers and students. Resources are not purchased because the school librarian likes it, or because it looks pretty in a catalog, or because it is a personal hobby of the school librarian or someone on the teaching staff.

This means that when a resource is challenged, the school librarian's role will be to guide the application of the selection principles to the resource in question. Statements of fact are always preferable to opinion so statements from published reviews are helpful. Even fiction resources can be judged as accurately representing the genre or, in the case of historical or science fiction, containing facts that are important curricular concepts. Fiction resources are also relevant, specifically in those curriculum standards that focus on encouraging students to read for pleasure.

The word "appropriate" always causes some concern. It is used at times as a catchall phrase that could mean anything from language to pictures to behaviors. When discussing challenged resources, all parties involved should make sure that they know specifically what the issues are. The following definitions of "appropriate" may help:

- Reading level. Is the resource appropriate as defined by reading level? Usually, the answer to this is yes, although there are times when materials are deliberately purchased that are far above or far below the majority of student reading levels in a school. The current focus on adding picture books to middle and high schools or on ensuring that high-level readers in upper elementary schools have books on their reading level addresses this concern. Schools with K–8 student populations have an especially difficult time selecting materials at all reading levels.
- Interest level. Is the resource appropriate as defined by interest level? Of course, this is one of several elements, but it could be argued that students are very interested in language, pictures, or behaviors of which adults disapprove. In reality, students may be more interested in NASCAR racing, the current NFL season, or the latest *American Idol* television update than they are in fiction set in middle school or high school.
- Intellectual level. Is the resource appropriate as defined by intellectual level? In other words, can the students for whom this resource is intended understand the content and context? This is different from reading level. One application of intellectual level may be whether or not the content can be applied to the state curriculum standards.
- Emotional level. Is the resource appropriate as defined by emotional level or maturity of the students? This particular definition of appropriateness will be the one that causes the most discussion, and there are times when all a committee can do is decide that for some students, this is emotionally appropriate, and for others, it may be emotionally inappropriate. Some students may be traumatized by nightmares after reading stories about ghosts and goblins. Some students may not be ready to read stories or facts that directly contest what their parents or church members believe.

Regardless of the answer to each of the above, they can be used to push the discussion of appropriateness from vagueness into proscribed categories so that each person around the table understands what specific points are under discussion.

School librarians select materials for the school community. It would be nice if the collection were as appropriate for each person in the school community as it is for the average student, but money, time, energy, and lack of available resources precludes any hope of doing this. The selection process should value each child and each parent equally. No one should receive more consideration because they may or may not object to a particular resource. No one receives less consideration because they may or may not speak the dominant language of the school. The goal is to stretch the collection to meet the needs and interest of each child. It's not easy, and it's no wonder that at times parents or other citizens are concerned over materials that do not match the needs and interests of their children.

REFERENCE

Dewey, J. (1905). *The School and Society*. New York: McClure, Phillips, & Company.

29

The Challenges of Challenges: What to Do?

Gail K. Dickinson

Why can't you just take it off the shelf because I say so? In truth, many resources are removed from the collection because one parent complained, or in some cases, because it was feared that a parent would complain. It is, therefore, helpful when questions are raised about a resource to clarify the circumstances. Here is one articulation of the different scenarios. More specific information can be found, along with a multitude of excellent support resources, at the ALA Office for Intellectual Freedom web pages (http://www.ala.org/aboutala/offices/oif).

Questioned: A resource is questioned when a parent or citizen (and sometimes an administrator, teacher, or staff person) expresses concern. This concern may be quietly raised in an email, shouted from across a table in righteous anger, or publicly stated to a newspaper or television camera. The proper response to inquiries from the media about the resource at this point is that a challenge has not been filed. The materials can be discussed with the complainant, but the resource will not be removed in this stage because there is no challenge. In some schools, especially when materials are questioned by classroom teachers or administrators, this stage can be emotionally difficult for the school librarian, but the administrator will need to be reminded that there is no challenge without the written form, and the challenged procedure cannot be initiated without it.

Challenged: A resource is challenged when the proper form is filled out and submitted. The district's board-approved challenged materials procedure then kicks into action, the committee is formed, and the resource moves through the process. The proper response to media inquiries during this scenario is that the district has an established process, and it is proceeding. The resulting decision is not yet known, but the administrator may note that the process is on schedule.

Banned: A resource is banned when the committee process is completed and the decision is made to remove the resource from the school. The option of limiting access to the resource should not be considered. Under normal access policies, instructional materials are open and accessible to everyone in the school community. Therefore, resources are in the collection or not in the collection, meaning they are either banned or they are retained. The proper response to media, parental, or student inquiries is that the school board has made a decision and the school will abide by it. Sometimes, students can be extremely emotional when a resource is removed. It's a difficult lesson in the democratic process for them, but if the process was followed, the decision must be followed unless the process has room for appeal by another parent.

A resource can only be removed from the shelf when it is banned. Just because a resource is questioned by one parent does not mean that it should be removed. Petitions with long lists of names are good input for the committee, but the decision cannot be based on one group of parents, no matter how large or small. The question is indeed one of parental rights and most states require schools to honor parental requests for alternative educational experiences. For example, if a parent feels strongly about their child reading *Macbeth*, then another Shakespearean play may be substituted. When a parent formally challenges resources, however, they are not asking for an alternative experience solely for their child, but for all of the children in the school. Other parents do not have the opportunity to make the choice; it has been made for them. Usurping the rights of all parents in the school to have a say in their child's education should not be taken lightly. For that reason, the committee process is crucial.

There are also legal considerations. It is said that the only time administrators learn about school libraries in their preparation programs is in a course on School Law. The applicable cases, *Tinker v. Des Moines* (1969) and *Pico v. Island Trees* (1982), provide the legal basis for why following the process is so important. In *Tinker v. Des Moines*, the right of students to due process was upheld with the phrase that notes constitutional rights do not stop at the schoolhouse door.

In *Pico v. Island Trees*, the U.S. Supreme Court affirmed that school boards could be sued for decisions made outside of board-approved processes. *Pico* is usually the basis for additional lawsuits in which administrators or school boards have removed materials at the questioning stage without allowing them to be formally challenged. In fact, in both *Pico* and a later case based in Olathe, Kansas, (*Case v. Unified S.D.* 1995) no formal challenge was ever presented. It is the role of the school librarian to note to the principal that it takes only one student or parent to sue if the resource is removed without the process as outlined in the policy manual, and that precedent and case law does not favor the school district in that case.

WHAT TO DO NOW?

Schools are sometimes seen as impenetrable fortresses by those who live and work outside of its walls. Approaching school personnel with a complaint takes energy, and sometimes that energy is worked up to the point of explosion. Fear of "the run-around" only makes the situation more explosive. It is important that the information given to parents is accurate and consistent.

SETTING THE STAGE

When the call, email, or frantic message from an administrator first comes, saying that a resource is being questioned or challenged, the school librarian should have a set response—to immediately write "the memo." There is no need to know why the material is being questioned. The purpose of the memo is to present facts about the resource, not to defend against specific issues. The one-page memo to the principal or instructional supervisor regarding the resource should be formatted as follows:

Paragraph 1: Write a brief plot summary of the resource. If the school librarian has not read, viewed, or listened to it, the plot can still be gleaned from summaries, review sources, or booktalk sites.

Paragraph 2: Embed the resource into the selection criteria. Quoting from reviews, explain factually how the resource meets selection principles, i.e., why it is accurate, authoritative, relevant to the curriculum, the four areas of appropriateness.

Paragraph 3: Review briefly the board-approved process for challenging materials, explaining each step.

Paragraph 4: Explain to the principal why the challenged materials process must be followed. The short answer is, of course, so that the district does not end up as a footnote in a school law text. The tone must be subtle, but factual. Court cases should be mentioned by name. The administrator should be familiar with *Tinker* and may have heard of *Pico.*

If the challenge becomes a media frenzy, which sometimes happens, pieces of the memo will be heard being calmly read on the evening news time and time again. The esteem of school librarians will rise dramatically from the perspective of the principal and superintendent.

IN THE LION'S DEN

When dealing with emotionally explosive situations, it helps to provide written documentation of school policy and procedures. If nothing else, it may provide an opportunity for a small window of time to explain the procedure. Almost all school boards have passed an approved selection policy and a procedure for challenging materials. This process usually begins with a form for concerned citizens to fill out. Although the policy or procedure that a district has approved may be flawed, it is the only allowable procedure. The case law surrounding challenged materials almost always is because the school or district did not follow the board-approved procedures. It may be informative and beneficial to the school library to have a file of policies and procedures from other districts even though they should not be used in your district. If challenges end up in the legal arena, the degree to which board-approved procedures were followed is a key component. Using another school's policy because "we liked this other one so much better" is not going to carry much weight.

Keep multiple copies of the school-board approved selection policy and challenged materials procedure in a desk drawer. Make sure that each of these has the date and policy number showing that they are official school board documents. Take copies, if appropriate, to a meeting with the complainant. Explain the process, and offer to let the complainant take the documents with them to read over.

MAKE THE CALL

We really do not know the number of questioned, challenged, or banned materials because most challenges are not reported, and sometimes the material is simply removed without incident. It is, however, the professional responsibility of school librarians to report challenges. Without this documentation, the top ten challenged materials list will continue to inaccurately reflect the number and titles of resources that are questioned, challenged, or banned.

WHAT WE DON'T KNOW

One interesting point that is raised occasionally and whispered about in corners is how long materials that are removed from the collections stay removed. Is it an eternal banishment? Or can removed materials be quietly replaced after several years, and after the challenging parents' children have safely moved on to another school?

Another question that is unanswered is how a new school librarian knows what has been banned in the past. There may not be a process to document past challenges. Think of this likely scenario. A new school librarian receives a request to update the biography section to include more diversity. They notice that the classic and often-studied *I Know Why the Caged Bird Sings* by Maya Angelou is not present. The new school librarian orders it, completely unaware that a public and rancorous challenge occurred the previous February.

There is little evidence in discussion lists or in the literature that any of the above occurs or is a problem if it does occur. Time rolls on, and even the most publicized challenge furor soon dies for lack of continued energy.

Challenges cannot be prevented, and they cannot be predicted. Concerned parents are probably not aware of nude rock stars on the cover of *Rolling Stone* magazine, and instead challenge Steinbeck's *The Grapes of Wrath*. An elementary library collection will be watched carefully to see if Harry Potter has made his insidious way onto the shelves, but other works making the top ten challenged lists every year such as Schwarz's *Scary Stories to Read in the Dark*, will be checked in and out with nary a ripple.

Because of this, it is useless for school librarians to deny students access to graphic novels, popular works, or specific topics and titles on the grounds that they are avoiding a challenge. They aren't, and instead they have diminished another bit of social capital for children who are in desperate need of the level playing field that schools are supposed to provide. True, some students and parents will buy resources that school libraries refuse to provide, but others won't, can't, or don't. Very few authors and speakers at a library conference stand with tears in their eyes and reminisce, saying, "_____was the best librarian . . . refused to purchase any resource any kid would remotely be interested in, wouldn't let us read anything above or below our AR level, and golly . . . if we had one overdue book, our checkout privileges were totally gone."

Fear of a challenge is not one of the selection principles. Lester Asheim said, "Censors look for what is wrong about a book; Selectors look for what is right" (1953). All schools and districts have censors that we may have to face, but the mirror may be where we face the strongest censor.

The role of the school librarian in this process is to gather the facts, share the importance of the school board approved process, defend the process, let the committee process work, and, hardest of all, accept the results.

REFERENCES

Angelou, M. (1970). *I Know Why the Caged Bird Sings.* New York: Random House.
Asheim, L. (1953). Not censorship but selection. *Wilson Library Bulletin, 28*(1), pp. 63–67.
Board of Education, *Island Trees Union Free School District no. 26 v. Pico*, 73 L.Ed.2d 435 (457 U.S. 853, 102 S.Ct. 2799 1982).
Case v. Unified School District no. 233, 908 F.Supp. 864 (D. Kan. 1995 1995).
Dewey, J. (1905). *The School and Society.* New York: McClure, Phillips, & Company.
Tinker v. Des Moines Independent Community School District, 21 L.Ed.2d 731 (393 U.S. 503, 89 S.Ct. 733 1969).

30

Can a School Library Be Challenge-Proof?

Helen R. Adams

Many school librarians fear facing a challenge to a resource in their libraries. Some even try to avoid a challenge by not selecting books that may be considered controversial. Library supervisors or principals who are also concerned about challenges may peruse the titles in a book order and cross out those that seem provocative or controversial.

Although there are books that have been challenged repeatedly in school libraries, no individual can know for certain what books or other resources will trigger a challenge. This fact is evident when checking the books listed by the American Library Association (ALA) as the "Frequently Challenged Books." Titles range from *The Kite Runner* by Khaled Hosseini to the Captain Underpants series by Dav Pilkey to *Go Ask Alice* by Anonymous to *Bridge to Terebithia* by Katherine Paterson. A diverse variety of books including *Adventures of Huckleberry Finn* by Mark Twain, *In the Night Kitchen* by Maurice Sendak, and *Arming America: The Origins of a National Gun Culture* by Michael A. Bellesiles have also been targets of censors (http://www.ala.org/advocacy/bbooks/frequentlychallengedbooks). The practice of self-censorship because of the fear of challenges is not a practical or ethical solution.

IS CHALLENGE-PROOFING A COLLECTION POSSIBLE?

Is there any way other than self-censorship that a school librarian can guarantee no resource will ever be challenged? The answer to that question is "no." In reality, any book or other library resource may be offensive to and questioned by a parent, principal, teacher, community member, or student. As discussed in the annual *State of America's Libraries,* challenges are most often initiated by parents and administration (ALA 2019). Since no one can predict which books or other resources will be challenged or who will express a concern, a more effective approach is to

Challenge-Proofing Your School Library Checklist

I have . . .	Met	Not Yet or District-Level Action	Next Steps

Personal Knowledge

Educated myself about how the First Amendment and court decisions affect minors' right to receive information in schools and libraries.

Reviewed American Library Association policy statements related to intellectual freedom and resisting censorship including the *Library Bill of Rights* and its interpretations and the *Code of Ethics* for the ALA.

Become a member of a state school library organization and participate in state conferences, workshops, and other professional development opportunities.

The Materials Selection Policy

Created a materials selection policy that includes a process for reconsideration of school library resources and requested that it be officially approved by the institution's governing body.

Posted the materials selection policy on the school's and the library's web pages to inform educators, patrons, and the community how school library resources are chosen.

Reviewed the reconsideration process and I am familiar with the steps and persons involved.

Worked with the principal and other administrators to clarify any steps or responsibilities in the reconsideration process that are not clear.

Arranged with administrators for opportunities to educate teachers, students, and parents about the selection and reconsideration of school library resources.

Considered how to proceed if the principal directs me as the school librarian to remove a library resource without following the reconsideration process.

Educating the Principal and Teachers

Proactively instructed administrators and teachers about materials selection, reconsideration of library materials, and how to respond to a complaint by a parent or other individual about a library resource.

Explained to new staff the school's library policies related to materials selection, reconsideration of a resource, circulation of resources, privacy of library records, interlibrary loan, Internet use, and others.

Annually reviewed with the principal the materials selection policy, how materials are selected, and district reconsideration procedures.

Shared with the principal and staff articles, websites, and other resources related to intellectual freedom in the school library and classrooms.

(*continued*)

Challenge-Proofing Your School Library Checklist (*continued*)

I have . . .	Met	Not Yet or District-Level Action	Next Steps
Selected professional materials related to censorship and made them available to staff.			
Planned collaboratively with teachers and students to create learning experiences incorporating minors' First Amendment speech rights.			
Selection of Materials			
Modeled best practices in selection of library resources by resisting outside pressures to avoid selecting materials considered by some to be controversial.			
Not permitted personal beliefs or values to interfere with selection of library resources.			
Teaching Students about Intellectual Freedom			
Incorporated into formal and informal student instruction, respect for the principles of intellectual freedom.			
Taught students about their First Amendment right to receive information in the school library.			
Educating Parents and the Community			
Described to parents and community members the process used to select library materials.			
Explained the reconsideration process for review of library resources about which a concern has been expressed.			
Practiced positive communication strategies with persons who express concern about a library resource.			
General Advocacy for the Library Program			
Built positive relationships with the principal, school staff, students, parents, and community members.			
Became knowledgeable about local media and provided positive information and photos about the school library program.			
Contacted legislators regarding the impact of proposed legislation on school libraries and patrons. (Adams 2008, Chapters 2, 3, 6, 9)			

take proactive steps toward creating a climate where the principles of intellectual freedom are understood and the legal right of minors to receive information in the school library is acknowledged.

Have school librarians become advocates for intellectual freedom and the First Amendment rights of minors in school libraries? Have they undertaken actions to prepare for a challenge before it occurs? The checklist provided here is an attempt to help school librarians develop a school culture where a challenge to a library resource can be managed successfully through school policy. School librarians can determine the vulnerability of their libraries to challenges by completing the "Challenge-Proofing Your School Library Checklist."

WHAT'S YOUR SCORE?

If more of your answers fall in the "not yet" column, begin to plan how to accomplish each task. Achieving every item on the checklist will take time, but the result will be the evolution of a group of knowledgeable allies who will support more readily the retention of a questioned title when a challenge occurs. It will also result in you being a school librarian who is confident, not fearful, when facing a challenge.

REFERENCES

Adams, H. R. (2008). *Ensuring Intellectual Freedom and Access to Information in the School Library Media Program*. Santa Barbara, CA: Libraries Unlimited.

American Library Association. *Frequently Challenged Books*. Retrieved from http://www.ala.org/advocacy/bbooks/frequentlychallengedbooks.

American Library Association. (2019). *State of America's Library Report 2019*. Retrieved from http://www.ala.org/news/state-americas-libraries-report-2019.

Part V

Filtering, Technology, and the Digital Divide

"The only way to protect children is with education.

You cannot depend on filtering.

You can't depend on creating a .xxx.

That's not going to work.

You have to make sure that parents and

their children really understand the Internet."

—*Emily Sheketoff, Executive Director of the ALA Washington Office*

31

Leadership: Filtering and Social Media

Judi Moreillon

Libraries that receive Library Services and Technology Act (LSTA) funds or Internet access through the Universal Service Fund E-Rate Program are required to comply with the Child Internet Protection Act (CIPA). This Act was passed in 2000 and the Supreme Court ruled that it was constitutional in 2003. Since then, legal and professional opinions about CIPA and Internet filtering, based on librarians' and their patrons' real-world experiences, are ever more wide-ranging.

NAVIGATING CIPA

In relationship to CIPA and filtering, there are, however, a few sure things for the school librarian:

- The purpose of the filter is to "protect against access" to materials that are obscene, child pornography, and anything "harmful to minors" under the age of seventeen.
- There is no obligation to use any particular filter.
- Filtering is inherently imperfect.
- A "good faith" effort constitutes compliance with CIPA, and therefore,
- Schools and libraries have some leeway in terms of selecting and modifying filtering technology (ALA 2009).

Since 2008, schools in the E-Rate Program must also specify that students are being taught how to appropriately use social networking sites and to guard against cyberbullying in their Acceptable Use Policies (AUPs). "With the new CIPA requirement, school librarians are in a position of strength to ensure that students receive regular digital citizenship education—a far more effective strategy than rigid filtering" (Adams 2012, 29).

Classroom teachers and school librarians know that a handful of students will choose to skirt the filter, and some will introduce inappropriate material into the academic environment. When teaching digital citizenship, the goal is to help youth make better choices and help schools maintain positive and appropriate learning environments. If CIPA is the law of the land for librarians serving children and youth, how, then, can school librarians take a leadership role in providing the least possible restrictions when accessing and publishing to the Internet?

WEBSITES

Banned Websites Awareness Day was born as an effort to spotlight the challenges inherent in Internet filtering (http://www.ala.org/aasl/advocacy/bwad). Originally sponsored by a dedicated group of high school librarians, the American Association of School Librarians (AASL) adopted this initiative to publicize the fact that censorship, which is often thought of exclusively in relationship to books, also happens when school district filters block students, teachers, and librarians from accessing educationally sound websites. Awareness is an important first step. Action is the logical next step.

What should school librarians do when a useful website is blocked by their district's filter? Working with district technology departments, librarians can most easily make a case for unblocking sites that support standards-based learning. The tricky part can be supporting students' access to information for personal knowledge that does not necessarily relate directly to mandated curriculum. In 2011, the American Civil Liberties Union (ACLU) launched the "Don't Filter Me" campaign, an inquiry into whether or not school filters were blocking access to Lesbian-Gay-Bisexual-Transgender (LGBT) information and organizations. A lawsuit followed and, ultimately, a federal district court ruled that a Missouri school district must "begin using a filtering system that blocks pornography without discriminating against LGBT-related content" (ACLU 2012).

School librarians are in a position to make every day in their schools and libraries banned websites awareness days. Taking action to ensure access for all students and teachers is at the heart of librarians' mission to serve the needs of all and protect the First Amendment rights of library users.

SOCIAL MEDIA

In many school districts, filtering extends to social networking sites such as Facebook, Twitter, YouTube, blogs, wikis, and more. When educators strive to make in-school learning more authentic and relevant to students' out-of-school technology-infused learning and living environment, their attempts to integrate social media are frequently pulled up short by the filter's block. How can educators use participatory culture tools and involve students in knowledge creation if the filter gets in the way?

This situation often leads to "connected" students rightly concluding that what they do in school is disconnected from what they do outside of school. In the Common Beliefs, the *AASL Standards Framework for Learners* note: "Information technologies must be appropriately integrated and equitable available" (AASL 2018a). Advocating for students' access to and appropriate use of social media websites during the school day when they can be guided in developing digital citizenship skills is part of the librarians' charge. Integrating these tools into learning and teaching can help motivate and inspire students to create knowledge and use the web to share their ideas with others.

Patrons of all ages using public library computers in the communities with which I am most familiar (in Tucson, Arizona and Denton, Texas) have access to blogs, Facebook, Pinterest, Twitter, wikis, and more. These sites invite participation in larger conversations that can make school-based learning more meaningful to students. If we are committed to the idea that 21st-century people, pre-K–12 students included, can and should be producers as well as consumers of information and ideas, school access to social media sites should not be different from access provided by the students' local public library.

A LEADERSHIP OPPORTUNITY

As with other aspects of digital citizenship, we can look to AASL's *National School Library Standards for Learners, School Librarians, and School Libraries* for support for our efforts to provide students with opportunities to practice essential learning skills required for their success. When school librarians work collaboratively with district-level information technology departments, everyone's goal should be to provide access to appropriate resources and social media tools in order to offer a rich and engaging menu of resources and tools for 21st-century learners. When we apply our knowledge of curriculum, instructional strategies, and technology resources and tools, we can help make in-school learning more relevant to students. Let's lead and make sure students and teachers have access to websites, including social media sites, to support curriculum as well as personal learning goals and needs.

REFERENCES

ACLU. (February 15, 2012). *Court Orders Missouri District to Stop Censoring LGBT Websites*. Retrieved from http://bit.ly/1a4DJF2.

Adams, H. R. (2012). The continuing saga of internet filtering. *School Library Monthly, 29*(3), pp. 28–29.

American Association of School Librarians (AASL). (2018a). *AASL Standards Framework for Learners*. Retrieved from https://standards.aasl.org/wp-content/uploads/2017/11/AASL-Standards-Framework-for-Learners-pamphlet.pdf.

American Association of School Librarians (AASL). (2018b). *National School Library Standards for Learners, School Librarians, and School Libraries*. Chicago: American Library Association.

American Library Association (ALA). (2009). *Children Internet Protection Act (CIPA) Legal FAQ*. Retrieved from http://www.ala.org/advocacy/advleg/federallegislation/cipa/cipalegalfaq.

32

Internet Filtering: Are We Making Any Progress?

Helen R. Adams

Congress approved the Children's Internet Protection Act (CIPA) in 2000 with the best possible motives—protecting children and young adults using the "Wild West" web. Unfortunately, the legislation is misinterpreted by many school districts and has created the unintended consequence of choking off access to valuable educational resources for students and teachers.

WHAT'S THE CURRENT FILTERING SITUATION IN SCHOOLS?

Many years after CIPA's implementation, the filters in many districts continue to be overly restrictive and block far beyond the requirements of shielding against *visual images* that are obscene, contain child pornography, or material harmful to minors as defined by federal law (FCC). The law does not require that districts filter text, audio, social media, or interactive web tools, although filtering software routinely bars access to these resources. To compound the problem, many schools make unblocking of mislabeled, but legitimate, websites a lengthy process.

In recent conversations with school librarians, their stories have not changed. Patty, a high school librarian in Wyoming, described the process for unblocking a website in her district this way:

> When students encounter a site that is blocked, they have an option to request that the page be unblocked. Since our students do not have separate logins when using school equipment, there is no way for the IT Department to know who initiated the request, so individual students are not notified of the status of their request.

> When a teacher requests that a site be unblocked, he emails our District Network Engineer, who reviews the request and then responds to the individual teacher. Regardless of whether an unblocking request comes from a student or a teacher, the response can take minutes, hours, or days. Our District Technology Department's workload means they cannot address the requests within a timeframe that meets the

real-time needs of teachers and students. (Patty, email message to author, November 16, 2015)

Patty, her students, and colleagues are not alone. Librarians across the country, including Rae Ann, an elementary librarian in Pennsylvania, continue to find the process for unblocking a website to be long and a hindrance to instructional preparation.

> Our web filtering can be described as pretty restrictive; however, we are able to request a website be unblocked. We have to submit an online work order to the technology department. Once the request is received, the techs will ask the teacher to *defend* the decision to unblock a site. Then, the Director of Technology needs to approve the decision. By this time, too much time has passed. Most elementary teachers (me included) will find an alternative website rather than endure a delay in finding information for a lesson. (Rae Ann, email to author, July 19, 2015)

Kristen, a high school librarian in Pennsylvania, brought up another way in which filters impact her teaching.

> Students who have their own devices at school and connect to the school's wifi are subject to the filter. When I'm using a new app with classes, I always have to check with technology [staff] to make sure it isn't blocked. But by the time we take this extra step, it's too late—we've already moved on from that lesson. (Kristen, email message to author, November 11, 2015)

Rae Ann was very forthright in her assessment of the cost of strict filtering.

> By having restrictive filters at school, we aren't teaching our students what to do in the real world. They will face situations where inappropriate websites and images appear on their phones, iPads, and other devices. Outside of school or a public library, our students may never encounter a filter while using the Internet. How will they know what to do? (Rae Ann, email to author, August 4, 2015)

ONE POSITIVE ADDITION TO CIPA

After CIPA was implemented in 2001, there was much discussion about teaching students about Internet safety rather than relying on filters. In 2008, the Protecting Children in the 21st Century Act added a provision to CIPA requiring schools receiving E-rate discounts for Internet access to include an instructional component in their Internet safety policies. Specifically, the policy must provide for educating minors "about appropriate online behavior" and "cyberbullying awareness and response" (FCC).

Districts take this obligation seriously. Karen, a high school librarian in North Carolina, explained that in her district, online safety and cyberbullying lessons are taught annually to elementary students in each grade over a period of several weeks. Middle and high school students are instructed in sixth and ninth grades using videos from iSafe (www.isafe.org) and engage in discussion of the content. To provide documentation, teachers are required to "verify online [to district administration] that students have received the information" (Karen, email to author, November 20, 2015).

WHAT HAVE ALA AND AASL DONE?

The American Library Association (ALA) and the American Association of School Librarians (AASL) have undertaken extensive efforts to combat excessive filtering in schools and libraries; and over the lengthy period since CIPA's enactment, these actions are easy to overlook. Here's a quick review:

- **2003**: ALA created the "Libraries and the Internet Tool Kit" and updated it in 2013 and 2020. Its purpose is to help librarians manage Internet use and educate their patrons.
- **June 2009**: The ALA Council approved "Minors and Internet Interactivity: An Interpretation of the Library Bill of Rights" (http://www.ala.org/advocacy /intfreedom/librarybill/interpretations/minors-internet-activity).
- **2010:** AASL established Banned Websites Awareness Day (http://www.ala .org/aasl/advocacy/bwad/) to remind administrators, school boards, parents, and the general public about restrictive filtering in schools and its impact on students' educational experiences.
- **2012:** AASL added questions about filtering to its national longitudinal survey "School Libraries Count!" Survey results revealed that 94 percent of schools use filters, and 73 percent of respondents disclosed that there is no differentiation between filtering for elementary students and high school seniors. Not surprisingly, 52 percent of school librarians reported that filters impact student learning by inhibiting student research, 42 percent stated that filters ignore the social process involved in learning, and 25 percent perceive that filters discourage online collaboration (AASL).
- **2014:** The ALA Office for Intellectual Freedom and the Office for Information Technology Policy published "Fencing out Knowledge: Impacts of the Children's Internet Protection Act Ten Years Later." The report provided a record of the extent of filtering in schools, its negative impact, and produced four recommendations to take action against the current filtering situation. The report and recommendations are available at http://www .ala.org/aboutala/sites/ala.org.aboutala/files/content/oitp/publications /issuebriefs/cipa_report.pdf.
- **2014**: "Minors and Internet Interactivity: An Interpretation of the Library Bill of Rights" was revised and renamed "Minors and Internet Activity." It speaks to the value of minors' use of web tools for academic pursuits and creative expression.
- **June 2015:** ALA Council approved "Internet Filtering: An Interpretation of the Library Bill of Rights." Written with input from public, academic, and school librarians, it lays out the weaknesses of filters, their impact on K–12 instruction and student learning, and asks schools to create a time-sensitive process for unblocking mislabeled websites.

These accomplishments were achieved through the work of many ALA and AASL committees and individuals with strong opinions about filtering and supporting students' First Amendment right to receive information in libraries. Yet years after the "Fencing out Knowledge" report was released, there is still no organized action on the recommendations including the two most important for K–12 schools:

- "Develop a toolkit for school leaders," and
- "Conduct research to explore the educational uses of social media platforms and assess the impact of filtering in schools" (Batch 2014).

WHAT CAN YOU DO?

Filtering is here to stay; and although ALA and AASL have taken positive action, restrictive filtering is still the norm in many schools. What is *your* role in affecting change? Here are a few ideas.

- Begin (or continue) a conversation about filtering in your school.
- Share the "Fencing out Knowledge" report findings on the impact of restrictive filtering on students' education with your administrators, colleagues, and parents.
- Advocate for reducing the level of filtering to meet CIPA's requirements but not affect access to Internet sites and interactive tools used for instruction and student research.
- Acknowledge minors' First Amendment rights by creating a system for students to request unblocking of mislabeled filtered websites that are not obscene, child pornography, or material harmful to minors (Adams 2020).
- Talk to AASL leaders about initiating action on the "Fencing out Knowledge" recommendations.

Your efforts, combined with allies in the library and education communities, can make a difference in reducing over-reliance on filters and moving schools toward an emphasis on instruction and developing students' personal decision-making online. Not only will this change produce a better learning environment, but it will also guide students to become responsible digital citizens.

REFERENCES

Adams, Helen R. (2020). "Internet Filtering and School Libraries." In Garnar, M. (Ed.), *Intellectual Freedom Manual*, 10th ed. Chicago: American Library Association.

American Association of School Librarians (AASL). (2012). *Filtering in Schools: AASL Executive Summary*. Retrieved from http://www.ala.org/aasl/sites/ala.org.aasl/files/content/advocacy/research/docs/AASL_Filtering_Exec_Summary.pdf.

Batch, K. R. (June 2014). *Fencing Out Knowledge: Revisiting the Children's Internet Protection Act 10 Years Later. Policy Brief No. 5*. American Library Association, Office for Information Technology Policy and the Office for Intellectual Freedom. Retrieved from http://www.ala.org/aboutala/sites/ala.org.aboutala/files/content/oitp/publications/issuebriefs/cipa_report.pdf.

Federal Communications Commission (FCC). *Guide: Children's Internet Protection Act*. Retrieved from https://www.fcc.gov/guides/childrens-internet-protection-act.

33

Equitable Access, the Digital Divide, and the Participation Gap!

Patricia Franklin and Claire Gatrell Stephens

Recently, when a district administrator was asked about providing an online resource for all high schools in the district, his response was not negative; however, he made clear that if the district provided this resource, funds from state monies would not be available for other school library collection development. Yet, other schools in the area offer the service and have found ways to pay for it without jeopardizing state monies for the school library's budget. This exemplifies how different school districts or even schools within one district can have varied levels of access available for students. This issue seems to be a common problem in school libraries across the country.

INEQUITABLE ACCESS

A few years ago, the terms "digital divide" and "equitable access" became popular ways of describing the differing levels of technology access available for students. Often, schools within the same district had vastly unequal levels of access. These same inequities often applied at home, too. Much has been written about the "haves and have-nots" in terms of technology access based on factors like economics, ethnicity, and education level. Although there have been improvements in closing this digital divide, new issues are surfacing.

MIT Professor Henry Jenkins points to the rise of what he calls the participation gap, the difference in educational experiences of students with and without technology access (NEA 2008). Simply put, students without computer and Internet access in the home have fewer chances to gain the digital literacy needed to function in our current world. These students may have access through school and public libraries, but time constraints, filters, and the ability to store and download information often limit access. Contrast this with the student who has a personal computer in their room and high-speed Internet access. The student with 24/7 access can use the computer for school assignments and spend many extra hours surfing the web. These students develop awareness and communication skills that may lead teachers to respond to them more positively than those without the same experiences.

The idea of a participation gap also leads to consideration of several areas of inequality that contribute to the problem. Inequities include the variety of hardware and software people use to access information, their ability to exercise autonomy in using the Internet, the skill level they bring to Internet use, and the amount of support users receive to learn technology use and integration (DiMaggio & Hargittai 2001). Further study needs to be done on the causes and effects of these problems, but school librarians should not wait to begin addressing these issues.

THE ROLE OF SCHOOL LIBRARIES

School libraries must embrace the changes facing students because of the vast amount of digital and portable information, the changes in the nature and sources of information, and the need for new workforce skills demanded by the global and technological economy. In his paper "Dangers and Opportunities," Doug Johnson suggests ways libraries can embrace the digital age. Even though school librarians may not be able to do all that is suggested or may not find ideas appropriate or workable in their particular schools, these ideas are still important to equitable access and technology participation. The following list of topics are adapted from Doug Johnson's "Top Seven Opportunities for Libraries in the Digital Age" (2007) and elaborated upon with ideas for what school librarians can do to update their programs and better meet the learning and technology needs of students.

- Look for opportunities to improve the school library facility. It is not just about books anymore. If a facility doesn't have enough computers or uses antiquated machines with unreliable Internet access, things need to change. School librarians can lobby the school administration, district personnel, or local community groups, or write grants to gain the financial means for improvements. Even small changes are positive and students will benefit.
- Create opportunities to educate. Increase efforts to collaborate with teachers to teach information skills to all students. Consider innovative approaches. Sponsor a technology club with the goal in mind of teaching students how to use common software and become sophisticated technology users. Be creative! The school library is not a traditional classroom setting; approaches to education should not be tied to traditional formats and programs.
- Embrace your changing role! Invest the time and energy needed to meet the demands of being a 21st-century school librarian. Students may have grown up with computers and the Internet, but they don't automatically possess wisdom and expertise about online resources. Studies document that the majority of people using search engines such as Google and Altavista use only one- to two-word search terms; try only one query, don't use advanced search features, don't proceed past the first page of results, and don't understand the difference between sponsored links and search results (DiMaggio & Hargittai 2001; Johnson 2007). School librarians can still be a source to help students access valid information from the web.
- Don't wait for them to come to you—get out there, go to them! Students live in a world of push technologies (Johnson 2007), for example, they sign up on a music service to automatically receive a new song when it debuts and it will automatically be pushed out to them for download when it becomes available. Consider making the school library a push organization. Boldly market services. Embrace new technologies such as podcasting. Update

the school library web page frequently. Do everything possible to demonstrate to students and teachers that using the school library services will lead quickly and easily to findable, valid resources.

- Diversify offerings, include the nontraditional. Maybe it is time to consider allowing students to use computers in ways currently prohibited. What about checking out recording equipment to students? Are audiobooks available for student checkout? Does the school library offer a place for group work/discussion? When is it open for students? Is there a way to alter the hours and better serve the school community? Are services offered to students who may not know how to use basic programs such as Microsoft's Office Suite or Google Drive? Are services offered for parents? (Often, the parents of digital divide students are uneducated technology users themselves so they can't support their children's efforts.) Maybe a change would benefit everyone, especially the students. Don't be afraid to think outside the box!

- Grow professionally. The significance of staying current has never been more crucial. If we are to maintain our relevance in a 21st-century school, then we must maintain our leadership role. Historically, school librarians have been among the first to bring new technologies to the world of education. There is no reason for this to stop because the technology is evolving so quickly. Keeping up-to-date on new trends in teaching and learning will help incorporate the newest technologies in ways that will benefit everyone.

Creating equitable access and bridging the participation gap in the school library is an important job. It happens strategically as school librarians plan, set goals, and establish programs. It happens daily when working with teachers to plan lessons and teach classes. It happens one-on-one when time is taken to work with a student struggling to use a computer to access information, type a paper, or create a digital presentation. In fact, in such a rapidly evolving world, it may be one of the most important things a school librarian does each day. School librarians shouldn't shy away from it; students' futures depend on such efforts.

RESOURCES

DiMaggio, P, & Hargittai, E. (Summer 2001). "From 'digital divide' to 'digital inequality': Studying internet use as penetration increases." *Working Paper Series 15*. Retrieved from https://pdfs.semanticscholar.org/4843/610b79d670136e3cdd12311f91f5 cc98d2ee.pdf?_ga=2.128727372.1553264040.1568818075-2019408512.15688 18075.

Johnson, D. (July 10, 2007). *Dangers and Opportunities: Challenges for Libraries in the Digital Age*. Retrieved from https://docs.google.com/document/d/1jmWpTZoz7 RmU_XjmrOsmOEibUKZsXNph7jGOw8zapbA/edit.

NEA. (March 2008). *The Participation Gap: A Conversation with Media Expert and MIT Professor Henry Jenkins*. Retrieved from http://www.nea.org/archive/15468.htm.

34

Bring Your Own Device (BYOD) and Equitable Access to Technology

Helen R. Adams

Countless recent online communications are devoted to managing use of personal technology devices in schools—and questions about these devices abound. Can faculty bring their own mobile technology to work? Are students allowed to connect personal devices to the school's network? Who assumes liability for damage or loss of a student-owned device? Less frequently asked is, how will students from impoverished families have equitable access to technology under a "bring your own device" (BYOD) policy?

EQUITY: AN ETHICAL DILEMMA

In public schools, instructional resources and technology should be available equitably to every student regardless of socioeconomic status. Under BYOD, schools face an ethical dilemma when some families are financially unable to provide personal technology for their children. The problem is real, and the statistics for poor and homeless Americans are astonishing:

- In 2017, 12.8 million or 17.5% of all children lived in poverty, with children of color experiencing higher rates than do white children (University of Wisconsin–Madison).
- In 2010, more than 18% of U.S. children had at least one unemployed or underemployed parent, compared with 9.1% in 2007 (Mishel 2011).
- In 2013, one in 30 or 2.5 million children were homeless, an annual increase of 8% (National Center on Family Homelessness 2014).

Some educators question whether all students should be restricted from using their personal technology in school because their economically disadvantaged peers do not have similar tools, and the disparity in the "real world" is often cited as justification.

PARENTS AND BYOD

Parents are partners with schools, and to gauge community support for BYOD, Jan, a technology director in the Midwest, disseminated a survey. Amid positive responses, parents had concerns about students' sense of responsibility; the potential for loss, theft, and damage; inappropriate use while in class; upgrades as technology changes; the potential for bullying; and families who cannot afford personal technology for school use. A few expressed apprehension about the emotional distress of students without personal devices, with one parent asking, "What if you are the one kid in a class without a laptop?" (Jan, email message to author, January 3, 2012). Although educators may propose sharing of students' personal devices in a classroom, some parents did not want their child to let others use their expensive technology. Still other parents preferred that the district buy the necessary hardware.

PROVIDING EQUITY IN A BYOD WORLD

As advocates for equitable access, school librarians must exercise leadership and urge study of strategies that will provide technology resources for all students. Before a BYOD plan is implemented, these ideas need to be considered:

- Share: Does everyone need an individual hardware item, or can a group share a school- or student-owned device? According to Scott Floyd, an instructional technologist in Texas, "Our students do a lot of collaborative work. It's the only way to prepare them for the work world they will enter. Many of our teachers in elementary levels will not allow a [personal] device to be used unless the student is willing to at least share their screen. Sometimes students with devices will let others take over the driving of it with monitoring by the student who owns it" (Scott Floyd, email message to author, January 8, 2012).
- Purchase/checkout: In addition to allowing student-owned technology in classrooms, purchase hardware that can be borrowed from the library by a teacher for classroom use by students without personal devices.
- Seek funding: Approach community groups or foundations, or seek grant opportunities to secure funding of mobile equipment for circulation to disadvantaged students in school.
- Community purchasing program: Set mobile device specifications and work with district hardware vendors to offer discounts on new technology for families (Roscorla, November 15, 2010).

Incorporating strategies for equity into BYOD programs creates a win-win situation for all students.

REFERENCES

Mishel, L. (September 8, 2011). Share of children with at least one unemployed or under-employed parent. *Economy Policy Institute*. Retrieved from https://www.epi.org /publication/share-children-unemployed-underemployed.

National Center on Family Homelessness. (November 2014). *America's Youngest Outcasts 2014: State Report Card on Child Homelessness. Executive Summary*. Retrieved from https://www.air.org/sites/default/files/downloads/report/Americas-Youngest -Outcasts-Child-Homelessness-Nov2014.pdf.

Roscorla, T. (November 15, 2010). Student devices save districts money. *Converge*. [No longer accessible].

University of Wisconsin–Madison. U.S. Poverty Rates by Age. *Institute for Research on Poverty*. Retrieved from https://www.irp.wisc.edu/resources/who-is-poor.

35

Baby Steps: Preparing for a One-to-One Device Program

Monica Cabarcas

One-to-one, or one device assigned to one student, is a growing phenomenon in schools across our nation. Some schools are already wading through the uncharted territory of tablet programs, laptop programs, or other pilots. Meanwhile, many school teachers are still checking out computer labs and laptop carts and the idea of a one-to-one program feels like something pulled from the tales of Never Never Land. This chapter shares the experiences of a Virginia middle school as it implemented such a program and focuses on future steps librarians and staff can take to further develop this meaningful shift.

SCHOOL-WIDE PLANNING FOR A GRADE-LEVEL PILOT

In the 2013–2014 school year, our school participated in a grade-level pilot program, issuing individual laptops to seventh-grade students. In order to make any pilot successful, members of the school community have to plan for an intentional change. At the time, I was an instructional coach working with teachers across content areas and worked with colleagues to solve problems. I had a first-row seat as the staff worked through the stages of troubleshooting, sharing philosophies, and developing policies and procedures that put everyone in the building on the same page.

The principal initiated the process of school-wide change in the spring of the previous school year. First, she restructured faculty meetings to include time for research on other pilots and any data they collected. Staff looked at feedback from pilots like Project Red and brainstormed adjustments and new ideas that were unique to our building needs. Then the principal looked for support at the county level, requesting laptops for teacher checkout. This allowed teachers to familiarize themselves with the devices their students would use. Teachers received professional development on Google apps for education and Blackboard, a course management system. Professional development was delivered school-wide, while other training was offered on a personal basis to meet the needs of an individual teacher or professional learning community.

In the fall of the pilot year, the principal strategically shifted all other devices and laptop carts to individual grade levels. It was almost as if the whole school had shifted to a school-wide one-to-one program overnight. The critical difference was that seventh graders had newer, higher functioning equipment that they were allowed to take home. Other grade levels had the former laptop carts that were older and less reliable and couldn't be taken home. Throughout the year, the seventh-grade team acted as a discussion panel sharing their experiences throughout the division. Teachers from other schools peppered them with questions on behavior management, Blackboard, flipped learning, Google apps, teacher planning, interactive assessments, and so much more. Their feedback helped other schools troubleshoot and plan for their own implementation programs.

By the 2014–2015 school year, our staff was prepared to implement this school-wide. With the full one-to-one integration underway, we made substantial changes to our technology procedures. Since we expected laptops to break down or be sent away for repair, the school instituted a loaner cart. This was housed in the media center and required a sign-in process. The school also formed a committee of grade-level team leaders with a technology integration focus. The team worked through procedures, adjusted expectations, generated professional development ideas, created student feedback surveys, and one lead teacher even developed an entire series of online cyber-safety lessons that students completed prior to bringing their devices home. All of these changes became entry points for collaboration between the librarian, teachers, and the administration.

IMPLICATIONS FOR THE SCHOOL LIBRARY PROGRAM

So what did all this change mean for the school library? The one-to-one program meant that the physical boundaries of the library were about to collapse and its territory was about to extend tremendously.

During the grade-level pilot, the Library Media Specialist (LMS) took several important steps. First, she began experimenting with her Virtual Learning Commons (VLC). Since students could use the databases from their classroom without necessarily visiting the media center, she began redesigning her landing page. The LMS selected Symbaloo, a digital bookmarking tool that presents itself as colored tiles on a grid versus a linear list of text and links, as an organizer for this page. We created a Symbaloo webmix, customized to student needs. It included carefully selected tools to which students and teachers needed quick access, including Discovery, Brain Pop, Duck Duck Go, Sweet Search, eBooks, databases, and our public library. This was critical because students would be using materials from their classrooms without her assistance. They needed to navigate independently and not get frustrated with a complicated click path. Second, since teachers had a school-assigned Google account, the LMS also experimented with creating a Google website and learned how to use Google forms to collect data tied to her goals. By the end of the year, we were experimenting with other educational web 2.0 tools such as Easel.ly to create infographics that could be tied to her annual report. The critical key to the LMS's success was diving right into the applications and programs that students would use. While she started with tasks related to her own professional development such as collecting student data or publicizing circulation statistics, she was learning skills that could be transferred into a daily lesson with ease.

In the 2014–2015 year, when the one-to-one program encompassed all three grade levels, the LMS further adapted her school library program. She restructured her learning space, removing all of the older, bulky desktops. She removed the study carrels, replaced them with flat tables, and only kept four flat screen desktops at standing work stations for quick catalog access and two laptops for guest use. The LMS maintained and updated her Symbaloo webmix and began adding tiles that featured pathfinders for students researching careers or current events in science. She also redesigned the database page on a Google site with descriptors and words in bold so students could easily determine the best resource to use whether they were working from home or school. The LMS's goals expanded to include collaboration with a history teacher who wanted to teach information skills through reference eBooks and databases. Together they collected preassessment data through Google forms and hoped to collect final data through a student-produced screencast of a successful database search. The LMS offered to curate resources for several teachers that were working on projects. When the library was overbooked, she streamlined digital resources so students could use them without a mini-lesson from her; and whenever possible, she offered to visit classrooms instead.

Once laptops reach the desk of every student, instructional design changes. The LMS sent our language arts department weekly resources via email that were timely and related to our one-to-one implementation and our Writing Workshop units. She also supported differentiation by teaching specific technology skills in small groups. At one point in the year, she took a small group of students and walked them through the steps of uploading book reviews to the library catalog. As our school dove deeper into the digital seas, the LMS responded to changing needs, found entry points to work with different professional learning communities (PLCs), and looked for new opportunities to support teachers and students. Her strategies fostered collaboration between teacher and librarian and served as a model for my own future service.

IMPLICATIONS IN THE CLASSROOM

Change in one sphere of the school has an immediate impact on the work completed in another sphere. I note the teacher changes just as much as the media center changes because the teacher-librarian relationship is a symbiotic one. Seventh-grade teachers involved in the pilot ventured on a steep learning curve. How would technology impact instruction?

The initial pilot required teachers to experiment with different learning tools and nearly every teacher's first steps began with uploading content to Blackboard. In the process, they discovered that everyone wanted to design their course their own way. Therefore, the school's principal required consistent landing pages that featured a school-wide agenda template. This helped sixth, seventh, and eighth graders navigate with some expectation of consistency as they switched from one digital learning space to another. Teachers were able to regularly incorporate additional educational resources such as: Quia, Newsela, and library databases. These tools were no longer restricted to days when they could sign out the laptop cart so they became a regular component of instruction. As a result, learning began to shift toward greater inquiry with fewer students passively consuming and more students creating. These changes were important. If students were already using web 2.0 tools regularly in the classroom, they no longer needed that "getting started" mini-lesson in the library. They needed mini-lessons that probed deeper and allowed more inquiry or opportunity for student creation.

When a staff undergoes a major shift in instruction, teachers need time to process, plan, and reflect, and that often means less time for everything else. In my case, I left coaching and joined the school's staff as a seventh-grade teacher in the year of the building-wide one-to-one integration. As I returned, I was quickly reminded of how little time there is for everything. Educators embarking on one-to-one need time to experiment, reflect, and adapt. The LMS should expect to see some moments of teacher excitement, frustration, and moments where a team is completely overwhelmed; being aware of this roller coaster of emotions can determine the success of an entry point.

On the curriculum development end, teachers at the school began searching for dynamic, web-based resources to upload to Blackboard. They wanted to take advantage of the technology and needed content that brought learning to life in a manner that was different from traditional lecture or Word documents. This growing need for dynamic instructional resources is formally captured through the Substitution-Augmentation-Modification-Redefinition progression, better known as the SAMR model (Schrock). The first two stages of this progression are often labeled the "enhancement model," where digital resources merely augment or substitute for traditional resource formats. (Using a Word document, for example, is not radically different from a photocopied document). The latter two stages are considered the transformative stages, where using a device actually changes the dynamic of learning into something deeper. Oftentimes, teachers simply have to start at the substitution level. Our teachers progressed rapidly, however. By the second year, they wanted simulations, carefully curated resources, and engaging content reading materials. Understanding the SAMR model can help a librarian understand a teacher's progression of growth, assess their readiness for new resources, and sell services more effectively in a one-to-one initiative.

ADJUSTING TO A GROWING TREND

When schools initiate a one-to-one program or even a modified one-to-one program, the educational landscape changes and the school library program must adapt. Both teacher and librarian have to learn new programs, applications, and search for new resources. It is important to acknowledge that it is okay to start at the substitution level of the SAMR model when you begin a one-to-one initiative. Sometimes, the educator's first step is simply learning the platform they are using to house curriculum. Collaboration at this level truly starts with a compassionate understanding of what each party is doing to adjust to the new change.

Below are entry points for any librarian whose school is about to embark on a one-to-one program. They come from my experiences and personal reflections of what I would do in my future service as a school librarian.

- Reexamine your virtual learning space. If this space is a virtual version of your library, does it fully represent the scope of your program?
- Experiment with the same platforms that teachers are expected to use.
- Join PLCs to learn about the digital problems and solutions teams are discussing.
- Anticipate the learning opportunities created when students no longer need "permission" to visit your physical library and can visit virtually throughout the day. Then plan ahead for student-friendly access.
- Create tutorials or flipped content as an alternative to a traditional face-to-face mini-lesson.
- Curate content-based resources that represent a mixture of text, simulation, interactive game, video, and audio.
- Consider joining your school's technology committee. If your school doesn't have one, is your administrator willing to start one? A collective party of teachers, librarian(s), and administrators is the best problem-solving force for working through building level technology procedures,

clarifying expectations, sharing ideas, and creating avenues of feedback or assessment.

- Sell new services. Sometimes librarians have to convince colleagues who are more reluctant. How will your services shift? Proactively plan for needs that might increase or services that should change.

Whether your school is currently in a pilot or about to start one, devices are headed your way. Technology will continue to enter our schools through BYOD policies or other initiatives. Even if it starts with one classroom or a grade level, the school librarian has to consider how increased access to a device shapes learning. In a one-to-one program, the virtual learning space becomes just as critical as the physical one. The way a librarian organizes, designs, and uses this platform to engage with learners determines the boundaries or extension of a program. What role can the library play in that learning? It is up to the school librarian to answer this question to initiate powerful change that is meaningful to our stakeholders.

REFERENCE

Schrock, K. *Resources to Support the SAMR Model.* Retrieved from http://www.schrockguide.net/samr.html.

Part VI

Student Privacy in the School Library

"Privacy, precisely because it ensures that
we are never fully known to others,
provides a shelter for imaginative
freedom, curiosity and self-reflection."

—Josh Cohen, Author and Psychoanalyst

36

Privacy: Legal Protections

Helen R. Adams

When was the last time you read the First Amendment? It's short, only 45 words. Here's what it says, "Congress shall make no law respecting an establishment of religion, or prohibiting the free exercise thereof; or abridging the freedom of speech"—that's our part—"or of the press; or the right of the people peaceably to assemble, or to petition the government for a redress of grievances" (National Constitution Center). How is the First Amendment relevant to our discussion of privacy? Although the First Amendment does not mention the word "privacy," courts have determined that minors have the right to receive information and ideas under the guarantee of free speech.

The Supreme Court stated in its well-known 1969 *Tinker v. Des Moines Independent Community School District* decision that students do not shed their constitutional rights at the schoolhouse gate. The Court also said that students need to have a wide range of information for intellectual growth (ALA "Notable First Amendment Court Cases"). This means that students have the right to read and research topics of personal and academic interest. However, if library users do not feel secure that their choice of research topics or reading will be kept confidential either by library staff or from inquisitive peers, they will not use the library. If they feel monitored, students' First Amendment rights are not supported, so protecting students' privacy in their use of school libraries is essential.

There is an important federal law that affects students' privacy in schools and the confidentiality of their records. The Family Educational Rights and Privacy Act, also known as FERPA, protects students' educational records and determines what information in those records may be disclosed. Under FERPA, an educational record is defined as ". . . records that are directly related to a student and that are maintained by an educational agency or institution or a party acting for or on behalf of the agency or institution" (U.S. Department of Education). FERPA gives parents the right to inspect and review their children's education records. Unlike state library records laws, FERPA was not written to shield library records, but rather to protect education records of students.

In recent years, the Family Policy Compliance Office, which oversees compliance with FERPA regulations, has issued guidance stating that library circulation records and similar records in a library are educational records under FERPA. FERPA generally requires institutions to protect the privacy of education records. How-ever, the law contains many exceptions that allow disclosure of students' educa-tion records without parents' consent (Scales 2009, 75).

FERPA permits release of information contained in student records to any school official who has a legitimate educational interest in the records. For exam-ple, this can be a teacher checking on a student's standardized test score. FERPA contains two other exceptions for disclosure of students' records. Records can be disclosed in health and safety emergencies, they can also be released in response to a court order or subpoena. As a result, FERPA permits disclosure of students' library records where state library laws and the ALA *Code of Ethics* would not (Scales 2009, 75).

States also have library records laws to protect the confidentiality of patron's library use. State library confidentiality laws always apply to public libraries and may apply to K–12 libraries. They may impose additional responsibilities on school libraries to protect student library records that go beyond FERPA's requirements. State library records laws vary in the types of libraries to which they apply, the records covered, and when records may be released. As a result, school librarians must read and interpret them carefully. For example, the New York State Library records law is very broad and protective in its coverage. It protects users' records in public, school, college, and university libraries and library systems. It protects library records including—and the law says it this way—but not limited to circula-tion records, computer database searches, interlibrary loan transactions, refer-ence queries, requests for photocopies of library materials, reserve requests, and the use of audio-visual materials. The records in New York State can only be released to library staff for conducting library business, to the library user them-selves, or with a subpoena or court order (State Privacy Laws).

On the other hand, Pennsylvania's library records law is very narrow and covers only circulation records. The information may only be released for proceedings in a criminal court case. State library records laws generally do not distinguish between adults and minors' rights. They simply refer to library users. However, in at least fifteen states including Wisconsin (where I live), Georgia, Ohio, and Vermont, the state laws allow parents and guardians to access library records of their minor children or wards (ALA, "State Privacy Laws").

What happens when FERPA and state library records laws seem to overlap, conflict with one another, or just be a tangled mess? Not being lawyers, how can we, school librarians, understand how these laws work? Separately or together? Which law, federal or state, has precedents? There are two possible courses of action to answer these questions. First, because of the complicated nature of state and federal privacy laws, when serious questions of minors' privacy arise, a school librarian should request that school administrators consult legal counsel. This is the best way to determine minors' legal rights under state library records laws and FERPA.

The second and more proactive strategy is to work with school administrators to create a school library privacy policy that extends the maximum privacy protec-tion possible. This is a good time for me to emphasize that my comments in this chapter are not to be considered legal advice. I am not an attorney and they are my opinion based on my reading and experiences as a school librarian.

For additional personal understanding of minors' legal privacy rights in school libraries, I recommend reading the essay, "The Law Regarding Privacy and Confi-dentiality in Libraries." It's written by Deborah Caldwell-Stone who is an attorney and who serves as the Director of the ALA Office for Intellectual Freedom. The essay is found in the current edition of the *Intellectual Freedom Manual* listed on the key privacy resources bibliography.

REFERENCES

American Library Association (ALA). "Notable First Amendment Court Cases." Retrieved from http://www.ala.org/advocacy/intfreedom/censorship/courtcases.

American Library Association (ALA). "State Privacy Laws Regarding Library Records." Retrieved from http://www.ala.org/advocacy/privacy/statelaws.

Scales, Pat. R. (2009). *Protecting Intellectual Freedom in Your School Library: Scenarios from the Front Lines*. Chicago: American Library Association.

U.S. Department of Education. "What is an education record?" Retrieved from https://studentprivacy.ed.gov/faq/what-education-record.

37

Practical Ideas: Protecting Students' Privacy in Your School Library

Helen R. Adams

Emily, a K–12 librarian, was surprised when her high school principal asked her who had checked out an eReader with specific titles loaded on it. A knowledgeable professional, Emily explained that divulging that information would infringe on the student's privacy, and that she protects borrowing records through provisions of their state's library records law, the federal Family Educational Rights and Privacy Act (FERPA), and the American Library Association (ALA) *Code of Ethics* (Emily, email message to author, November 2, 2012).

CIRCULATION, BOOK RESERVES, AND BROWSING PRIVACY

Many conversations take place daily in the circulation area in school libraries. Kelly, a K–12 librarian in Pennsylvania, recounted:

> With my elementary students, I do book check-in and check-out individually which gives me a chance to greet all the students that enter my library personally, as well as maintain their privacy. I have duct taped an "X" on the floor indicating where K–2 students should stand when I call them to check in. I talk with them as I check in their books. They love it. It gives them a chance to share something special with me. I use the same process for check-out. (Kelly, online exchange with author, May 5, 2013)

With this simple system, Kelly has created an "island of privacy," using it to demonstrate to young students their right to privacy in the library.

According to Cheryl, a Pennsylvania middle school/high school librarian:

> Often as my middle school students are checking out books, they say things like, "I'm checking this one out because . . . (insert reason here)." Yesterday when a girl was

checking out two books, she explained one was for her English independent reading and the other was a graphic novel she wanted to try. I reminded her that I am happy she's checking out books and that she doesn't have to tell me her reasons for doing so. She gets to choose and read whatever she wants without judgment from me. (Cheryl, online exchanges with author, February 27 and May 8, 2013)

Cheryl's comments reflect best practice in carrying out Article III of the ALA *Code of Ethics*, which advocates that librarians protect library users' privacy (ALA 2008).

Jessica, an elementary librarian in New York, shared her recent changes related to reserves:

Our third graders frequently ask me to put a book on hold. I used to say, "when Johnny brings it back, you can borrow it." This, however, infringes on "Johnny's" privacy. I now say, "when the book is returned, you will be notified and can borrow it." (Jessica, online exchange with author, May 9, 2013)

School librarians can also protect students' privacy when browsing. Design quiet nooks with a comfy chair and make books on hot button topics readily available on a small table nearby (Adams 2013, 139). For students who don't want to be seen perusing specific Dewey areas, conveniently set baskets filled with books on sensitive issues around the library.

EDUCATING STUDENTS ABOUT PRIVACY

Teaching students about their privacy rights when using school libraries is one of the responsibilities of school librarians. Cheryl begins each school year with an orientation for sixth- and seventh-grade students.

During library orientation, I let students know that it's no one's business what they read (except their parent/guardian). It's not their friend's concern or other peers' either. I make it very clear that I don't judge students or make assumptions about them based on the books they check out. Just because they borrow a book on drugs, doesn't mean I think they must be doing drugs. I point out that I don't share [titles of] books they have checked out with other teachers or students. I have book covers they may use if they are uncomfortable checking out a particular book and having others see it. A few students have accepted my offer to borrow [stretchable fabric] book covers. Most were "freebies" from the military recruiters and are plain camo colored, but others are the school color. They return the book, and I get the cover back. (Cheryl, online exchanges with author, February 27 and May 8, 2013)

PRIVACY POLICIES ARE KEY

One of the best ways to protect students' privacy and the confidentiality of their library use records is to have a board-approved privacy policy. The ALA recommends that every school library have a policy that describes how students' privacy is protected, when their library records may be disclosed, and to whom. The policy should cover circulation records for all types of materials including eBooks. ALA also counsels that the policy should include references to state library records law where it is strong and guidelines for the exceptions when student "education records" (including library records) may be released under FERPA (ALA 2019). Educating the school community about the privacy policy is one way to observe ALA's Choose Privacy Week, held annually during the first week in May.

SCHOOL LIBRARY PRIVACY RESOURCES

- American Library Association (ALA). *Choose Privacy Week*. Retrieved from http://chooseprivacyweek.org.
- American Library Association (ALA). (2016). "Library Privacy Guidelines for Students in K–12 Schools." Retrieved from http://www.ala.org/advocacy/privacy/guidelines/students.
- American Library Association (ALA). (2019). "Privacy and Confidentiality Q&A." http://www.ala.org/advocacy/intfreedom/privacyconfidentialityqa.

REFERENCES

Adams, H. R. (2013). *Protecting Intellectual Freedom and Privacy in Your School Library*. Santa Barbara, CA: Libraries Unlimited.
American Library Association (ALA). (2008). *Code of Ethics of the ALA*. Retrieved from http://www.ala.org/tools/ethics.
American Library Association (ALA). (2019). *Privacy and Confidentiality Q & A*. Retrieved from http://www.ala.org/advocacy/intfreedom/privacyconfidentialityqa.

38

Protecting Your Students' Privacy: Resources for School Librarians

Helen R. Adams

Privacy and confidentiality are traditional core values for school librarians, but the legal and ethical considerations involved are among the most difficult to understand and apply in school libraries. Fortunately, there are many online resources that a school library professional can use to become knowledgeable about protecting students' privacy.

2016—AN OUTSTANDING YEAR FOR SCHOOL LIBRARY PRIVACY TOOLS

In 2016, the American Library Association (ALA) privacy advocates took giant steps to create tools to provide advice and direction for school library privacy issues. In April, ALA published "Library Privacy Guidelines for Students in K–12 Schools" (http://www.ala.org/advocacy/privacy/guidelines/students). Aimed at helping school librarians protect their students' privacy, this document addresses why privacy is important; having a library privacy policy; conducting an audit of library privacy procedures; creating safeguards for collecting, retaining, and sharing students' data; establishing safeguards for data sharing with teachers, parents, and third parties such as vendors; working with learning management systems; and educating students about their privacy rights and respecting the rights of others. A list of significant supporting resources is appended to the document.

Four additional guidelines were published in August 2016. Depending on your situation, they offer nuggets of valuable information:

Library Privacy Guidelines for Public Access Computers (http://www.ala.org /advocacy/privacy/guidelines/public-access-computer)
Library Privacy Guidelines for Library Websites, OPACS, and Discovery Services (http://www.ala.org/advocacy/privacy/guidelines/OPAC)
Library Privacy Guidelines for Library Management Systems (http://www.ala .org/advocacy/privacy/guidelines/library-management-systems)

Library Privacy Guidelines for Data Exchange between Networked Devices and Services (http://www.ala.org/advocacy/privacy/guidelines/dataexchange).

In the fall of 2016, ALA volunteers created action-oriented checklists that correspond to the five library privacy guidelines. The checklists give librarians a starting point for proactively protecting their users' privacy with prioritized levels of actions—Priority 1, 2, or 3—with Priority 1 being the least demanding. Each tier increases the effort and knowledge required by a librarian. "The checklists are intended to help libraries of all capacities take practical steps to implement the principles that are laid out in the Privacy Guidelines," said Michael Robinson, chair of the ALA Intellectual Freedom Committee Privacy Subcommittee. "They break up what can seem to be overwhelming privacy issues into a more discrete set of actions and allow librarians to quickly identify the areas for improving privacy practices in their libraries" (Michael Robinson, email message to author, December 7, 2016).

In the "Library Privacy Checklist for Students in K–12 Schools," Priority 1 actions are basic and include steps such as only collecting minimal personally identifiable information about each student, configuring the circulation system to delete unnecessary student borrowing history, and creating internal library procedures to protect students' library use. Priority 2 activities raise the bar to a more proactive level, encompassing educating teachers, administrators, and other staff about students' privacy rights and initiating privacy instruction for students. Priority 3 actions require the greatest engagement by a school librarian but also provide the strongest protection for students' privacy. One key step includes working collaboratively with other stakeholders to create a library privacy policy to be approved by the governing body and communicated widely. The privacy checklists were published in early 2017 and are available on the Choose Privacy website (http://www.ala.org/advocacy/privacy/checklists).

2016 CHOOSE PRIVACY WEEK SPOTLIGHTED YOUTH PRIVACY

Annually since 2009, the ALA Office for Intellectual Freedom (OIF) has observed Choose Privacy Week (CPW) during the first week of May. CPW creates a dedicated time for school librarians to educate faculty and students about personal privacy and privacy as a national issue. In 2016, youth privacy issues finally received primary attention. The CPW theme centered on respecting individuals' privacy, emphasizing youth privacy, and using the tagline "Respect me, respect my privacy." CPW blogs focused on topics such as resources for teaching privacy to K–12 students, protecting students' personal information when using school online electronic resources and apps, and student data management involving state legislation and local district actions. The 2016 CPW webinar featured three presenters including Erin Berman, one of the developers of the San Jose Public Library's Virtual Privacy Lab (https://www.sjpl.org/privacy), a free online tool that, through a series of questions, creates a personalized list of resources to increase the individual's knowledge about online privacy and security. The free hour-long webinar is still available for viewing on demand (http://www.ala.org/advocacy/intfreedom/webinar/privacy2016).

FREE ONLINE PRIVACY INFORMATION SOURCES

Authoritative current information on privacy is available from a number of familiar ALA sources. For a general background on privacy in libraries, check out the "Privacy and Confidentiality Q & A (http://www.ala.org/advocacy/intfreedom/privacyconfidentialityqa) developed and updated by ALA's Intellectual Freedom Committee on a regular basis. Relevant information on school library privacy is found in Section IV, Questions 28–31. Don't miss the ALA Privacy Tool Kit (http://www.ala.org/advocacy/privacy/toolkit) for a very thorough coverage of privacy including the impact technology has on privacy. OIF privacy information and news can also be found on social media including Facebook and Twitter.

The OIF's blog (https://www.oif.ala.org/oif) is a one-stop source of thoughtful posts on a myriad of intellectual freedom and privacy topics. In addition to posts by OIF staff, there are contributing (volunteer) bloggers that rotate from year to year often including school librarians. The site also hosts an extensive archive of news on Banned Books Week from many sources.

The "Intellectual Freedom News," a compilation of links to news articles from U.S. and global media sources about privacy, book challenges in schools and libraries, filtering issues, access to information, the First Amendment, copyright, and other relevant topics is published weekly. Sign up at the ALA website (http://ala.informz .net/ala/profile.asp?fid=3430) to receive the free electronic round-up via email.

ALA's Choose Privacy Week (https://chooseprivacyeveryday.org/) website has a large number of current and archived privacy resources. One of the most useful links for school librarians is "Students' & Minors," located under "Resources." Another helpful area is "Privacy in the News," which is updated daily. The Library Privacy Guidelines and their corresponding checklists are also archived on the site for easy retrieval. In 2017, there was a complete redesign of the site and its content.

A NEW SUBSCRIPTION RESOURCE

In May 2016, OIF debuted *The Journal for Intellectual Freedom & Privacy* (JIFP), a new source of in-depth privacy articles for librarians. Published quarterly online, it is an "expansion" of *The Journal of Intellectual Freedom*, a print magazine available from 1952–2015. Although subscription-based at $50 per year, the inaugural issue is available online for no charge (https://journals.ala.org/index.php/jifp/index).

OIF STAFF ASSISTANCE WITH PRIVACY ISSUES

In addition to the online resources listed throughout this chapter, OIF staff, especially director Deborah Caldwell Stone, are available to answer questions about library privacy for minors in a school setting. Anyone may contact the OIF (http://www.ala.org/aboutala/offices/oif) for assistance, ALA or AASL membership is not required.

FINAL THOUGHTS

Protecting your students' privacy in the library and informing the school community—administrators, teachers, support staff, students, and parents—is one of your responsibilities under the ALA *Code of Ethics*, Article III, which urges librarians to "protect each library user's right to privacy and confidentiality . . ." (ALA). Using these resources will help you meet your ethical and legal responsibilities.

ADDITIONAL RESOURCES

- Center for Information Policy Research—http://cipr.uwm.edu/
- Let's Encrypt certificate program—https://letsencrypt.org/about/
- Tor browser—https://www.torproject.org/projects/torbrowser.html.en

REFERENCE

American Library Association (ALA). *Code of Ethics*. Retrieved from http://www.ala.org /advocacy/proethics/codeofethics/codeethics.

39

How Circulation Systems May Impact Student Privacy

Helen R. Adams

When automation systems were first installed, school librarians thought only of the convenience and the release from the drudgery of filing checkout cards and typing overdue lists. Original concerns with student privacy and computerized circulation records centered on the retention of information that the school librarian and patron assumed was deleted. When an item was checked in, it was believed that the link between the patron and the book or other library resource borrowed was broken; this, however, is erroneous. By checking a book's "copy status," library staff can determine the current borrower and, depending on software configuration, learn who checked it out previously—from the most recent person to a staff-designated number of earlier borrowers. These records remain in the system indefinitely, unless purged. Some school librarians want this type of information; it allows them to trace recent borrowers if damage is discovered after the item is returned. Conversely, it can also be a privacy issue as it can be used to determine who is reading selected types of books.

None of us imagined how these circulation program features would change and improve to the point of becoming a greater threat to the privacy of school library users. Today's programs allow easy access to data once available only through laborious use of a separate utility program or hand collation. Patron checkout histories, beginning with the first item borrowed by the student through the current time, are now readily available at the click of a mouse. Pat, a middle school librarian in Washington, agreed to provide information for this chapter on condition of anonymity. He said that by selecting "checkout history," he is able to view every title checked out by a student, its barcode number, and the date of checkout (Pat, email to author, October 2, 2007).

While Pat can disable this feature to protect the circulation history of the student, he is reluctant to do so. He said, "I have had occasion to use this information in conjunction with classroom teachers looking for the truth about what certain students claim they have read versus what they have actually checked out. I do not share the entirety of the list, only sharing the YES or NO on titles in question" (Pat, October 2, 2007). He sees yet another positive side of the checkout history

142

feature when he states, "I have had students ask me what they checked out in the past. One in particular comes to mind. She is a migrant student and reads voraciously. When she found out she had checked out fifty-two books in one year, she crowed about it to her friends and bragged about how well she was doing. To me, that is worth it" (Pat, October 2, 2007).

According to Gwen, a middle school librarian in Virginia who also agreed to provide information for this chapter under condition of anonymity, students are able to access their own circulation records from any Internet accessible computer (Gwen, email to author, October 4, 2007). This means they can learn what items are checked out, when they are due, and put others on reserve. Are there any privacy concerns associated with this new freedom for students? In some schools such as Gwen's, patron library numbers are the same as student lunch numbers. While this may make it easier for students to remember, it also means that the number has a greater opportunity to be learned by others. To Gwen's knowledge, students have not shared their patron library numbers nor played tricks on each other by checking out "interesting" items to one another (Gwen, October 4, 2007).

Why should the advances in automation systems concern school library professionals? The ALA *Code of Ethics* states in Article III, "We protect each library user's right to privacy and confidentiality with respect to information sought or received and resources consulted, borrowed, or transmitted" (ALA). School librarians must take steps to ensure that the readily available information about student patrons' use of library resources is protected from teacher and administrator inquiries, parent and student volunteers, and students who may be at the circulation computer involved in self-checkout of their library materials.

There are a number of ways school librarians can protect student circulation records including:

- Develop a Privacy Policy that states who has access to library patron records and the circumstances under which records may be released.
- Use a password to protect circulation records with differing levels of access "rights" assigned to students, volunteers, and library staff (Gwen, October 4, 2007).
- Make a conscious effort to purge circulation records on a regular basis. Note: For specifics, read chapter 40 of this book, "Retaining School Library Records."
- Teach ALL students to respect the confidentiality of library records—their own and those of others.

Additionally, Pat trains student assistants about library privacy and provides each with a brochure that includes guidelines for being a volunteer (Pat, October 2, 2007). Key points relating to the confidentiality of library records include:

> Student aides are not to use the circulation program to look at other students' information, either personal or academic. Library aides will not give out information about other students' library circulations to anyone. (Pat, October 2, 2007)

If we are serious about students' privacy when they use the school library and its resources, we must consider how the automation system and each upgrade may affect the confidentiality of library records, and take proactive measures to protect them. Our students are depending on us!

REFERENCE

American Library Association (ALA). *Code of Ethics*. Retrieved from http://www.ala.org /tools/ethics.

40

Retaining School Library Records

Helen R. Adams

What should you keep and for how long? Are you a saver? Many of us are, but this may not be a good trait when it comes to keeping library records that include personally identifiable information about patrons. The purpose of library records is to manage library resources efficiently. However, once statistical data such as how many books were circulated during a school year has been obtained, the raw information that connects a user to an item or service should be erased, shredded, or expunged.

Library records may include but are not limited to circulation records; interlibrary loan records; public access computer/Internet sign-up lists or automated sign-ups, temporary files, cookies, and use records created during Internet searching; reference interviews and email queries; and server logs. School library and technology staff should develop a schedule and specific guidelines to destroy nonessential, personally identifying data or files of library records that are no longer needed.

There are two important concepts regarding library records. The first is that library records should be kept for as long as they are needed and then destroyed. The shortest possible retention of records helps ensure patron privacy. The second important concept is to retain minimal library records. After all, you cannot produce those library records that are no longer available, nor can those records be vulnerable to unauthorized disclosure.

Retention periods for records are a matter of local policy unless dictated by state or federal law, state records retention schedules, or contracts. Before creating a school library records retention policy, the school librarian must be aware that most states have a record retention schedule for school districts. This schedule lists the records that districts must retain and the length of retention. While school library records may not be specifically mentioned, the state document will give an overview of the types of records that must be retained and may provide some useful insights for developing a library records retention policy. If the type of library record is not specifically noted and there is no broad language that may include the record, school library staff may presumably dispose of the information.

Unexpected retention of data may produce a threat to the confidentiality of patron library records. School librarians may not be aware that many circulation systems can be configured to retain additional book checkout history on previous borrowers of a library resource. This feature allows staff to learn the names of the last one or more persons to check out a particular book. While it may not be easy to obtain the information, it can be done. Library automation vendors state it is not their place to determine if checkout history data should be retained; this is a local decision. Therefore, it is very important that school librarians be knowledgeable about how their circulation systems operate and what types of confidential data may be retrievable.

A case was made for creating two policies—a "Confidentiality of School Library Records Policy" and a "School Library Privacy Policy." Creating a "School Library Records Retention Policy" would also be useful to protect the privacy of library patrons and the confidentiality of their library records. According to Deborah Caldwell-Stone, director of the American Library Association's Office for Intellectual Freedom, "Record retention policies assure that records due to be erased or shredded actually are erased and shredded, and they also provide evidence of the library's everyday practices should anyone question why a record has not been retained" (Adams 2005, 112–113). Items to be included in a retention policy include the concept of destruction of unnecessary records on a regular basis, record disposal will follow local school policy as well as state and federal laws, and guidelines for record destruction should be provided for each type of record. A sample "School Library Media Program Records Retention Policy" with guidelines for record retention can be found in the book *Privacy in the 21st Century: Issues for Public, School, and Academic Libraries* (Adams et al. 2005, 112–113).

It is very important to be prepared for a record request. If the school library does not hold or no longer retains the record or information requested, the matter ends there. If records exist, library staff should never destroy the record after receiving a records request. Library staff and administrators, in conjunction with district legal counsel, will determine the proper course of action.

REFERENCE

Adams, H. R., Bocher, R., Gordon, C., & Barry-Kessler, E. (2005). *Privacy in the 21st Century: Issues for Public, School, and Academic Libraries*. Santa Barbara, CA: Libraries Unlimited.

41

The Age of the Patron and Privacy

Helen R. Adams

Does the age of the patron make a difference in extending privacy rights?

The American Association of School Librarians (AASL) no longer has a separate position statement on the privacy rights of children and youth; however, that concept is now included in "Privacy: An Interpretation of the Library Bill of Rights," which states: "ALA and its members recognize that children and youth have the same rights to privacy as adults" (ALA 2019). The ALA *Code of Ethics* does not distinguish between minor and adult patrons. State library records laws and the Family Educational Rights and Privacy Act (FERPA) do not differentiate between younger and older students unless the student is determined to be an adult (defined in state and federal legislation at varying ages of 16, 17, and 18).

Should age be considered when granting privacy rights to students in an elementary library? Here are some questions to consider. Do young children know that they have privacy rights in school libraries, and are they concerned about their privacy? Does it matter if the school librarian calls out the names of children because they have unreturned library books? Is it a serious breach of privacy for the child if a peer overhears the name of the overdue item? Does it compromise a child's privacy if a teacher assists in locating a student's overdue book? These examples may seem like innocuous situations where a child's right to privacy need not be stringently enforced.

On the other hand, compromising privacy may be a slippery slope. While elementary students may have difficulty remembering to return books or even the titles they checked out, they are worthy of our respect as future citizens. Where will they learn about their rights to privacy in a library unless we begin teaching them now? It is my belief that one of the expectations of privacy for students in a school library is that all will be granted the right to read and borrow free from scrutiny, regardless of age.

In a practical sense, how can a school librarian maintain privacy for elementary age library patrons while still teaching them about their responsibility to return borrowed materials? When a book is overdue for several weeks, sending a friendly nonthreatening note home about overdue items including the title of the book, date due, replacement cost, and school librarian contact information is one way to enlist parent assistance in the return of books and still address privacy concerns. Parents of young children will likely be receptive to this type of gentle reminder.

Many children's lives are very complicated. Their overdue materials may be found in many different places. By obtaining the cooperation of parents, the overdue materials will probably be returned quickly. It is a win-win situation with little loss of privacy for the child and includes a lesson in accountability.

Can an elementary teacher become involved in the hunt for a missing book and still preserve the privacy of the child involved? The answer is yes, although it is very important that the school librarian communicates to teachers the need to protect the child's privacy to the fullest degree possible by not "exposing" the titles and corresponding students' names to the entire class. In the majority of states, library records of any age patron are protected by state law.

Here is a manageable strategy for making teachers partners in the search for missing library books and still maintaining student privacy. A list can be sent by the school librarian to a teacher stating that a number of books are missing and including the names of the children who checked them out. The teacher may then speak discreetly to the children with missing books, help them check their desks or backpacks, check to see if the books were lent to friends, thereby moving the search to other students' desks and backpacks. If not located, a full classroom search may be instituted. If the books are found and returned to the school library, there is a win-win situation with little loss of confidentiality for those involved.

The school librarian should take advantage of opportunities to teach elementary students about their rights to privacy and confidentiality in a library. If a student is searching for a particular title and it is not on the shelf, they may ask who has checked out the item. The school librarian can explain that the name of the person who has borrowed the item is private, but the school librarian will put the item on reserve for the student. By taking this action, the school librarian is demonstrating that each child has the right to read what they choose and can share that information if they wish. But YOU as the school librarian will not divulge who has checked out the title being sought.

As school librarians, our goal is to make the principles of privacy and confidentiality work in a practical way in a school library. The previous examples demonstrate ways to help young children be responsible in the borrowing of materials and, at the same time, learn how library staff can guard the privacy of those who check out materials. In reality, there are few secrets among elementary children about what they are checking out. Yet, it is in these situations that school librarians begin to train young children about their right to privacy in a library.

REFERENCE

American Library Association (ALA). (2019). "Privacy: An Interpretation of the Library Bill of Rights." Retrieved from http://www.ala.org/advocacy/intfreedom/librarybill/interpretations/privacy.

42

The Troubled Student and Privacy

Helen R. Adams

When should a school librarian consider violating a student's privacy? Although school library professionals should extend the maximum amount of privacy to students, there may be times when library staff must use common sense rather than American Library Association (ALA) policy and ethics statements because of a concern for the student's welfare. For example, if a sudden change in personality, dramatic switch in friends, a move toward isolation, or a fixation with information on risky or criminal activity is observed, then other action might be considered. The first action is to talk to the student casually but confidentially. If, after a period of time, the school library professional is still concerned, they may seek advice from the school's guidance counselor, who is also bound by confidentiality. The counselor is an excellent choice for a confidant because they may already know the child, have obtained similar reports from other sources, and have training and experience on how to proceed in such a situation.

A guidance counselor may look at a student's grades, record of absences, and recent disciplinary actions, as well as inquire casually among the teachers of the troubled student to see if any changes have been noticed. At times, friends of a student who may be talking about suicide may confide in a teacher, and that information is reported to the counselor. With the collective background information, the counselor will likely choose to speak directly with the student. The school library professional's observations may help in determining what is concerning the student and keep them safe. Because of confidentiality, it is unlikely that the library professional will ever learn the result of reported observations, but can feel confident that someone with the necessary resources is taking the concerns seriously.

If the situation, however, appears to be related to a school safety issue, the school librarian may speak directly to the principal. A principal is responsible for the health and safety of all students and staff. If there are indications that the student is actively engaging in potentially dangerous or threatening behavior, the principal may contact the parents and/or police immediately to protect the well-being of the school community.

A second instance for violating privacy of school library users may occur if the school librarian observes indications of possible child abuse. All states have child protection laws that require educators to report suspected maltreatment of children.

For example, in Pennsylvania, the Child Protective Services Law (23 Pa. C.S., Chapter 63) establishes definitions of child abuse, who is required to report abuse, and the procedures to be followed (Pennsylvania Department of Public Welfare).

Aside from the circumstances outlined above, a school library professional must remember that there are very strong professional policy statements, such as the *Library Bill of Rights* and the *Code of Ethics* of the ALA, which urge library staff to guard the privacy of library users. This is especially true in terms of scrutinizing what a student is reading. In this case, the school librarian must accept that they are not the "information" police. Minors have the right to receive ideas and information from their school library as part of their First Amendment rights, and they should not be subjected to probing inquiry if they are investigating topics that may be personally distasteful to the school librarian. Only parents have the right to limit or restrict their children's choice of reading—whether in a public or school library setting.

The Children's Internet Protection Act (CIPA) requires that educators monitor students' Internet use. Observing a student looking at a page on bomb-making or guns could elicit several possible reactions. It is possible the student accidentally found the information, or it may be research for a presentation for how easy it is to find weapons-type information on the Internet. The school librarian should avoid jumping to a false conclusion that a student is planning to build a bomb or use a weapon for criminal purposes.

Situations in which a school library professional may violate a student's privacy with just cause are rare. School librarians should think carefully before taking actions that can compromise a student's privacy because students depend on the discretion of school library staff. In most instances, the school librarian should strive to protect student privacy following state library records confidentiality laws, and the *Library Bill of Rights* and the *Code of Ethics* of the ALA.

REFERENCE

Pennsylvania Department of Public Welfare. *Child Abuse Referrals*. Retrieved from https://www.compass.state.pa.us/CWIS/Public/ReferralsLearnMore.

43

Confidentiality and Creating a Safe Information Environment

Chad Heck

At a recent conference session, I was presenting various intellectual freedom scenarios. One of the most interesting was a hypothetical about a student coming into the school library and checking out many books on suicide, including self-help books. The question discussed was what steps the librarian should take after such an occurrence. There were impassioned responses on both sides of the issue, with some librarians wanting to seek immediate help for this student, while others wanted to respect the confidentiality of checking out materials in the library. One thing was certain; both of these camps had care and concern for the safety of students.

As school librarians, we are often put in tricky situations that librarians in other institutions do not find themselves in. We act *in loco parentis*, or in the place of parents, in our role as teachers, whereas other professional librarians do not. We also have mandatory reporting requirements in most states, obligating us to report if a child is facing abuse or harm. It is incredibly difficult to navigate whether a report should be filed in any given situation, and most err on the side of caution, and rightfully so. However, filing a report of suspected abuse or imminent harm based solely on the materials a student has checked out may have unintended consequences for a library that may cause further harm to our students.

Article VII of the *Library Bill of Rights* states that "all people . . . possess a right to privacy and confidentiality in their library use" and "libraries should . . . protect people's privacy, safeguarding all library use data, including personally identifiable information" (ALA 2019). We have a duty to our patrons to keep their library records, including which materials they check out, confidential. As mentioned above, we also have a duty in many states as teachers to report any suspicions of harm or abuse of students. We can reconcile this by always taking the approach of making no assumptions about students based on materials they access. If a student checks out a self-help book on suicide, there should be no assumption that that student is suicidal. That student could be checking this book out for a health class report or doing some research on how to help a friend. If the library's policy is to report to administrators or counselors when a student checks out sensitive material, eventually students would no longer view the library as a safe place to access these materials—a very damning unintended consequence of a well-intentioned librarian. We want our students to feel safe to access the materials they need to access without fear of being reported.

So what should a well-intentioned librarian do? First, if there are signs of abuse or suicidality *other* than the materials checked out, a report is not only justified, it is mandatory. Second, as librarians, we are the ultimate curator of resources. If a student is checking out books on a sensitive topic, it is absolutely appropriate to suggest to the student that they check out other resources on the topic including stopping by and talking to a school counselor or mental health professional. This should be done in such a way that is assumption-free about a student's status, but offering other sources of information for the student. Third, the library should maintain an up-to-date, information-rich environment on sensitive issues. Patrons may not feel safe checking out print materials on these issues, so inventorying and replacing lost and stolen copies is important. In addition, having consumables such as bookmarks and flyers nearby or even right next to these materials on the shelves in some of these sections could be a tremendous help. Finally, and most importantly, developing relationships with students as the librarian as a trusted and safe person makes all the difference in every aspect of what we do.

REFERENCE

American Library Association (ALA). (2019). *Library Bill of Rights*. Retrieved from http://www.ala.org/advocacy/intfreedom/librarybill.

44

Privacy Solutions for Cloud Computing: What Does It Mean?

Annalisa Keuler

School librarians have long believed in an ethical obligation to protect the privacy rights of students when using the school library. Librarians have a professional obligation to protect students' privacy and to teach students how to keep their information private. In the wake of the sweeping use of cloud computing by school districts around the country, librarians must now extend this obligation to support privacy protection beyond the library walls. Can schools protect students' privacy while storing more and more data in the cloud? Policy makers and legislators are just beginning to scratch the surface of this complicated and evolving issue.

STUDENT DATA

"How to Protect Student Data in Education" sums up three main types of identifiable student data: personally identifiable information, de-identifying data, and aggregate data (edSurge 2014). Personally identifiable information is anything that can identify individual students. This could be grades, schedules, images, student work, and so on. De-identifying data would be individual student data with any identifying information removed. Lastly, aggregate data is information about students in groups, but would not have identifying information (edSurge 2014).

By understanding the types of student information that may be shared through cloud services, it becomes apparent how important it is to have strict privacy policies to protect students from having this information shared with a third party. The Family Educational Rights and Privacy Act (FERPA) provides specific information about parents' rights in relation to student records (Family Policy Compliance Office 2014).

CLOUD COMPUTING

There is much more to cloud computing than just using Dropbox or Google Drive. The cloud includes any web-based service that requires users to submit and transfer information. Donna Williamson, Technology Director for Mountain Brook City Schools (Alabama), cites mobility, cost, efficiency, and recovery as the main reasons cloud computing works for many school districts over traditional hardware models (Williamson, personal communication with the author, November 3, 2014). However, security and privacy risks can arise when storing data hosted in the cloud. These include data breaches, data loss (which can occur "by users who unknowingly expose information by sharing or sending information"), password reuse, and collection of personally identifiable data (Consortium for School Networking 2013).

Another concern includes the use of educational software applications by teachers. Librarians can help teachers understand that each app they require students to use has its own privacy policy. Many of these programs employ an information acquisition technique, commonly called "data mining," and sell the information to a third party. Teachers may use these apps with the best of intentions, but school librarians should make educators aware of the potential pitfalls that may accompany their use. So, as Williamson asks and answers, "Do we need to throw out cloud-based services? No. We just need to get smart" (Williamson, November 3, 2014).

CREATING A DATA GOVERNANCE POLICY

The Alabama Legislature passed legislation in October 2013 that every school system is required to have a data security and privacy policy. Many schools, including Mountain Brook City Schools in Mountain Brook, Alabama, are answering this call for student privacy by drafting a data governance policy (see References for a link to Mountain Brook's policy). Bills have also been passed around the country to address the issue of privacy in schools. Due to the ever-changing nature of the information in this policy, it is critical for school districts to continually update this policy and communicate these changes to the public.

Because of this policy, Mountain Brook City Schools is also reexamining software services in use districtwide and requesting a Memorandum of Agreement (MOA). This will ensure that these vendors are aware of and adhere to the new policy. But, reaching out to vendors will take some time. In some cases, it has taken up to six months to get them to sign on. To assist with this, the Future of Privacy Forum and The Software and Information Industry Association announced in October 2014 that many leading K–12 software service providers, including Edmoto, Follett, and Microsoft, are signing a pledge committing themselves to the privacy of student information. As of 2019, 386 service providers have signed the pledge (Future of Privacy Forum and The Software and Information Industry Association 2019).

QUESTIONS TO ASK

School districts have a long way to go before they can confidently grapple with these issues. School librarians, however, may begin to position themselves as thoughtful leaders in the ongoing privacy debate by posing and providing affirmation to the following questions: Does your school have a data governance policy? Has this policy been communicated effectively to the students and parents? Do you know what the policy states and how can librarians make sure that students' data is protected? Students and parents place their trust in schools to protect children and their privacy. Donna Williamson put it plainly: "It is our responsibility to do everything we can to honor and respect that trust" (Williamson, November 3, 2014).

REFERENCES

Consortium for School Networking (CoSN). (Winter 2013). Security and privacy of cloud computing. *EdTechNext: Emerging Technology for K–12 Education.* Retrieved from http://cosn.org/sites/default/files/pdf/ETN-CloudSecurity.pdf.

EdSurge. (2014). *How to Protect Student Data in Education.* Retrieved from https://www.edsurge.com/news/2014-07-21-how-to-protect-student-data-in-education.

Family Policy Compliance Office. (June 2, 2014). *Family Educational Rights and Privacy Act.* U.S. Department of Education. Retrieved from http://www2.ed.gov/policy/gen/guid/fpco/ferpa/index.html.

Future of Privacy Forum and The Software and Information Industry Association. (2019). *Student Privacy Pledge: K–12 School Service Provider Pledge to Safeguard Student Privacy.* Retrieved from http://studentprivacypledge.org/?page_id=45.

Mountain Brook Schools. (October 2014). *Data Governance Policy.* Retrieved from https://www.mtnbrook.k12.al.us/Page/9007.

Part VII

Access, Equity, and Diversity

"It's important to have diverse characters in books
because books give kids mirrors and windows.
Books create empathy. If we don't have diversity,
if we're only showing things from one perspective,
how are we creating empathy?"

—*Angie Thomas, Author*

45

Library Access on a Fixed Schedule

Ernie Cox

School librarianship has advocated for flexible scheduling for a long, long time. However, it appears the fixed schedule will forever be part of the professional landscape. This reality creates a tension between leading "library classes" and fostering a culture of wide access to information. In many cases, the balance tilts toward a restrictive-access approach that limits the library experience for kids. A recent survey of Iowa teacher-librarians showed that the norm in many elementary settings was one library visit per week and a low limit on checkouts per child (one to two books) (Johnson & Donham 2012). If access to the resources, services, and trained personnel of a school library is important, we must find ways to make it work even in a fixed-schedule environment. Here are five ways to begin opening up access to better serve children:

1. Open Anytime

Has the fixed schedule approach created a situation where kids are visiting the library once a week during a set period of time? Take a few days to analyze how well this is working from the student perspective. Imagine a second-grade student checking out the next A–Z Mystery on Monday. By Wednesday, they are done and ready for the next installment. Do we really want them to wait until next Monday? That is four whole days of not reading! How is a once-a-week visit (for a few minutes) creating a culture of serving readers?

At Prairie Creek Intermediate, teachers allow students to visit on a pass. We talk about expectations for library visits using the building-wide common language of Positive Behavior Interventions and Support (PBIS). Kids know appropriate voice levels to use when a class is in session in the library. They know to stay focused on finding what they came to get. As the teacher-librarian, we should invest in growing independent users of the library. If a student is struggling, I will invite them to come back when I know I'll have time to devote to that individual student.

2. Unlimited Checkouts (or at least a robust limit)

In the Iowa survey mentioned earlier, Johnson and Donham (2012) ask, "How can we design circulation practices and policies to support literacy in young

157

readers?" In a climate of accountability and fiscal shortfalls, teacher-librarians need to evaluate how well our programs demonstrate an understanding of literacy and learning. Are we providing indispensable services to our school? In the early years of school, a large volume of reading from a wide variety of texts builds the foundation for academic success. A common approach to checkout is a sliding scale with first grade getting one book, second grade getting two books, and so on. If a first grader is only checking out one copy of the Elephant and Piggie series at a time, what does this say to kids, teachers, and parents about the relevance of the library? This one book per grade policy is the inverse of what would make the most impact—a first grader should have the five-book limit. That fifth grader can probably make a week of reading from one book.

One concern about this liberal checkout policy is loss of materials. Johnson and Donham (2012) ask, "How can we determine an appropriate threshold for loss of resources justified by the importance of access?" Every school is unique and the answer to this question will vary, but it is one we need to answer with data-informed decision-making. Where does loss occur now and to what extent? How much is it worth in replacement costs if the volume of overall reading expands? In one of our elementary schools at College Community, a librarian offered summer book checkout. Of the 3,000+ books circulated in May, all but 10 of them were returned in August. This seems like a small price to pay to have provided that much summer reading. The policy at Creek is simple and straightforward, allowing for a case-by-case application:

- Check out the books and materials you need and can be responsible for reading and returning in 2 weeks.
- Need more than 2 weeks' worth? You're welcome to renew library materials once.

The renewal function has also been entrusted to kids. This eliminates a recurring action by an adult that kids can easily manage instead.

3. Self-Check and Self-Service

A small technical shift can make a big difference in changing the culture of the school library. Most automated library systems have the capability of setting up a checkout-only account. This enables checkout for accounts with no issues (overdue, and so on). Students use school-issued library cards to check out their selections. Two quotes from Creek students highlight how this service empowers students with authentic ownership of the process:

> When you have your whole class there you can do the self checkout and you can have more time to read. (Alayna, fifth grade)

> The self checkout is really cool because it feels like shopping for books and scanning my card is like using a credit card. (Allie, fifth grade)

A majority of our students make great use of this power. When visiting as a whole class, students can make selections, check out a book, and grab more reading time. They are motivated to keep their accounts in good standing so this feature remains available to them. Students can also login from any device to see what they have checked out, renew titles, place holds, and build to-be-read lists. This has saved countless hours of adult time and built more ownership of the library experience. It takes an investment to train students to use all of these features. The return is well worth it.

4. All Out Reader's Advisory

Students still need the expert guidance of the librarian but this can be delivered in a variety of ways. Traditional tools like displays, bulletin boards, signage, and maps can be helpful. Going digital can make anytime reader's advisory (RA) possible. Readalike book lists in the automated library catalog can respond to current high demand titles. In Iowa, we have access to TeachingBooks http://www.teachingbooks.net through our Area Education Agencies. TeachingBooks provides a wealth of digital content about books with custom QR codes that can be printed and placed on shelves or displays. Create brief booktalks for a library YouTube channel. A few of these each week will result in a growing library of engaging RA. Have these video booktalks available on public computers in the library (headphones attached!). Form a teachers' book group to cultivate awareness of new developments in children's literature among staff. The librarian cannot be the sole provider of adult reading advice. Invest in training library associates to guide kids toward their next book. Moving fiction into genre categories can provide a built-in RA function. Collaborate with the art teacher to have student-created genre signs. Students can also get in on the work of RA (see below).

5. Toward a Participatory Space

All of these changes will spark excitement among students. As the old paradigm of checkout limits and fixed library days fades into the distance, a whole new range of possibilities open up. Get kids involved in recommending books to one another. Encourage kids to complete a shelf talker card for a recently returned book they enjoyed. Not only does this provide information for students, it provides the librarian with another level of detail about how children are responding to reading. Offer discrete maker activities that can accumulate over time. We're preparing to host a storytelling table with LEGO story starter kits. Kids can contribute to the growing narrative a few blocks at a time. Provide a stop motion story challenge. In an envelope, provide a few sheets of construction paper, a marker, scissors, and a one-page guide to using stop motion apps. Invite kids to create a fifteen-second super-short story. Host these on the library YouTube channel too (they will be in great company with your booktalks). Survey students about their experiences in the library. Are they finding books they want to read? Do they feel welcome in the library? Evaluating our impact using circulation numbers alone tells a small part of the library story. Embrace and elevate student perspectives to improve and advocate for programs.

While the fixed schedule may be here to stay, the student experience does not have to suffer.

REFERENCE

Johnson, L., & Donham, J. (2012). Reading by grade three: How well do school library circulation policies support early reading? *Teacher Librarian, 40*(2), pp. 8–12.

46

Using Assistive Technology to Meet Diverse Learner Needs

Stephanie Kurtts, Nicole Dobbins, and Natsuko Takemae

Implementing new and advanced technology for instruction and access to the curriculum for the increasingly diverse student populations in our schools can be a daunting task for even the most tech-savvy school personnel. This task can be even more challenging when devices, tools, and systems associated with assistive, or adaptive, technology are part of an individualized education program (IEP) for students with disabilities. School librarians should be knowledgeable about how assistive technology (AT) becomes part of a student's learning. Being a member of the team of classroom teachers, administrators, specialists, and parents who are striving to meet the needs of children who learn differently and require instructional accommodations or modifications to the curriculum using AT can be an essential role for school librarians.

LEGISLATION AND ASSISTIVE TECHNOLOGY DEFINED

While all students can benefit from the implementation of technology into the delivery of effective instruction, students with identified educational disabilities may have individualized education plans that require devices, tools, or systems as part of their instruction. The Individuals with Disabilities in Education Act (IDEA) 1990 (P.L. 101-476) defined assistive technology, mandated schools to provide AT devices and services for students with disabilities, and addressed what those would be for an individual student's individualized education plan (Assistive Technology Training Online Project 2005). Further legislation, IDEA 1997 (P.L. 105-17), reinforced students' rights to receive AT devices and services addressed on IEPs, and allowed students to use these AT devices and services outside school settings (Office of Special Education and Rehabilitative Services 2003).

One thing that has been consistent across the legislation is the definition of assistive technology. IDEA 2004 defines an assistive technology device as "any item, piece of equipment, or product system, whether acquired commercially off the shelf, modified, or customized that is used to increase, maintain, or improve functional capabilities of a child with a disability" (U.S. Department of Education 2011). In addition, IDEA 2004 supports the uses of AT devices and/or services in order to encourage students' maximized access to learning. This also includes training and technical assistance for service providers and educators so that AT can be selected, acquired, and utilized in a way that a student's needs are met (U.S. Department of Education 2011). As such, the technology associated with serving students with disabilities has evolved. A variety of devices have been invented, reinvented, and advanced.

With over 5,400,000 children receiving special education services across the country, increasingly in general education classrooms and in inclusive educational settings, the need for effective and innovative technology-based programs that respond to individual student needs is critical (U.S. Department of Education 2005). The school librarian can provide a valuable service for teachers, related service providers, and families in integrating media resources to assist in the delivery of instruction and providing access to the curriculum while using instructional AT tools and devices. School librarians are in a unique position to do this based on their comprehensive understanding of the curriculum, expertise in the areas of instructional technology, and the ability to locate a variety of resources (Gavigan & Kurtts 2010).

UNIVERSAL DESIGN FOR LEARNING AND THE TOOLS OF ASSISTIVE TECHNOLOGY

The evolution of AT includes the creation of more sophisticated educational software as well as more responsive and unobtrusive assistive devices. Technology can enhance the academic and social success of the students as well as provide a link between the information taught by the teacher and the expected academic and social behaviors the student is expected to perform (Reisberg 1990).

Curriculum that considers the specific needs of students with disabilities and makes use of technology should include appropriate content as well as the method of instruction. Universal Design for Learning (UDL) can enhance the use of technology integration and assistive technology for all students, including those with disabilities. UDL transforms instruction from the outset in order to broaden the definition of the learners who are expected to succeed in the general education environment without "adding-on" accommodations or modifications (Pisha & Coyne 2001).

By implementing the principles of UDL along with the use of assistive technology, teachers can rethink how they plan instruction for their students and their needs in the classroom. Teachers who understand the principles of UDL in lesson planning consider diverse students' needs to be the result of normal variance within a heterogeneous population rather than isolated instances of difference or disability (McGuire, Scott, & Shaw 2006). Lessons planned using innovative strategies supported by UDL indicate that teachers anticipate a wide range of learning styles and abilities in the classroom, and are prepared to adapt instruction that will most effectively meet all students' needs (Kurtts, Matthews, & Smallwood 2009). By definition, the UDL lesson is flexible and deliberately multifaceted in order to engage all students as they work to meet curricular goals through multiple and varied interactions with instructional materials and activities (Gavigan & Kurtts 2009; Orkwis 2003).

Assistive technology tools and devices are an integral part of the implementation of UDL principles across instruction. AT tools and devices can be low-tech, mid-tech, and high tech. Low-tech tools, which could be used by all students in the classroom, thus enhancing access to the curriculum, might include specialized writing tools, pencil grips, planners, raised-line paper, or highlighting pens and tapes. Mid-tech tools, also used by all students, might include timers, spell checkers, tape recorders, digital recorders, calculators, and alternative keyboards. Low, mid, and high-tech tools can serve as assistive technology when indicated in an IEP as a tool to provide access to instruction or can also serve to enhance engagement with the curriculum (Gavigan & Kurtts 2009).

FOCUS ON HIGH-TECH TOOLS

High-tech AT tools are becoming more common as advanced and specialized technology becomes increasingly available to classrooms and all students. School librarians may be frequently called upon to provide assistance in implementing the use of the tools and should have the opportunity for training in the use of the technology tools.

While the sheer numbers of high-tech tools and devices are too numerous to list here, school librarians and teachers may be familiar with touch screens, adapted computers, software programs, portable keyboards, audiobooks, word processing software, word prediction software, instruction websites, and communication (Hitchcock & Stahl 2003). Through these tools, school librarians can lead collaborative activities with teachers as they work to improve learning outcomes for students with disabilities or diverse learning needs.

Preparation for school personnel in the use of high-tech tools is a must for the most effective implementation of instruction supported and enhanced by the technology. School librarians may be the key to this training and assistance, encouraging collaboration between educators while enhancing the implementation of UDL principles and the use of AT tools with innovative technology-based strategies to improve outcomes for all students.

REFERENCES

Assistive Technology Training Online Project (ATTO). (2005). *Assistive Technology Legislation. Web.* [No longer available].

Gavigan, K., & Kurtts, S. A. (2009). AT, UD, and thee: Using assistive technology and universal design for learning in 21st century media centers. *Library Media Connection, 27*(4), pp. 54–56.

Gavigan, K., & Kurtts, S. A. (2010). Together we can: Collaborating to meet the need of at-risk students. *Library Media Connection, 29*(3), pp. 10–13.

Hitchcock, C., & Stahl, S. (2003). Assistive technology, Universal Design, Universal Design for Learning: Improved learning opportunities. *Journal of Special Education Technology, 18*(4), pp. 45–52.

Kurtts, S. A., Matthews, C., & Smallwood, T. (2009). (Dis)Solving the differences: A physical science lesson using Universal Design. *Intervention in School Clinic, 44*(3), pp. 151–159.

McGuire, J. M., Scott, S. S., & Shaw, S. F. (2006). Universal Design and its application in educational environments. *Remedial and Special Education, 27*, pp. 166–175.

Office of Special Education and Rehabilitative Services. (2003). *IDEA '97: The Law.* Retrieved from https://www2.ed.gov/offices/OSERS/Policy/IDEA/regs.html.

Orkwis, R. (2003). *Universally Designed Instruction* (ERIC digest No. E641). ERIC Clearinghouse on Disabilities and Gifted Education. Retrieved from https://files.eric.ed.gov/fulltext/ED475386.pdf.

Pisha, B., & Coyne, P. (2001). Smart from the start: The promise of Universal Design for learning. *Remedial and Special Education, 22*, pp. 197–203.

Reisberg, L. (1990). Curriculum evaluation and modification: An effective teaching perspective. *Intervention in School and Clinic, 26,* pp. 99–105.

U.S. Department of Education, Office of Special Education and Rehabilitative Services, Office of Special Education Programs. (2005). *26th Annual (2004) Report to Congress on the Implementation of the Individuals with Disabilities Education Act, 1.* Washington, D.C., pp. 20–47.

U.S. Department of Education. (2011). *Building the Legacy: IDEA 2004.* Retrieved from https://sites.ed.gov/idea/building-the-legacy-idea-2004.

47

Online Accessibility Tools

Heather Moorefield-Lang

School librarians are here to plant and grow a love of learning in each student and also to offer information access to all students in an equitable manner (American Association of School Librarians 2009). Each and every day, students with a wide range of skills and abilities come to the school library. Having knowledge of online tools for those students who might be known as differently abled is advantageous for everyone in our community.

The following are some of my favorite tools that feature accessibility options.

Flipgrid: https://info.flipgrid.com/

A great online tool and app to gather conversation topics and discussions with your students, peers, and community. Using this tool is simple: post a topic and your students, audience, and/or peer educators respond via video. The administrator (you) selects a response time of 90+ seconds and your responders can answer from anywhere using just about any device. Accessibility is promoted in multiple ways. First your students can answer via video, which means they do not have to type out an answer, as is typically the case with a traditional discussion board. Try this as an alternative method of assessment in a classroom environment. Each video is also transcribed for viewers to read and listen for better absorption and comprehension of content. Flipgrid is appropriate for K–12+ audiences and this online tool can be used for any learning or professional development scenario to enhance discussion, learning, and collaboration.

Mysimpleshow: https://www.mysimpleshow.com/

Mysimpleshow is a video creation tool that focuses on explainer videos. If you need to focus on learning or teaching resources, educational ideas, or instructional materials then mysimpleshow has you covered. It's a great tool for students to use with projects. Using mysimpleshow is easy. Sign in, create a script, and the program chooses images and illustrations to explain your script or idea. Then as the creator, you can choose a voice to narrate your video or you can choose to do the voiceover yourself. Captions are also available for accessibility purposes. So not only are you visually explaining a concept but your videos are also captioned for all viewers. A great tool for digital storytelling, short videos, and class/library tours and introductions.

YouTube Closed Captioning: https://www.youtube.com/

If you have a Gmail account, you now have a YouTube account as well. Loading and sharing videos has never been easier, but what makes YouTube even more exciting is the user-friendliness of the site. Simply load your video via My Channel and then edit content in your Video Manager. There are a variety of editing options, but for accessibility purposes, the most important is closed captioning. Video creators can caption their own videos or YouTube will automatically do the captioning.

Ted-Ed: https://ed.ted.com/

TED-Ed is TED's initiative for young people and education. TED-Ed's mission is based on celebrating the ideas of teachers and students internationally and supporting learning. They offer a platform to help teachers create interactive video lessons as well as a library of original, animated videos. Finding videos is easy. Search by content, student level, video duration, language, and more. Each video has captioning for accessibility, multiple choice questions, guided discussion questions, and learning content. A great location to find short videos for any topic in your classroom.

Google offers a wide range of online tools, apps, and materials related to accessibility with an entire website dedicated solely to accessibility at https://www .google.com/accessibility/. The site takes users through the types of tools Google has to aid in accessibility for both the web as a whole as well as for many of their individual products. Check the site for all things accessible in the world of Google (see Chapter 48 for more on Google Accessibility).

REFERENCE

American Association of School Librarians. (2009). *Empowering Learners: Guidelines for School Librarians*. Chicago: American Library Association.

48

Google Accessibility for Your Library

Heather Moorefield-Lang

The overarching job and goal of a school librarian essentially stays the same over time—regardless of technology, trends, and new developments. School librarians work to plant and grow a love of learning in each student and strive to offer information access to all students in an equitable manner (American Association of School Librarians 2009). Every day, students with a variety of skills and abilities come into the school library. Having knowledge of online tools for those students who might be known as "differently-abled" is advantageous for all.

Google offers a wide variety of online tools, apps, and materials. What you may not know is that Google now has an entire site dedicated solely to accessibility (https://www.google.com/accessibility/). The site is broken down into the categories of communication, productivity, and on-the-go for easy site navigation. The entire website takes users through the types of tools Google has to aid in accessibility for the web as a whole as well as for many of their individual products. The following are a few personal favorites:

YouTube Closed Captioning

If you have a Gmail account, you now have a YouTube account as well. Loading and sharing videos has never been easier, but what makes YouTube even more exciting is the user-friendliness of the site. Simply load your video via My Channel and then edit content in your Video Manager. There are a variety of editing options but for accessibility purposes the most important is closed captioning. Video creators can caption their own videos or YouTube will automatically do the captioning and content can be edited. Either way, video content has now become more approachable for all viewers.

Google Hangouts

This amazing web conferencing tool has become a staple in many libraries for author visits, interviews, meetings, office hours, and more. Captioning is now an option offered on the toolbar in Google Hangouts. It can happen two different ways. At no cost, users or attendees in a Google Hangouts session can download or type in captions. For a fee, an outside entity can be paid to caption a Google Hangout session. Google Help also offers a Sign Language Interpreter App for Google Hangouts. There are quite a few options in this particular communication tool.

Google Search

Navigate and search the Internet hands-free. Speak your search terms and criteria aloud for a web exploration. Options for web results to be read aloud to students and library users are also now available. Google accessibility offers helpful pages and step-by-step guides to aid librarians and our patrons when they are away from library spaces.

Google Docs

A favorite option offered by Google is the voice typing feature in Google Docs. Users simply start a new document, click on tools, voice typing, and the microphone, and say aloud their papers and written documents. This is useful for a variety of reasons. Students with different abilities in learning and comprehension might find speaking their typing a more successful way to deliver written assignments. Students with differing physical abilities may find it easier to speak a paper than type it. Sometimes, it's just nice to talk out an idea rather than type it. Regardless of why it's being used, the option is amazing and the opportunities for use are endless.

These are only a selection of some of the tools available via Google Accessibility. There are many others for your laptops and mobile devices. Teaching our students is not a one-size-fits-all scenario. There are many wonderful tools and online resources that can aid all of our students. These tools will get you started and hopefully get you thinking about concepts and methods in accessibility for all students who enter your library. Share these with your teaching colleagues!

REFERENCE

American Association of School Librarians. (2009). *Empowering Learners: Guidelines for School Librarians*. Chicago: American Library Association.

49

Deaf ≠ Silenced: Serving the Needs of the Deaf/ Hard-of-Hearing Students in School Libraries

Kimberly Gangwish

Although the number of students who are deaf/hard-of-hearing (HoH) may be small within a single school or district, the unique learning needs of this population cannot be ignored. To ensure that students who are deaf/HoH have the same access as hearing students to resources and programming designed to meet their learning needs, school librarians must consider the needs of these students in all aspects of library services.

Equitable access means that *all*—not some—students have the right to become educated and information literate. A common belief of the American Association of School Librarians (AASL) is that school librarians should be "committed to inclusion and equity" (AASL 2018). But in many cases, "equitable" is considered in terms of funding or technology. Equitable access is more than that; it requires that all students have equal opportunity to learn. School librarians have a responsibility to support successful learning for every student, preparing each for the information-rich world in which they will study and work.

Approximately two to three out of 1,000 children are born in the United States with hearing loss and one in eight people aged twelve and older suffers loss in both ears (National Institute on Deafness and Other Communication Disorders 2015). According to the Center for Hearing and Communication, "15% of children between the ages of 6–19 have a measurable hearing loss in at least one ear" and "approximately 3 million children in the U.S. have a hearing loss." There are four key areas in which the work of school librarians can result in better access and learning opportunities for this population of students:

1. First, school librarians need to consider students who are deaf/HoH in their collection development decisions.
2. The implementation and use of technology can also help provide equitable access for these students.
3. School librarians can consider how they teach and incorporate instructional strategies that meet the learning needs of the deaf/HoH more effectively.
4. Finally, school librarians need to become leaders in their schools and districts about services, materials, and teaching methods for students who are deaf/HoH.

COLLECTION DEVELOPMENT

Students should be able to see themselves and their lives reflected in a school library collection. Most school libraries have materials related to diverse cultures and groups of people. But would a student who is deaf/HoH find materials relevant to their life and challenges? Does the collection have books—both fiction and nonfiction—featuring deaf characters, authors, and issues? As school librarians develop their library collections, they should include books that reflect the lives of students who are deaf/HoH. In young adult fiction, this might mean books with deaf characters, such as *Strong Deaf* by Lynn McElfresh, *Read My Lips* by Teri Brown, *Tone Deaf* by Olivia Rivers, *You're Welcome Universe* by Whitney Gardner, and *The Silence Between Us* by Alison Gervais. In nonfiction, consider adding books that deal with deaf issues and culture, such as *Angels and Outcasts: An Anthology of Deaf Characters in Literature* by Trent Batson and Eugene Bergman or *Train Go Sorry: Inside a Deaf World* by Leah Hager Cohen. Book lists featuring deaf characters, authors, and culture can be found from several sources. Resources from the Laurent Clerc National Deaf Education Center of Gallaudet University and the Young Adult Library Services Association (YALSA) are great starting points. Also consider adding audio books to the collection for those students who benefit from amplification devices. A review list of young adult titles featuring deaf characters can also be found on my website, ksgangwish.net.

TECHNOLOGY

Technology can be used to ease the frustration levels of struggling students, especially the deaf/HoH. These students may be challenged by learning and/or reading comprehension difficulties and may become frustrated with trying to learn in a hearing environment. Consider using technology tools to facilitate the learning of students who are deaf/HoH. For example, teach students to use features of research databases to support their individual needs, including searching by reading level or using visual search methods. Access to information at the appropriate reading level is a critical component in providing equal opportunity for classroom success.

Closed caption technology can also benefit students who are deaf/HoH. An easy way to provide this is the closed captioning service of YouTube. When searching in YouTube, look for the closed captioned symbol in the description for videos. Do you use school- or teacher-created videos? YouTube can help add closed captioning to those as well. Create a YouTube account and upload the videos to the account. Then in Video Manager, edit videos to include subtitles/closed captioning. Although the translation is not always perfect, it does offer another opportunity to provide information to students who are deaf/HoH in a familiar format. A step-by-step guide is available on YouTube.

INSTRUCTIONAL STRATEGIES

Think about how you instruct students, and whether you take into consideration students who are deaf/HoH. When I analyzed my own teaching style in relation to students who are deaf/HoH, I realized that what I do is designed to meet the needs of my hearing students—not my students who are deaf/HoH. For example, I use a projected image to show what I'm teaching, I verbalize the content, and I tend to walk around the area, all at the same time. The only item of benefit to students who are deaf/HoH is the projected image. Even if a student who is deaf/HoH reads lips, when an instructor moves around the room, the student either has to choose to focus on the screen or the teacher. Add in the possibility that they may also have an interpreter to watch, and the frustration level likely increases and the opportunity for learning decreases.

How can school librarians address this? Provide alternatives to allow these students to access the same content in multiple ways. Develop handouts with screenshots and clear instructions concerning the lesson. Allow opportunities for learning independently and at students' own pace.

Challenge yourself to develop videos created with both closed captioning and American Sign Language interpretation. These videos offer students who are deaf/HoH visual support and interpretation, which is helpful for students whose reading comprehension may make the use of closed captioning alone difficult. iMovie is one program that allows the creation of these videos using the subtitle and picture-in-picture steps. A step-by-step guide for this process can be found on the Apple website.

LEADERSHIP IN THE SCHOOL

School librarians should become leaders in their schools and districts to support the needs of students who are deaf/HoH, as well as to provide professional development for teachers and administrators. School librarians are in the unique position of being able to work with every curricular area in their school. This provides the opportunity to inform other teachers about the unique needs of these students, to introduce library resources that support their needs, and to share strategies that work in different class settings. Along with special education teachers or specialists, school librarians can learn about strategies and then model and guide other staff members in effective methods of teaching students who are deaf/HoH. School librarians can also help to inform the student population about deaf/HoH culture through books, information, dialog, and programming.

Equitable access means that every student has the right to materials and instruction that meet their needs. Addressing collection development, technology use, and instructional strategies will allow school librarians to better meet the needs of all students, including students who are deaf/HoH. School library standards demand equal access and opportunity for all students. In order to provide that access across the school, school librarians need to become leaders in their schools and districts in providing effective methods of teaching and interacting with students who are deaf/HoH.

REFERENCES AND RESOURCES

American Association of School Librarians. (2018). *National School Library Standards for Learners, School Librarians and School Libraries*. Chicago: American Library Association.

American Association of School Librarians. (2018). *AASL Standards Frameworks for Learners*. Chicago: American Library Association.

Apple Inc. *iMovie 11: Add a Picture-in-Picture Clip*. Retrieved from http://support.apple.com/kb/ph2243.

Bill of Rights for Deaf and Hard of Hearing Children. Retrieved from http://nad.org/issues/education/k-12/bill-of-rights.

Brown, T. (2008). *Read My Lips*. New York: Simon Pulse.

Center for Hearing and Communication. *Statistics and Facts about Hearing Loss*. Retrieved from http://chchearing.org/facts-about-hearing-loss.

Education Rights for Deaf Children. Retrieved from https://www.equalrightstrust.org/content/world-federation-deaf-policy-education-rights-deaf-children.

Gallaudet University. *Books about Deaf Culture*. Retrieved from https://www3.gallaudet.edu/Documents/Clerc/Books-DeafCulture.pdf.

Gardner, W. (2017). *You're Welcome, Universe!* New York: Alfred A. Knopf.

Gervais, A. (2019). *The Silence Between Us*. Grand Rapids, MI: Blink.

Laurent Clerc National Deaf Education Center, Gallaudet University. https://www.gallaudet.edu/clerc-center.

Little, D. (April 15, 2013a). Deaf and hard-of-hearing characters in YA fiction. *YALSA: The Hub*. Retrieved from http://www.yalsa.ala.org/thehub/2013/04/15/deaf-and-hard-of-hearing-characters-in-ya-fiction.

Little, Dena. (April 15, 2013b). Serving deaf or hard-of-hearing teen patrons. *The YALSA Blog*. Retrieved from http://yalsa.ala.org/blog/2013/04/15/serving-deaf-or-hard-of-hearing-teen-patrons.

McElfresh, L. (2012). *Strong Deaf*. South Hampton, NH: Namelos.

National Institute on Deafness and Other Communication Disorders. *Quick Statistics*. Retrieved from http://www.nidcd.nih.gov/health/statistics/pages/quick.aspx.

Rivers, O. (2016). *Tone Deaf*. New York: Sky Pony Press.

YouTube. *Add Your Own Subtitles and Closed Captions*. Retrieved from http://support.google.com/youtube/answer/2734796?hl=en.

50

Serving Homeless Children in the School Library

Helen R. Adams

According to the Institute for Children & Poverty, it is estimated that there are over 1.35 million homeless children in 600,000 families in the United States and another 3.8 million adults and children in "precarious" housing situations (https://www .icphusa.org/faq/). The Department of Education reported that over 1,354,363 homeless students were enrolled by local public education agencies in the 2016–2017 school year, an increase of over 50,000 from the 2015–2016 school year (National Center for Homeless Education 2019).

PROVIDING AN EDUCATION FOR HOMELESS CHILDREN

In 1987, Congress passed the McKinney-Vento Homeless Education Act, which requires schools to provide a free, appropriate education to homeless children. The federal law established the "Education of Homeless Children and Youth" (EHCY) program in all states. State educational agencies apply for funding to ensure that all homeless children, including preschool education, receive an education comparable to their housed peers. Because of the downturn in the U.S. economy and weather-related disasters such as hurricanes, floods, tornadoes, and fires, many districts have homeless students. School districts can apply for grants, administered through their states, to support student enrollment and placement, referrals for support services, outreach activities, transportation, school supplies, before and after school as well as summer education programs, and coordination among local service agencies (National Coalition for the Homeless 2009).

The McKinney-Vento Act defines homeless students as "Children and youth who lack a fixed, regular, and adequate nighttime residence" (McKinney-Vento 2002). The law further describes the situations in which these students find themselves:

Chapters 50 originally appeared as a 2-part series. See sources chapter for more information.

- "Sharing the housing of others due to loss of housing, economic hardship, or a similar reason
- Living in motels, hotels, trailer parks, or camping grounds due to lack of adequate alternative accommodations
- Living in emergency or transitional shelters
- Abandoned in hospitals
- Awaiting foster care placement
- Living in a public or private place not designed for or ordinarily used as a regular sleeping accommodation for human beings
- Living in cars, parks, abandoned buildings, bus or train stations, or similar settings
- Migratory children . . . living in the above circumstances" (McKinney-Vento 2002).

Under the federal law, school districts are responsible for such actions as appointing a district-level homeless liaison, enrolling students identified as homeless even if medical and academic records are not available, providing transportation to the school if requested by the parents or guardian, and ensuring that district policies and procedures have no barriers for homeless students (Wisconsin Department of Public Instruction 2017).

WHAT DOES BEING HOMELESS MEAN TO CHILDREN?

Because of their mobility and precarious living conditions, homeless children and young adults face many educational challenges. Moving from school to school or not being enrolled for extended periods disrupts their social network and interrupts their learning. The impact of frequently changing schools or not attending school regularly results in their being "nine times more likely to repeat a grade, four times more likely to drop out of school, and three times more likely to be placed in special education programs than their housed peers" (National Coalition for the Homeless 2009).

According to Mary Maronek, education consultant for the Wisconsin EHCY program, "Children who are homeless face problems daily that housed children don't experience. These issues may include: developmental delays, emotional difficulties, more health problems with lack of access to health services, exposure to violence, less cultural experiences than their housed peers, and concerns about meeting basic needs . . . Also, many children may be suffering from trauma due to their homelessness" (Mary Maronek, email interview with author, August 10, 2010).

Patty, an urban elementary school librarian in the Midwest, described the effects of homelessness on her students:

A student who becomes homeless may show signs that students undergoing any type of emotional stress will show. He or she may become listless and not seem to care about school-related or library-related activities, or may become depressed and isolate himself or herself, or may become easily angered and lash out at others verbally or physically . . . again, any of the signs associated with extreme distress. These signs cause me to go to a student's classroom teacher both to let the teacher know about the behavior I observed and to see if the teacher has any suggestions or insights that will help me understand what the student is experiencing.

Sometimes students will share their [housing] situations with me. It often happens if there are library materials that are overdue, and I am asking the student where the materials are. It is very difficult for a student who comes home from school to find the door to his or her apartment bolted by the landlord and all of the family's belongings locked inside. Sometimes landlords just throw everything away including library books. The student has no control over this . . . so it's difficult to restrict access to library materials for something [unreturned books] the student cannot fix.

Sometimes a student will share if we are privately discussing his or her behavior. I will often ask why the student is acting in a certain way, and the student may explain his or her living situation, usually tearfully.

For me, it is important to remember that homelessness for an elementary student is not his or her fault. School, especially the school library, may be the only thing a homeless student can count on as a place that is safe, comfortable, and full of books, magazines, online resources, and more that can bring enjoyment and respite from the daily stresses in his or her life" (Patty, email to author, August 12, 2010).

RESPONSIBILITIES OF LIBRARIANS

All homeless children and young adults have the same legal right to an education as their housed classmates. Libraries promote access to resources and services, and the American Library Association's "Library Services to the Poor" states:

> The American Library Association promotes equal access to information for all persons, and recognizes the urgent need to respond to the increasing number of poor children, adults, and families in America. These people are affected by a combination of limitations, including illiteracy, illness, social isolation, homelessness, hunger, and discrimination, which hamper the effectiveness of traditional library services. Therefore, it is crucial that libraries recognize their role in enabling poor people to participate fully in a democratic society, by utilizing a wide variety of available resources and strategies.

Since the economic downturn began, homelessness is occurring more frequently from metropolitan areas to suburbs to rural localities to small towns and cities across America. In December 2008, a company in Wisconsin closed its plant. Approximately 4,000 General Motors and satellite business employees lost their jobs in Janesville, Wisconsin, and the economic ripple in the community of 60,000 created financial hardship for many families (https://granta.com/janesville-wisconsin/). As a result, the School District of Janesville is serving an increasing population of students who are homeless.

SCHOOL POLICIES AND HOMELESS STUDENTS

According to Ann Forbeck, a homeless liaison for the School District of Janesville:

> Many students in poverty and homeless students especially, live in chaos and focus only on surviving from day to day. In that environment, it is very difficult for families to keep track of important papers, like birth certificates and school records. It is rarely on the radar for these families to take care of getting library books back to school on time, if at all.
>
> I have run into situations where students were denied access to school records or permission to graduate due to an unpaid fee for a missing book [NOT in Janesville]. These are the kind of policies that cause homeless students to give up on their education. It is also illegal to discriminate against students who are homeless. [. . .] I have worked with high school students who left school books in unsafe places where they had stayed temporarily, and they have been afraid to go back to those residences to retrieve the books. It is very important that school libraries have policies that allow for students to have access to the materials without penalizing them for situations that are beyond their control. (Forbeck 2010)

"Economic Barriers to Information Access: An Interpretation of the Library Bill of Rights" states, "Libraries should examine policies and procedures, particularly those involving fines, fees, or other user charges, and actively move toward eliminating any that may create potential barriers to access or academic achievement." School librarians must balance their fiduciary responsibility to maintain a collection with open access for all students.

SCHOOL DISTRICT EFFORTS

Janesville school librarians have developed policies that fulfill *Library Bill of Rights* principles and consider homeless students' needs. Kathy Boguszewski, Janesville Library Media and Instructional Technology Coordinator, affirmed:

> We encourage all children to check out books. We want the children to become better readers, and to become better readers they need to read. The key is getting books in the hands of students. If items do not come back, due to many circumstances, they [librarians] do what they can to encourage the students to return materials. But what does not come back is just the cost of doing business. I know I can speak for all our school librarians. Literacy is our business. We do not limit access to materials or checkouts. (Boguszewski 2010)

To enable some students to complete homework, the school district placed computers and printers in two homeless shelters (Forbeck 2010). Boguszewski agrees this action is helpful but asserts, "I would like to see all of our school libraries open beyond school hours. The homeless shelters are not an ideal learning environment. Our libraries are" (Boguszewski 2010).

PRACTICAL STRATEGIES FOR SCHOOL LIBRARIANS

School libraries have traditionally been safe havens for at-risk students and can also make a difference in the lives of students who are homeless. According to Mary Maronek, "School librarians or any school staff should not assume, because of age or grade level, the understanding a student may have on any subject. Nor should they assume that a child can take homework home, and s/he has the resources to complete school assignments" (Maronek 2010).

Practical strategies school librarians can use to help homeless students include:

- Welcome new students and provide a library map, brochure describing library usage policies, a brief tour, and orientation to library resources.
- Assign a library buddy for elementary students.
- Stock basic school supplies commonly needed to complete assignments.
- Set clear, consistent rules that provide structure to library use (adapted from Wisconsin Department of Public Instruction 2011).
- Provide individual support and frequent encouragement to students as they seek resources and work on assignments.
- Provide the one-on-one attention homeless students often desire (Maronek 2010).
- Respect students' privacy in library usage and personal confidences.
- Help students plan where library books can be stored safely, and provide a calendar showing the day library books are due (Forbeck 2010).
- Seek ways to give students books to keep. Janesville elementary school librarian Karen Forst recounts, "I give away books nearly every week. After story time, I choose two students to answer story-related comprehension questions, and they are allowed to choose a book to keep ("forever and ever!" as some little ones say). I also post trivia questions with books as the prize and ask third to fifth graders Dewey questions with book rewards (Forst 2010).

- Seek alternate ways to replace lost/damaged books such as asking a local service organization to establish a small fund for that purpose or offering students the option to work in the library to pay for a fine or book replacement (Adams 2008, 69).
- Select books on poverty and homelessness to enable homeless students to see themselves in the collection and their housed peers to learn about those conditions.
- Share lesson plans and resources with teachers about students living in poverty and experiencing homelessness.

LIBRARIANSHIP WITH COMPASSION

Providing library resources and service to students who are homeless is a mix of applying professional ethics, recognizing students' First Amendment right to receive information in a school library, and meeting a legal requirement to provide an education equal to that of housed students. Ann Forbeck says it best when she states, "There are no easy answers to helping homeless students succeed in school. However, it is possible to change punitive policies regarding lost and late books with compassion for the very difficult lives of students who are homeless or living in poverty" (Forbeck 2010). So, to contribute to this effort, school librarians can start by reviewing and fine-tuning library policies. They can then greet homeless students in the school library with a friendly smile, they can offer a safe space with resources, and they can establish flexible policies.

REFERENCES

Adams, H. R. (2008). *Ensuring Intellectual Freedom and Access to Information in the School Library Media Program.* Santa Barbara, CA: Libraries Unlimited.

American Library Association. *Economic Barriers to Information Access: An Interpretation of the Library Bill of Rights.* Retrieved from http://www.ala.org/advocacy/intfreedom/librarybill/interpretations/economicbarriers.

American Library Association. *Library Services to the Poor.* Retrieved from http://www.ala.org/aboutala/offices/extending-our-reach-reducing-homelessness-through-library-engagement-7.

Boguszewski, Kathy. Email to author, August 12, 2010/email to Nancy Anderson, August 9, 2010.

Forbeck, Ann. Email to Kathy Boguszewski, August 16, 2010.

Forst, Karen. Email to Nancy Anderson, August 22, 2010.

Institute for Children & Poverty. *Quick Facts: National Data on Family Homelessness.* Retrieved from http://www.icpnyorg/index.asp?CID=7.

Maronek, Mary. Email interview with author, August 9–10, 2010.

McKinney-Vento Homeless Education Act. (2002). Retrieved from https://nche.ed.gov/mckinney-vento.

National Center for Homeless Education. (2019). *National Overview.* Retrieved from http://profiles.nche.seiservices.com/ConsolidatedStateProfile.aspx.

National Coalition for the Homeless. (September 2009). *Education of Homeless Children and Youth.* Retrieved from http://nationalhomeless.org/factsheets/education.html.

Patty (elementary librarian). Email message to author, August 12, 2010.

Wisconsin Department of Public Instruction. (February 2011). *How Teachers Can Help Homeless Students.* Retrieved from https://dpi.wi.gov/sites/default/files/imce/homeless/pdf/teach_help_hmls_stud.pdf.

Wisconsin Department of Public Instruction. (2017). *Education for Homeless Children and Youth.* Retrieved from https://dpi.wi.gov/homeless.

51

Literature as Mirrors, Windows, and Sliding Glass Doors

Lucy Santos Green and Michelle Maniaci Folk

We love our lit and, fortunately, the impact a book can have continues far beyond the rituals we enjoy as we settle in and begin turning pages. The concept of books serving as windows and mirrors for readers resonates with many of us. We see this phrase often in blog posts, tweets, and comments from authors, educators, and librarians. Despite being three decades old, Rudine Sims Bishop's words have not lost their importance. One could, in fact, argue that Dr. Bishop's words are more essential than ever.

> Books are sometimes windows, offering views of worlds that may be real or imagined, familiar or strange. These windows are also sliding glass doors, and readers have only to walk through in imagination to become part of whatever world has been created and recreated by the author. When lighting conditions are just right, however, a window can also be a mirror. Literature transforms human experience and reflects it back to us, and in that reflection we can see our own lives and experiences as part of the larger human experience. Reading, then, becomes a means of self-affirmation, and readers often seek their mirrors in books. (Bishop 1990, 1)

Bishop explains mirrors are essential because "when children cannot find themselves reflected in the books they read, or when the images they see are distorted, negative, or laughable, they learn a powerful lesson about how they are devalued in the society of which they are a part" (Bishop 1990, 1).

Bishop continues by describing how windows are just as important because "books may be one of the few places where children who are socially isolated and insulated from the larger world may meet people unlike themselves" (Bishop 1990, 2). Author Jacqueline Woodson brings up an interesting and additional benefit of providing windows. Not only do these introduce us to new experiences, windows help us "find a place in those people and in the story where they are, [and where we and] they share a common ground" (Weatherford 2018).

As stewards of the reading experience, we owe our school community an honest, impassioned effort to guarantee this happens for the students who walk through our doors, and that this effort goes beyond multicultural literature.

We need to focus on other groups that we may be leaving out. An excellent source to begin this process is We Need Diverse Books (WNDB), an organization with a simple mission of "putting more books featuring diverse characters into the hands of all children," and an honorable vision of "a world in which all children can see themselves in the pages of a book" (2018). WNDB defines diversity as "all diverse experiences, including (but not limited to) LGBTQIA, Native, people of color, gender diversity, people with disabilities, and ethnic, cultural, and religious minorities" (2018). Their website (https://diversebooks.org/) has a helpful list of books that allow readers to see themselves or develop empathy for others.

As school districts continue to draw our attention to trauma-informed care, we may even consider looking for books that will appeal to students struggling with homelessness or poverty, children whose parents are incarcerated or suffer from addictions, and those who have witnessed gun violence.

The Cooperative Children's Book Center (https://ccbc.education.wisc.edu/) publishes an annual, annotated list dating back to 1980, of what their librarians on staff consider to be the best books called *Choices*. CCBC librarians are experienced in evaluating multicultural literature and are committed to providing teachers and librarians with a diverse collection of titles. Each publication of *Choices* includes an essay on publishing industry trends librarians have observed over the past year, including statistics on multicultural literature and books about diverse topics.

As you continue to develop your school library's collection, remember you are curating mirrors and windows for your students. You are empowering them, through their love of literature, to become part of a rich and diverse global community. As Jacqueline Woodson says: "We're trying to figure out how to connect with people and work together and make a better world. I mean that's what education is, [it] is about understanding" (Weatherford 2018).

REFERENCES

Bishop, Rudine Sims. (Summer 1990). "Mirrors, Windows, and Sliding Glass Doors." *Perspectives: Choosing and Using Books for the Classroom,* 6(3), pp. 1–2.

Weatherford, Carole Boston. "Transcript from an Interview with Jacqueline Woodson." *Reading Rockets.* July 4, 2018. Retrieved from http://www.readingrockets.org /books/interviews/woodson/transcript.

52

Collection Development for Readers: Providing Windows and Mirrors

Mary Frances Zilonis and Chris Swerling

Rudine Simms Bishop, a professor at Ohio State University, coined the phrase "windows and mirrors" (1990) capturing the importance of mirroring children's life experiences in the books they read. Books can also provide a window for those outside a culture. Through the pages of a book, readers can (and should) see life from someone else's perspective.

Since 1985, the Cooperative Children's Book Center (CCBC) has documented the number of children's books written and illustrated by African Americans. That year, it was eighteen. By 1994, the report had expanded to include books by and about African Americans and other ethnicities including Latino, Asian/Pacific Americans, and First Nations. Their yearly report on children's literature publishing trends, entitled *Choices* (https://ccbc.education.wisc.edu/books/choices.asp), should be required reading for every school librarian.

In Fall 2016, the National Center for Education Statistics projected 50.4 million students would be enrolled in PK–12 public schools, with whites making up less than half—24.6 million—of that enrollment. Of the 3,400 books examined in 2015 by the CCBC, 106 were by African Americans (authors and/or illustrators) and 269 were about African Americans. Fifty-eight were by Latino (authors and/or illustrators) and eighty-two were about Latinos. Asian Pacific and Asian/Pacific Americans showed the greatest gain: 176 books authored and or illustrated with 113 titles about Asian Pacific and Asian/Pacific Americans (CCBC 2015). There has been some gain in representing our diverse society in children's books but not enough to provide "windows and mirrors" for students of color.

Enter the school library! Creating a collection filled with titles reflective of our diverse society *and* that provide "windows and mirrors" for *all* children is a challenge. Limited budgets and, sadly, limited title selections that quickly go out of print, need to be overcome. The statistics above should communicate a sense of urgency. More diverse children's titles are published now than ever before. But there are also more children of color in our schools than ever before. Population and publishing are not keeping pace with each other.

Marley Dias, an African American sixth-grade student and avid reader from New Jersey was frustrated with her reading choices. She shared her frustration with her mother who responded, "What are you going to do about it?" Thus was launched the #1000blackgirlbooks movement. By the time Marley's story was broadcast on *CBS This Morning* in February 2016, Marley had collected more than 1,300 books featuring African American girls.

With titles that act as "windows," children begin to see themselves as part of a global community. Through characters like themselves (as well as unlike themselves), children not only learn different perspectives, they also develop a sense of empathy. Reading books that act as "mirrors" empowers and enhances self-esteem, especially for children in underrepresented ethnicities. It sends a powerful message that they are valued. The school library can be a place where all students can feel safe and acknowledged, and where they can discover themselves. When children see characters who resemble themselves, their family, and their friends in books, they are more likely to be motivated to read.

The We Need Diverse Books Campaign (http://weneeddiversebooks.org) started in 2014. It initiated an important conversation about diversity and children's publishing. The impact is visible in the increase in the number of diverse children's titles published over the last two years. But the momentum needs to continue and grow. In comparison to the number of students of color enrolled in our schools nationwide, there are still relatively few books available that accurately reflect our nation's diversity, providing the essential "windows and mirrors" for all readers. As you use your budget dollars for collection development this year, we echo the question posed by Marley's mother: *What are you going to do about it?*

REFERENCES

Bishop, R. S. (1990). Mirrors, windows, and sliding glass doors. *Perspectives, 6*(3), pp. ix–xi.

CBS. (February 18, 2016). An 11-Year Old Book Lover's Drive for Change. *CBS News.* Retrieved from http://www.cbsnews.com/news/1000blackgirlbooks-social-media -book-drive-movement-black-characters.

Cooperative Children's Book Center. *Publishing Statistics on Children's Books about People of Color and First/Native Nations and by People of Color and First/Native Nations Authors and Illustrators.* Retrieved from https://ccbc.education.wisc.edu /books/pcstats.asp.

National Center for Education Statistics. *Fast Facts: Back to School Statistics.* Retrieved from http://nces.ed.gov/fastfacts/display.asp?id=372.

53

Building School Library Collections with Windows and Mirrors

Mary Frances Zilonis and Chris Swerling

School librarians must view books in the collection with a critical eye for stories told from within a culture, written in an authentic voice. Consider examining your school library collection for diversity. What percentage of your collection mirrors what you know (or may learn) about the cultures and families of your student body? How current are the titles in both fiction and nonfiction? You will yield informative data as you analyze, review, and reflect on your collection through a lens focused on diversity. Unfortunately, there is no digital tool to easily analyze your collection in this way, but there are a few strategies you can try to create a picture of representation and needs.

One place to start is with your materials about countries. Do they reflect the cultures represented in your school and are they up to date? If not, this is an immediate gap to fill. Next, look at your folklore section. Check titles for authenticity. Are there notes as to the story's origin and source materials? Is the country of origin specified—or is it labeled more generally, such as "African folktale"? Remember, Africa is not a country; it is a continent with many countries, each with a unique heritage that should be acknowledged in the literature that children read.

Another area to review is fiction. Both picture books and chapter books need to be reviewed for stereotypes. Stories written in the 1960s and 1970s often portrayed cultures and settings in exaggerated, "exotic" terms and with blatant stereotypes. Shifting to nonfiction, are your biographies up to date? Are the cultures represented reflective of people that the students know?

Studying the diversity of your collection will likely necessitate a hands-on review of titles. Make a list of multicultural search terms. Use them to search your catalog and uncover diverse titles in relevant areas. Exactly how many titles do you have that reflect the demographics and ethnicities of your school? Are these titles current, relevant, and authentic? Use diversebookfinder.com, funded through the U.S. Institute for Museum and Library Services. Search their online database of thousands of picture book titles with characters of color that have been published in the United States. In addition, diversebookfinder.com tracks trends beyond their main focus of representations of Black, Indigenous People, and People of Color also analyzing representations of social, sexual, ethnic, and religious identity in children's picture books. Sign up—and use—the newly added Collection Analysis Tool (CAP) feature. Once you have an account, you can upload your picture book collection data. You will receive a report that analyzes who is represented and how—useful for identifying the strengths of your picture book collection as well as to identify areas in which to focus your collection development efforts. Need guidance in selecting titles? Boston University's African Studies Center provides an excellent article with guidelines for selecting titles, entitled "A Guide to Selecting Multicultural Literature: Separating the Wheat from the Chaff" (http://www.bu.edu/africa /outreach/selection_guide/). For a more in-depth discussion of what to avoid, read "Examining Multicultural Picture Books for the Early Childhood Classroom: Possibilities and Pitfalls" by Jean Mendoza and Debbie Reese. Their recommendations, such as looking out for "popular but problematic books" are applicable to titles for all ages (2001).

How does the number of Newbery Award titles in your collection compare to the number of Coretta Scott King Award titles? Another starting point for collection development is increasing the number of titles that have won awards specifically created to promote titles by diverse authors and illustrators, and/or about a specific culture. Lists of Coretta Scott King, Pura Belpré, and other awards can be found on the ALA Youth Media Awards website (http://www.ala.org/news/mediapresscenter /presskits/youthmediaawards/alayouthmediaawards).

Finally, as you build a "windows and mirrors" library collection with diverse characters or themes, consider asking these questions:

- **Characters**: What characters and what ethnicities are portrayed as successful and play a major role in the book?
- **Language**: Does the dialog and text look like and sound like the daily life of the represented culture?
- **History**: Are historical events and encounters portrayed accurately or are they fictionalized to make a more appealing (and possibly less accurate) story?
- **Illustrations**: Are the illustrations stereotype-free? Do they accurately reflect the culture of an identified ethnic group? Do they enhance the text?
- **Author/Illustrator**: Do they have a background or access to the background of the culture to write and/or illustrate authentically? Are research notes available?
- **Emotional Response of the Reader**: Would a child whose heritage is reflected in the book's pictures and pages feel proud? Does the book aid children from outside the represented culture to gain appreciation and understanding?
- For more detailed criteria, read "Beyond Good Intentions: Selecting Multicultural Literature," by Joy Shioshita (https://www.leeandlow.com /educators/race/beyond-good-intention-selecting-multicultural-literature).

As you apply your knowledge to build your collection, be aware that having only one title in a school library representing any culture or group can unwittingly create misconceptions. Chimamanda Ngozi Adichie speaks movingly on this topic in her popular TED Talk "The Danger of a Single Story" (https://www.ted.com/talks /chimamanda_adichie_the_danger_of_a_single_story?language=en). Review your titles carefully, then grow and share your collection with students!

REFERENCES

Brown, B. B. A Guide to Selecting Multicultural Literature: Separating the Wheat from the Chaff. *Boston University Pardee School of Global Studies, African Studies Center.* Retrieved from http://www.bu.edu/africa/outreach/selection_guide.

Mendoza, J., & Reese, D. (2001). Examining multicultural picture books for the early childhood classroom: Possibilities and pitfalls. *Early Childhood Research and Practice, 3*(2), Retrieved from http://ecrp.uiuc.edu/v3n2/mendoza.html.

54

Moving Diverse Books from Your Library Shelves and into the Hands of Readers

Mary Francis Zilonis and Chris Swerling

Developing a collection with diverse titles is challenging. Diverse titles are often published by small or independent companies, and may or may not be reviewed in traditional library review sources—or remain in print very long. The following will guide you to some of the best resources for expanding the diversity of your collection.

Lee and Low (https://www.leeandlow.com/) is the largest multicultural children's book publisher in the United States. Minority owned, their mission is simple: to publish contemporary diverse stories for all children. They make a special effort to work with unpublished authors and illustrators of color.

In response to an editor's proclamation, "there is no market for black children's books," Wade and Cheryl Hudson started Just Us Books (http://justusbooks.com/) in 1987. Over thirty years later, the publishing company is still going strong.

There are many excellent resources online. Here are some of our favorites:

- Multiculturalism Rocks https://multiculturalism.rocks/
- Teaching for Change https://www.teachingforchange.org/books/multi cultural-childrens-books
- ¡Colorín Colorado! http://www.colorincolorado.org/books-authors/multi cultural-literature
- Center for the Study of Multicultural Children's Literature https://www .csmcl.org/
- Windows Mirrors Doors http://mirrorswindowsdoors.org/
- Anti-Defamation League. Books Matter: People, Identity and Culture http:// www.adl.org/education-outreach/books-matter/people-identity-culture .html

If your diverse titles remain sitting on your library shelves, they are not serving as "windows and mirrors." You need to actively promote titles with students and teachers. Here are some strategies:

#1: Take Five at a Faculty Meeting: Ask for five minutes to booktalk five diverse titles. Set a goal of checking them out on the spot.

#2: Highlight Diverse Materials: Create a place on your library website to feature diverse titles. Highlight an author, illustrator, a new title, a timely title, or student reviews.

#3: Create a Diversity Resource Page: Highlight diverse resources in your collection. Include authors and illustrators of diverse books. Provide links to their websites, video clips, book trailers, awards, and booklists. Be sure to add a link to teachingbooks.net and their Teach Diverse Books resources (https://www.teachingbooks.net/show.cgi?f=literacy_diverse).

#4: Initiate a Staff or Student Book Club: Make the theme reading books from and about diverse cultures. Focus on reading award-winning titles by authors of color.

#5: Provide Professional Development about Diverse Literature. Teachers love to browse and talk about new books. Develop a workshop that will introduce authors and illustrators of diverse children's literature.

#6: Be Active in Curriculum Development. As new units are written and old units revised, add your voice to suggest diverse titles.

#7: Create a Diverse Literature Criteria Checklist to Raise Awareness. Be sure to include the caveat that titles should be bias and stereotype free. Diverse characters should be primary in their roles and authentically presented. For help in developing criteria consult:

- K–12 Reader: Ten Tips for Selecting Multicultural Books for Reading Instruction http://www.k12reader.com/ten-tips-for-selecting-multicultural-books-for-reading-instruction/
- Anti-Defamation League: Assessing Children's Book Collections Using an Anti-Bias Lens http://www.adl.org/assets/pdf/education-outreach/Assessing-Children-s-Book-Collections.pdf

#8: Reach out to Parents. Parents are always seeking titles to share with their children. Host a parent coffee hour or attend a PTO meeting. Display a range of diverse titles. Encourage parents to start a family book club featuring diverse titles.

#9: Promote the Awards! Let staff (and students) know about the Coretta Scott King Award, Pura Belpré Award, Asian Pacific/American Award for Literature, and others. Go beyond ethnicity and promote the Schneider Family Book Award that honors authors and illustrators whose works feature characters with special needs and those that recognize the LGBTQ community: Stonewall Award (http://www.ala.org/glbtrt/award/stonewall) and the Rainbow Book List (http://glbtrt.ala.org/rainbowbooks/).

#10: A Picture Speaks a Thousand Words! Obtain appropriate permissions, then take photos of your staff and students reading diverse children's titles to display in the school library.

Make "windows and mirrors" a visible theme in your library. Create a permanent display as a visual reminder to read diverse books. Start the conversation about diversity and invite students and staff to contribute.

55

Serving Rainbow Families in School Libraries

Jamie Campbell Naidoo

As shifting demographics in the United States testify to a rising number of children and families from diverse backgrounds, it is essential for school librarians to create inclusive collections, environments, and curricula that take into account various forms of diversity, including children or caregivers who identify as lesbian, gay, bisexual, transgender, and queer/questioning (LGBTQ). According to U.S. Census data analyses and targeted studies of the LGBTQ population, approximately 2 to 3.7 million children and teens are raised in LGBTQ families, otherwise known as rainbow families, and over 125,000 same-sex couples raise children in almost every community in the nation (Gates 2013; Gates 2015). Rainbow families can include children, teens, and/or caregivers who identify as LGBTQ.

In November 2014, the United Nations Children's Fund (UNICEF) reaffirmed the universal rights of children and caregivers in *all* families, including rainbow families, and emphasized that they should not be discriminated against. Specifically, the organization notes, "All measures to protect LGBT children and LGBT parents should be enforced in a manner that truly is in the best interests of children, and does not simply silence the victim or drive the discussion underground" (UNICEF 2014, 1). School librarians can uphold UNICEF's position by facilitating open and honest discussions and providing print and digital collections inclusive of LGBTQ topics. In doing so, librarians help to normalize the experiences of individuals in rainbow families. The subsequent sections explore strategies for creating welcoming spaces as well as suggestions for building diverse collections of LGBTQ materials.

CREATING WELCOMING ENVIRONMENTS

Students in rainbow families have similar informational needs as other students. These include accurate, current information about LGBTQ topics as well as the ability to find this information within the library's catalog; inclusive language in library programs and discussions; and opportunities to encounter LGBTQ individuals/

characters via library displays and collections. School library environments also should be free of homophobic and transphobic attitudes and practices.

Initially, school librarians may be hesitant to include LGBTQ topics because of their own concerns about developmental appropriateness or for fear of administrative/parental backlash. Often, LGBTQ themes are erroneously thought to be about sex. In reality, a children's book about a gender nonconforming child or a child with two mothers is no more about sex than any other children's book depicting children's emotions and family compositions. The Welcoming Schools website (http://www .welcomingschools.org/) provides an extremely helpful section on how to respond to student's tough questions about LGBTQ topics and how to introduce them into the curriculum. School librarians might also consider lesson plans or activities for International Family Equality Day or International Day against Homophobia and Transphobia. This allows librarians to celebrate all types of family diversity and be inclusive of rainbow families too.

Another way to be inclusive of rainbow families is to introduce the character Allie the Ally (http://allietheally.tumblr.com/aboutallie) in the library as soon as school begins. Created in 2011 by James Hubert Blake High School's Gay-Straight Alliance in Silver Spring, Maryland, Allie is the inclusive version of the book character Flat Stanley. She can be printed out and posted in library displays, used during library events, or included in the curriculum in such ways as "Allie the Ally's List of Recommended Family Friendly Books." Allie can also be displayed around the school to designate it as a rainbow family inclusive environment.

School librarians might consider partnering with local rainbow family parenting groups, LGBTQ organizations such as PFLAG, or community centers such as the LGBT Center of Raleigh, North Carolina, or the Magic City Acceptance Center for LGBTQ youth in Birmingham, Alabama. Through partnerships with these organizations, librarians can gain a better awareness of the local rainbow family culture as well as an understanding of the community services offered to these families. A successful partnership would also allow the school librarian to bounce ideas off other like-minded, culturally sensitive professionals.

No matter how a school librarian chooses to introduce LGBTQ topics into the curriculum, the most important point to remember is sensitivity. A librarian would not ask a student with a disability or from a particular ethnic group to speak for their entire cultural group and the same holds true for students in rainbow families. While a student in a rainbow family is the expert of their own experiences, they cannot speak for all individuals in rainbow families. It is extremely critical that librarians avoid *outing* or calling unwanted attention to these students. A teen may not want their classmates to know that they have two fathers, identifies as trans, or is bisexual. When having a discussion about family compositions, circumvent the urge to identify students in the school who are in rainbow families and do not call on them to testify about their experiences.

Selected Resources for Welcoming Rainbow Families in Schools

- **COLAGE: People with a Lesbian, Gay, Bisexual, or Transgender Parent:** Offers booklists, brochures, and web resources to support children in rainbow families such as "Tips for Making Classrooms Safer for Students with LGBTQ Parents." https://www.colage.org/resources/tips-for-making-classrooms-safer -for-youth-with-lgbtq-parents/

- **GLSEN (Gay, Lesbian, & Straight Education Network):** Provides suggestions for making schools a safe space for rainbow families and offers curricular guides and lesson plans related to bullying, diversity, and bias. https://www.glsen.org/activity/inclusive-curriculum-guide
- **Open to All: Serving the GLBT Community in your Library:** Developed by the Rainbow Round Table (RT) of the American Library Association, this toolkit includes recommendations for collection development and program considerations for serving rainbow families. http://www.ala.org/rt/sites/ala.org.rt/files/content/professionaltools/160309-glbtrt-open-to-all-toolkit-online.pdf
- **Trans Student Educational Resources:** Youth-led organization dedicated to helping educators better understand gender nonconforming and transgender students. Includes a helpful infographic of The Gender Unicorn that explains various terminology related to gender, as well as other useful infographics on diversity within the trans community. http://www.transstudent.org/graphics
- **Welcoming Schools:** Sponsored by the Human Rights Campaign Foundation, this comprehensive website includes lesson plans, librarian and teacher tips, extensive bibliographies of books for all ages covering a broad spectrum of LGBTQ topics, and other resources for creating welcoming school environments for rainbow families. http://www.welcomingschools.org/

COLLECTION DEVELOPMENT CONSIDERATIONS

School librarians developing collections inclusive of rainbow families have a variety of considerations to think through. These include selecting quality books representing diverse characters and findability within the collection. Over time, a growing body of LGBTQ children's and teen books has been published on a variety of topics and themes such as bullying, living within rainbow families, coming to terms with one's sexual orientation, and celebrating gender expression. The majority of these books are for young adults but children's books are becoming more common by way of non-U.S. imports, self-published titles, and small press publishing. Although rainbow families are more likely to be racially and ethnically diverse than other families, with nearly 40 percent of the caregivers and 50 percent of the children identifying as nonwhite, most books representing LGBTQ characters and families do not capture this diversity (Gates 2013). When comparing LGBTQ children's books to young adult novels, it becomes clear that older readers have more opportunities to see reflections of diversity in their books than their younger counterparts. More diverse LGBTQ children's books are needed such as Megan Lambert's *Real Sisters Pretend* (2016), which features two racially diverse adopted sisters living with a biracial lesbian couple.

While a school librarian may not feel qualified to select LGBTQ titles, several print and digital curricular resources and bibliographies are available to assist in locating the best materials with LGBTQ content. Created by LGBTQ organizations or curated by passionate librarians, many of these resources divide recommended titles into age groups or by material type (picture book, novel, digital resource, and so on) and suggest a variety of educational uses. Numerous book awards for LGBTQ youth literature can provide librarians with a solid core collection of print materials to begin their collections.

Recommended Resources for Locating LGBTQ Children's and YA Materials

- **"I'm Here. I'm Queer. What the Hell Do I Read?"** Created by writer and speaker Lee Wind, this blog, for both teens and librarians, provides a wealth of information about LGBTQ young adult books. http://www.leewind.org/
- *LGBTQAI+ Books for Children and Teens: Providing a Window for All.* Christina Dorr and Liz Deskins. ALA Editions, 2018.
- *Rainbow Family Collections: Selecting and Using Children's Books with Lesbian, Gay, Bisexual, Transgender, and Queer Content.* Jamie Campbell Naidoo. Libraries Unlimited, 2012.
- *Representing the Rainbow in Young Adult Literature: LGBTQ+ Content since 1969.* Christine Jenkins and Michael Cart. Rowman & Littlefield Publishers, 2018.
- **YA Pride:** (Formerly GayYA) Blog focused on criticism of LGBTQIA+ representation in young adult books. Includes a growing "master list" of tween and teen books. http://www.yapride.org/

Book Awards

- **Lambda Literary (Lammy) Awards:** Awarded by the Lambda Literary Foundation, these celebrate the best in literary fiction and nonfiction books that represent LGBTQ experiences. http://www.lambdaliterary.org/complete-list-of-award-recipients/
- **Rainbow Book List:** Presented annually by the American Library Association's Social Responsibility Roundtable (SRRT) and Rainbow Round RT, this booklist includes LGBTQ children's and teen titles. http://glbtrt.ala.org/rainbowbooks/rainbow-books-lists
- **Stonewall Book Award—Mike Morgan and Larry Romans Children's and Young Adult Literature Award:** Administered by the Rainbow RT, this award recognizes children's and YA books representing rainbow families. http://www.ala.org/rt/glbtrt/award/stonewall
- **Rise: A Feminist Book Project for ages 0-18:** (Formerly the Amelia Bloomer List) Established by the Feminist Task Force of the SRRT, this booklist identifies youth books that have strong feminist content relevant for gender-nonconforming children. http://ameliabloomer.wordpress.com/

The ability to locate LGBTQ books in the school library collection is an equally important consideration that librarians need to address. Often, precataloged materials from vendors will not include relevant LGBTQ subject headings or will use terminology foreign to students. Some astute librarians will edit the MARC records to include subject headings and keywords familiar to students to assist in findability. Other librarians will decide to mark LGBTQ titles with spine labels that identify them as such. The latter is an extremely problematic practice as it calls attention to anyone reading LGBTQ books. As such, students in rainbow families or their allies may not embrace these books for fear of being outed. The best option is to edit MARC records to identify LGBTQ content while maintaining patron privacy.

Another concern when building an LGBTQ collection is creating a balanced collection that represents all perspectives and viewpoints. While some librarians might be tempted to do this by acquiring books with anti-gay or homophobic content, in reality the best way to balance the collection is to include quality books with heterosexual and cisgender characters. Purchasing anti-gay materials is not only detrimental to the self-esteem of student in rainbow families but also a violation of the library's collection development policy. Most policies require at least two positive professional reviews of a particular title before it can be included in the collection. No homophobic titles currently meet this criterion. An extremely helpful tools for school librarians defending intellectual freedom and providing access to LGBTQ youth materials is the Defending Intellectual Freedom: LGBTQ+ Materials in School Libraries toolkit (https://standards.aasl.org/project/lgbtq/) created by the American Association for School Librarians (AASL). This resource uses the AASL Standards for school librarians to outline services for LGBTQ+ students and provides information for school librarians needing support to address book challenges and censorship attempts related to LGBTQ+ materials in school systems.

CONCLUDING THOUGHTS

Students in rainbow families are often not welcomed in classroom and school libraries. As noted in the GLSEN (the Gay, Lesbian & Straight Education Network) School Climate Survey, students in rainbow families are bullied at a much higher rate and are more likely to commit suicide than heteronormative students, cisgender students, or those in traditional families (Kosciw et al. 2014). If ever there was a time in our nation's history to embrace rainbow families in the library, it is now. Armed with some of the resources and suggestions above, school librarians can be well on their way to providing this much needed and long overdue overture.

REFERENCES

Gates, G. J. (2013). *LGBT Parenting in the United States*. Williams Institute, UCLA School of Law. Retrieved from http://williamsinstitute.law.ucla.edu/wp-content/uploads/LGBT-Parenting.pdf.

Gates, G. J. (2015). Marriage and family: LGBT individuals and same-sex couples. *The Future of Children, 25*(2), pp. 67–87.

Kosciw, J., Greytak, E., Palmer, N., & Boesen, M. J. (2014). *The 2013 National School Climate Survey: The Experiences of Lesbian, Gay, Bisexual, and Transgender Youth in our Nation's Schools*. GLSEN. Retrieved from http://www.glsen.org/sites/default/files/2013%20National%20School%20Climate%20Survey%20Full%20Report_0.pdf.

Lambert, M. (2016). *Real Sisters Pretend*. Illus. by Nicole Tadgell. Gardiner, ME: Tilbury House.

United Nations International Children's Emergency Fund (UNICEF). (November 2014). *Eliminating Discrimination against Children and Parents Based on Sexual Orientation and/or Gender Identity. Position Paper no. 9*. Retrieved from http://www.unicef.org/media/files/Position_Paper_Sexual_Identification_and_Gender_Identity_12_Nov_2014%283%29.pdf.

56

Whose History Is It?: Diversity in Historical Fiction for Young Adults

April M. Dawkins

Before I became a high school librarian, I was a history teacher. I love history—the real people, their stories, the conflicts, the drama. However, I often struggled to help my students love it as much as I did. Many students see history as dry and uninteresting, filled with rote memorization of facts. However, when students can see people who are like them as historical figures who make a contribution to the world, history can become much more impactful.

Once I became a high school librarian, I was always on the lookout for excellent and appealing historical fiction. Finding historical fiction that represented diverse viewpoints, cultures, ethnicities, and religions was difficult. Across the board, prominent recommended reading lists neglect to include diverse authors, viewpoints, and historical figures in a ratio that reflects our society's reality. For example, of the 171 informational texts recommended in the Common Core State Standards, only eighteen are by authors of color. The lives of the poor and nonwhite are rarely part of the story, despite the fact that more than half of the children in the United States today fit into those categories (Gangi & Benfer 2014). Considering the fact that the best readers are those who make personal connections with text, this situation seems to stack the deck against many of the children served by school libraries (Copeland & Martin 2016).

AWARD-WINNING DIVERSE HISTORICAL FICTION

One challenge in supporting diverse historical fiction collections is finding quality historical fiction written for children and young adults. The need for diverse materials has been widely discussed; however, diversity in specific genres has not really been addressed. Often, school librarians use awards lists to determine which titles should be included in their collections. Therefore, I decided to examine two awards to see if diverse historical fiction titles were being recognized.

I conducted a content analysis of the Michael L. Printz Award for Excellence in Young Adult Literature (awarded by the Young Adult Library Services Association, http://www.ala.org/yalsa/printz) and the Young Adult Library Services Association's Best Books lists for the period from 2000 to 2016 (http://www.ala.org/yalsa/booklists/bbya; http://www.ala.org/yalsa/best-fiction-young-adults). I chose to begin with awards issued in 2000 because that was the inaugural year for the Printz Award.

In a typical award year, the Printz will recognize three to five books. During this time period, the Printz recognized a total of 77 books as winners or honorees. Of the 77, 12 were historical fiction titles. Of those 12 titles, 7 represented a diverse perspective.

During the same time period, the Best Books for Young Adults (BBYA) recognized a significantly higher number of books. (Note that in 2011, BBYA became the Best Fiction for Young Adults [BFYA]. Prior to that time, the list included both fiction and nonfiction). During those years of fiction and nonfiction recognition, the list included as many as 95 titles. In the first three years of the change to a fiction-only list, the BFYA recognized between 99 and 112 titles. That number decreased significantly in 2015 and 2016 when the list included 58 and 64 titles respectively. From 2000–2016, the list has included a total of 1,459 titles. Of that number, 174 have been historical fiction titles. Of those 174 historical fiction titles, 80 have been diverse.

With both sets of honored books, I examined historical fiction books and recorded the ethnicity and religion of the main characters and the historical and geographic setting of the titles. It is important to note that the diversity in the historical fiction titles on these lists included racial, ethnic, religious, and geographic diversity; however, no historical fiction titles dealt with diversity in sexual identity. Additionally, almost all of the historical fiction titles about African Americans on these lists deal exclusively with slavery, the Civil War, or civil rights.

While the relatively high proportion of diverse historical fiction titles on these lists is encouraging, the overall publication of diverse titles is significantly lower. In their 2015 statistics, the Cooperative Children's Book Center (CCBC) notes that of the 3,400 books received by the center, only 15% reflect diverse perspectives (CCBC 2016). The statistics that the CCBC collects do not reflect the genres included or the authenticity or accuracy of the depictions of diverse people.

FINDING ADDITIONAL SOURCES FOR DIVERSE HISTORICAL FICTION

Much of the historical fiction that is published is about European history or about U.S. history from a white perspective. So, where do we look?

The Cooperative Children's Book Center at the University of Wisconsin–Madison is an excellent general source on children's and young adult books. In addition to collecting publication data they have resources for locating multicultural materials including a list of small publishers who specialize in producing books by and about people of color.

An excellent source for reviews and perspectives about the portrayal of indigenous peoples in children's and young adult books is the American Indians in Children's Literature blog started by Debbie Reese in 2006 (https://americanindiansinchildrensliterature.blogspot.com/).

Because it is often difficult to find non-U.S.-centric historical fiction titles, another place to find diverse historical fiction is the titles that receive the Batchelder Award. This award is presented annually to an outstanding book originally published outside the United States in a language other than English, and translated into English for U.S. publication (http://www.ala.org/alsc/awardsgrants/bookmedia/batchelderaward).

EVALUATING QUALITY IN DIVERSE HISTORICAL FICTION

Once we find diverse historical fiction, there are two areas to examine: the historical aspects and the portrayal of diversity.

To evaluate the historical aspects of the title, consider:

- Are the historical events rooted in historical fact?
- Are the characters who are real historical figures portrayed realistically?
- Has this author developed an expertise in this time period/location/events?
- If there are little or no actual events or people, are the historical setting and culture accurately portrayed?

In judging the diverse nature of the title, ask:

- Are the characters portrayed in a stereotypical way? (If so, this may be problematic).
- Is the dialogue authentic?
- Does this author know the culture, religion, ethnicity?
- Does this author identify as a member of the culture, religion, ethnicity?

This final criterion is one that has garnered widespread debate: can someone who is an outsider accurately portray someone else's culture, ethnicity, or religion? Yes, it can be done. However, this is why school librarians need to carefully evaluate diverse materials using the first three criteria listed above.

COLLABORATING WITH HISTORY TEACHERS

Having diverse historical fiction in your school library collection is great, but because historical fiction can be a tough sell for teens, librarians must highlight these titles and advocate for teachers to use them. The use of historical fiction in history or social studies classes provides young people with a broader, more inclusive view of history. The first discussion to have in a teacher collaboration is what type of historical fiction they would like to use. Historical fiction can be either novels rooted in a historical period with few if any historical events or figures in them, or the books can portray historical figures and events in a way that provides insight into personalities and nuances of the time. You will want to tailor your selections for individual assignments based on the desired outcomes of the classroom teacher.

One of my favorite assignments as a student in a history class involved reading a historical fiction novel. We were studying the Roman Empire, and the teacher had everyone read *I, Claudius* by Robert Graves. The assignment involved choosing one character from the novel and then conducting research to determine the accuracy of the author's portrayal of that character. A similar project could easily be done in history classes today. Students could examine the historical accuracy of a historical fiction title from multiple perspectives including the characters, geographic setting, and historical events. Characters could be examined from two different perspectives: if the character was a real historical figure, was that portrayal accurate? Or, if the character was not a real person, what was the accuracy of the character portrayal in terms of culture, ethnicity, or religion? This type of research requires students not only to find the historical information, but also to judge the accuracy of the author's usage of historical fact.

Many students are aware of the Holocaust as a historical event, but may not make connections with other genocides that have happened throughout history. In a sociology class that is studying genocide, students might use historical fiction as part of a comparative study of 20th-century genocides, including those in Armenia, Germany, Rwanda, and Cambodia.

A geography class might use a historical fiction title in which the main character undergoes a journey. Students could plot the journey on a map, determine if the descriptions of the physical geography are accurate, and decide if the journey would have been possible in the time allotted in the book by studying the transportation of the period.

CONCLUSION

As school librarians, we have the opportunity to help our students become more engaged with history by including diverse historical fiction titles in our collections and advocating for the use of diverse perspectives in history and social studies classes. Tyrone Young, writer and director of the documentary *Filling the Gap*, explains that "history becomes easier to understand when students are able to relate or empathize with the struggles and achievements of other people" (Williams 2011).

REFERENCES

Cooperative Children's Book Center (CCBC). (2016). *Publishing Statistics on Children's Books about People of Color and First/Native Nations and by People of Color and First/Native Nations Authors and Illustrators.* Cooperative Children's Book Center. Retrieved from https://ccbc.education.wisc.edu/books/pcstats.asp.

Copeland, C., & Martin, M. (2016). Camp Read-a-Rama® and fully-engaged literacy learning: Implications for LIS education. *Journal of Education for Library and Information Science, 57*(2), pp. 112–130.

Gangi, J. M., & Benfer, N. (September 16, 2014). How Common Core's recommended books fail children of color. *The Washington Post.* Retrieved from http://www .washingtonpost.com/blogs/answersheet/wp/2014/09/16/howcommoncoresre commendedbooksfailchildrenofcolor.

Williams, J. (2011). About filling the gap: Written and directed by Tyrone Young. *School Library Monthly, 28*(3). Retrieved from http://slc.librariesunlimited.com/Home /Display/1967323.

57

Progressive Collection Development = A Foundation for Differentiated Instruction

Judi Moreillon

Differentiated instruction (DI) is a way of planning for teaching and learning. Educators who differentiate instruction advocate for beginning where students are; they are proactive about designing learning experiences so that content can be learned in multiple ways (Tomlinson 2001). Some learners come to school with advanced skills while others come with inadequate preparation. Some come with open minds while others come from more closed-minded environments. More and more learners are diagnosed with various learning disabilities; some have physical disabilities that require individual accommodations. More and more students attend school as second language learners and come from a wide range of cultural backgrounds. Students' learning needs are ever more diverse. A one-size-fits-all approach is not effective in today's classrooms and libraries.

School librarians who honor, support, and advocate for this diversity have many ways to contribute to differentiating instruction in order to meet students' diverse needs. Collection development and resource integration into the classroom curriculum are ways that librarians can build a firm foundation for DI because the materials that students use to access and learn content are essential DI components. Instructional resources must motivate students—make them curious about an idea or problem so they want to know more. Readers must be able to relate to the content and "see" how it is relevant to their experiences. They must use their own or build their background knowledge to begin adding to, modifying, or replacing what they already knew about a concept or dilemma.

MIRRORS, WINDOWS, AND DOORS

Rudine Sims Bishop wrote that "if literature is a mirror that reflects human life, then all children who read or who are read to need to see themselves as part of that

195

humanity" (1993, 43). Offering materials in which students can "see" themselves in the texts they read is one way to differentiate resources. In addition, literature and texts can also serve as windows into the lives of those who have different cultures, abilities, or sexual orientations than the readers themselves. Taken together, mirrors and windows can open doors to understanding. All children and youth deserve to read literature and texts that reflect the diversity of a global society.

"Culturally responsive collection development" is a term and strategy librarians apply to indicate that they build collections that reflect and support the cultural backgrounds of students (Moreillon 2015). Several researchers have examined book collections to determine whether or not school library collections provided resources for specific groups of children and young adults. They have also looked closely at the stereotypes that are portrayed in certain types of literature and noted issues with appropriate and positive representation.

SEEING THEMSELVES AND LEARNING ABOUT "OTHERS" IN PRINT

Sandra Hughes-Hassell, Elizabeth Overberg, and Shannon Harris conducted an analysis of lesbian, gay, bisexual, transgender, and questioning (LGBTQ)-themed literature available to teens in 125 high school libraries in one Southern U.S. state. The researchers used a core collection of 21 recommended titles to evaluate these collections. "Noticeable was the absence of nonfiction titles focused specifically on LGBTQ issues such as sexual health, bullying, or gay rights" (Hughes-Hassell, Overberg, & Harris 2013, 12). In addition to providing information for students' personal use and raising social issues that could lead to critical discussions, these resources should be available to support the curriculum. (The state in which this study was conducted had adopted a comprehensive reproductive health and safety program that addresses contraception, safe sex, and healthy relationships.)

The researchers also noted a lack of biographies about LGBTQ individuals in these collections. Biographies are needed to provide role models expressly for LGBTQ students. They are also important as a means to inform heterosexual students of the accomplishments of notable LGBTQ people. Learning about themselves and about others is an essential aspect of adolescence and all students should be supported in their personal as well as academic growth.

Unfortunately, literature can also perpetuate stereotypes that undermine the goal of affirming and advocating for each person's right to be diverse. Many librarians have purchased and promote graphic novels as important resources for visually oriented students as well as alternatives to other genres that may be less accessible or appealing to youth. Marilyn Irwin and Robin Moeller conducted two studies of how individuals with disabilities are portrayed in the "best" graphic novels as determined by librarians' book reviews (2010) and on a graphic novel best-seller list (2012). In both cases, the depictions of characters with disabilities perpetuated negative stereotypes. It is true that such depictions, when duly noted, can be used to spark readers' critical thinking and engender thoughtful discussions. At the same time, when librarians differentiate the library collection, they must weigh pros and cons and consider how the resulting diversity contributes positively to students' social, emotional, and cognitive development.

INTERCULTURAL UNDERSTANDING THROUGH GLOBAL LITERATURE

School librarians must also consider that today's learners are living in a global society that extends far beyond students' personal and family cultures to a wider and more diverse world. In order to ensure that multiple voices and perspectives are represented in the resources the library provides, librarians can develop a collection that includes global literature. Global literature includes books set in non-U.S. cultures, or those written by immigrants about living in the United States or in their home countries, or those written by authors who live and work in the United States and another country. These resources can help readers connect with others who live within and beyond our country's borders.

The Longview Foundation grant-funded "Global Literacy Communities" project involved twenty-five prekindergarten to high school educator study groups from nineteen U.S. states that met regularly for one to three years to learn through global literature. In their study groups, educators used global literature to further develop their *international* understanding and strove for something more—*intercultural* understanding. Intercultural understanding "extends beyond nationality and politics to include informed problem solving and social action activities that necessitate an appreciation of the full range of issues, including the values and beliefs of everyone involved. Intercultural understanding creates the potential to move from curiosity about a culture to a deeper understanding of others that allows us to live and work together as global citizens" (Corapi & Short 2015, 4). The educators who participated in these study groups prepared themselves to authentically and accurately share global literature with children and youth.

MAXIMIZING THE POSITIVE IMPACT OF THE LIBRARY COLLECTION

When librarians practice progressive collection development, they have the potential to positively impact curriculum. However, they can guarantee that impact by co-planning and co-teaching in order to integrate library resources for the benefit of all students. When librarians take students' home and individual cultures into account and use them as background knowledge in lesson design, they are maximizing opportunities for diverse resources to motivate students and support their learning. When librarians further develop their collections with global literature and integrate it into the classroom curriculum, they help prepare students to be thoughtful and successful global citizens.

Collaborating librarians cannot overestimate the importance of their work as literacy stewards who provide the resource foundation for DI. With their knowledge of literature, librarians can support teachers' teaching and help motivate students to engage in deep and meaningful learning. Providing multiple resources that serve as mirrors and windows can make DI a reality. Diverse resources are an essential first step in opening doors for all students to succeed.

REFERENCES

Bishop, R. S. (1993). Multicultural Literature for Children: Making Informed Choices. In Harris, V. J. (Ed.), *Teaching Multicultural Literature in Grades K-8*, pp. 37–54. Boston, MA: Christopher Gordon.

Corapi, S., & Short, K. G. (2015). *Exploring International and Intercultural Understanding through Global Literature.* Longview Foundation, Worlds of Words. Retrieved from http://wowlit.org/Documents/InterculturalUnderstanding.pdf.

Hughes-Hassell, S., Overberg, E., & Harris, S. (2013). Lesbian, gay, bisexual, transgender, and questioning (LGBTQ)-themed literature for teens: Are school libraries providing adequate collections? *School Library Research, 16*, pp. 1–18. Retrieved from http://www.ala.org/aasl/sites/ala.org.aasl/files/content/aaslpubsandjournals/slr/vol16/SLR_LGBTQThemedLiteratureforTeens_V16.pdf.

Irwin, M., & Moeller, R. (2010). Seeing different: Portrayals of disability in young adult graphic novels. *School Library Research, 13*, pp. 1–13. Retrieved from http://www.ala.org/aasl/sites/ala.org.aasl/files/content/aaslpubsandjournals/slr/vol13/SLR_SeeingDifferent.pdf.

Moeller, R., & Irwin, M. (2012). Seeing the same: Follow-up study on the portrayals of disability in graphic novels read by young adults. *School Library Research, 15,* pp. 1–16. Retrieved from http://www.ala.org/aasl/sites/ala.org.aasl/files/content /aaslpubsandjournals/slr/vol15/SLR_SeeingtheSame_V15.pdf.

Moreillon, J. (November 30, 2015). Intercultural understanding through global literature. *Building a Culture of Collaboration*® (blog). Retrieved from http://www.school librarianleadership.com/2015/11/30/intercultural-understanding-through -global-literature.

Tomlinson, C. A. (2001). *How to Differentiate Instruction in Mixed-Ability Classrooms.* Association for Curriculum Supervision and Development.

Annotated Bibliography

This resource list is a place to begin finding information to support your efforts to champion the rights of students in schools. The place to begin is always the American Library Association's (ALA's) Office for Intellectual Freedom that has a rich variety of information, resources, and tools for libraries of all types.

ALA'S ONLINE RESOURCES

The Library Bill of Rights
http://www.ala.org/advocacy/intfreedom/librarybill

> This is the foundation upon which libraries are built. The Library Bill of Rights was first adopted in 1939, and updated in 2019 with the addition of Article VII on Privacy and Confidentiality. This site includes the Bill of Rights and Interpretations of the Library Bill of Rights.

Office for Intellectual Freedom
http://www.ala.org/aboutala/offices/oif

> Established in 1967, the Office for Intellectual Freedom implements ALA policies about intellectual freedom. The goal of the office is to educate librarians and the general public about the nature and importance of intellectual freedom in libraries. The resources page on their website has wonderful support for libraries including Toolkits for a variety of issues:
> * Defending Intellectual Freedom: LGBTQ+ Materials in School Libraries (https://standards.aasl.org/project/lgbtq/)
> * Selection & Reconsideration Policy Toolkit for Public, School, & Academic Libraries (http://www.ala.org/tools/challengesupport/selectionpolicytoolkit)
> * Libraries and the Internet (http://www.ala.org/advocacy/intfreedom/iftoolkits/litoolkit/librariesinternet)
> * Open to All: Serving the GLBT Community in Your Library (http://www.ala.org/glbtrt/tools)
> * Privacy (http://www.ala.org/advocacy/privacy/toolkit)

Advocacy
http://www.ala.org/advocacy/

> ALA's advocacy resources includes sections on:
> - Advocacy & Public Policy
> - Banned Books
> - Equity, Diversity & Inclusion
> - Intellectual Freedom
> - Literacy
> - Privacy
> - Public Awareness

The Intellectual Freedom section has one area of particular interest to school librarians: Schools and Minors' Rights—http://www.ala.org/advocacy/intfreedom/minors. You'll find ALA policies and statements related to this subject along with links to publications and webcasts.

PRINT RESOURCES

Adams, Helen R. 2013. *Protecting Intellectual Freedom and Privacy in Your School Library*. Santa Barbara, CA: Libraries Unlimited.

> This excellent resource provides practical tips on supporting access and protecting privacy in school libraries. Each of the nine chapters include introductory essays, key ideas, resources, and discussion questions.

Ewbank, Ann Dutton. 2019. *Political Advocacy for School Librarians: Leveraging Your Influence*. Santa Barbara, CA: Libraries Unlimited.

> Ewbank's book is a practical guide for school librarians as they begin to advocate for school library access for all children. It provides tips and ideas for working at the local, state, and national level.

Fletcher-Spear, Kristin, and Kelly Tyler, eds. 2014. *Intellectual Freedom for Teens: A Practical Guide for Young Adult & School Librarians*. Chicago: ALA.

> This book provides practical on how to prepare for challenges to materials through policy develop and preparing a plan to respond. Additionally, this resource explains how to craft a defense of a challenged material as well as developing a media message.

Magi, Trina, et al., eds. 2015. *Intellectual Freedom Manual*. 9th ed. Chicago: ALA.

> Updated periodically, this is the essential resource on intellectual freedom and libraries. While it includes all of the ALA policy statements and core documents, it also includes summaries on key issues such as access by minors to controversial materials and advocacy.

Miller, Donalyn, and Colby Sharp. 2018. *Game Changer! Book Access for All Kids*. New York: Scholastic.

> This slim volume provides insight into the impact of increased access to reading materials. It is filled with practical tips for school librarians and other educators.

Naidoo, Jamie Campbell, and Sarah Park Dahlen, eds. 2013. *Diversity in Youth Literature: Opening Doors through Reading*. Chicago: ALA.

This volume collects content from on topics related to themes in diversity including African American, Latino, Asian as well as homelessness and many others. Additionally, the book includes help in selecting and evaluating quality diverse literature.

Office for Intellectual Freedom. n.d. *Choose Privacy Week Resource Guide.* Chicago: ALA.

This resource guide created by the Office for Intellectual Freedom includes lessons, programming ideas, and other resources to help implement privacy programs in a variety of types of libraries.

Pekoll, Kristin. 2019. *Beyond Banned Books: Defending Intellectual Freedom throughout your Library.* Chicago: ALA.

This resource provides case studies in a variety of library settings about challenges to access unrelated to books including bookmarks, reading lists, databases, programs, displays, and more.

Scales, Pat R. 2009. *Protecting Intellectual Freedom in Your School Library: Scenarios from the Front Lines.* Chicago: ALA.

This resource includes case studies on a variety of intellectual freedom issues that might arise in school libraries. Additionally, Scales has provided sample policies and explanation of important statutes and decisions related to intellectual freedom.

Scales, Pat R. 2015. *Scales on Censorship: Real Life Lessons from School Library Journal.* New York: Rowman & Littlefield.

This collection of questions and answers from Scales' long-running *School Library Journal* column on intellectual freedom provides information about the real-world challenges of defending intellectual freedom and access in schools.

Sources

Adams, Helen R. "Advocating for Intellectual Freedom with Principals and Teachers." *School Library Media Activities Monthly*, 25, no. 6, February 2009. *School Library Connection*, schoollibraryconnection.com/Home/Display/2200347.

Adams, Helen R. "Bring Your Own Device (BYOD) and Equitable Access to Technology." *School Library Monthly*, 28, no. 8, May 2012. *School Library Connection*, schoollibraryconnection.com/Home/Display/1967208.

Adams, Helen R. "Can a School Library Be Challenge-Proof?" *School Library Monthly*, 26, no. 4, December 2009. *School Library Connection*, schoollibraryconnection.com/Home/Display/2146280.

Adams, Helen R. "Computerized Reading Programs: Intellectual Freedom." *School Library Monthly*, 28, no. 2, November 2011. *School Library Connection*, schoollibraryconnection.com/Home/Display/1967341.

Adams, Helen R. "Fewer School Librarians: The Effect on Students' Intellectual Freedom." *School Library Monthly*, 27, no. 6, March 2011. *School Library Connection*, schoollibraryconnection.com/Home/Display/2010156.

Adams, Helen R. "IF Matters: Intellectual Freedom @ your library®: Serving Homeless Children in the School Library—Part 1." *School Library Monthly*, 27, no. 3, December 2010. *School Library Connection*, schoollibraryconnection.com/Home/Display/2010358.

Adams, Helen R. "The Intellectual Freedom Calendar: Another Advocacy Plan for the School Library." *School Library Monthly*, 27, no. 7, April 2011. *School Library Connection*, schoollibraryconnection.com/Home/Display/2010130.

Adams, Helen R. "Intellectual Freedom Leadership: Standing Up for Your Students." *School Library Connection*, May 2018, schoollibraryconnection.com/Home/Display/2147959.

Adams, Helen R. "Intellectual Freedom 101: Core Principles for School Librarians." *School Library Monthly*, 30, no. 2, November 2013. *School Library Connection*, schoollibraryconnection.com/Home/Display/1967014.

Adams, Helen R. "Internet Filtering: Are We Making Any Progress?" *School Library Connection*, April 2016, schoollibraryconnection.com/Home/Display/2009316.

Adams, Helen R. "The Materials Selection Policy: Defense against Censorship." *School Library Media Activities Monthly*, 24, no. 7, March 2008. *School Library Connection*, schoollibraryconnection.com/Home/Display/2200901.

Adams, Helen R. "The 'Overdue' Blues: A Dilemma for School Librarians." *School Library Monthly*, 26, no. 9, May 2010. *School Library Connection*, schoollibraryconnection.com/Home/Display/2203360.

Adams, Helen R. "Practical Ideas: Protecting Students' Privacy in Your School Library." *School Library Monthly*, 30, no. 6, March 2014. *School Library Connection*, schoollibraryconnection.com/Home/Display/1966933.

Adams, Helen R. "Privacy Matters. How Circulation Systems May Impact Student Privacy." *School Library Media Activities Monthly*, 24, no. 6, February 2008. *School Library Connection*, schoollibraryconnection.com/Home/Display/2200960.

Adams, Helen R. "Privacy Matters. Retaining School Library Records." *School Library Media Activities Monthly*, 23, no. 5, January 2007. *School Library Connection*, schoollibraryconnection.com/Home/Display/2226254.

Adams, Helen R. "Privacy Matters. The Age of the Patron and Privacy." *School Library Media Activities Monthly*, 23, no. 7, March 2007. *School Library Connection*, schoollibraryconnection.com/Home/Display/2207732.

Adams, Helen R. "Privacy Matters. The Troubled Student and Privacy." *School Library Media Activities Monthly*, 23, no. 4, December 2007. *School Library Connection*, schoollibraryconnection.com/Home/Display/2207249.

Adams, Helen R. "Protecting Students' Rights and Keeping Your Job." *School Library Monthly*, 28, no. 6, March 2012. *School Library Connection*, schoollibraryconnection.com/Home/Display/1967255.

Adams, Helen R. "Protecting Your Students' Privacy: Resources for School Librarians." *School Library Connection*, April 2017, schoollibraryconnection.com/Home/Display/2071402.

Adams, Helen R. "Reaching Out to Parents." *School Library Monthly*, 27, no. 8, May 2011. *School Library Connection*, schoollibraryconnection.com/Home/Display/2010100.

Adams, Helen R. "Serving Homeless Children in the School Library—Part 2." *School Library Monthly*, 27, no. 4, January 2011. *School Library Connection*, schoollibraryconnection.com/Home/Display/2010331.

Adams, Helen R. "What Is Intellectual Freedom?" *School Library Media Activities Monthly*, 24, no. 1, September 2007. *School Library Connection*, schoollibraryconnection.com/Home/Display/2207466.

Brown, Kathryn K. "Unrestricted Checkout: The Time Has Come." *Library Media Connection*, 31, no. 2, January 2013. *School Library Connection*, schoollibraryconnection.com/Home/Display/1948838.

Burns, Elizabeth A. "Understanding Advocacy for Effective Action." *School Library Monthly*, 31, no. 7, May 2015. *School Library Connection*, schoollibraryconnection.com/Home/Display/1967057.

Cahill, Maria. "Library Books and Reading-Level Labels: Unfettered, Guided, or Constrained Choice?" *School Library Connection*, November 2017, schoollibraryconnection.com/Home/Survey/2129179.

Carnesi, Sabrina. "Challenging Opportunities: Dealing with Book Challenges." *Library Media Connection*, 33, no. 2, October 2014. *School Library Connection*, schoollibraryconnection.com/Home/Display/1949182.

Cox, Ernie. "Library Access on a Fixed Schedule." *School Library Connection*, August 2016, schoollibraryconnection.com/Home/Display/2029152.

Dawkins, April M. "Creating Reconsideration Policies That Matter." *School Library Connection*, March 2020, schoollibraryconnection.com/Home/Display/2209716.

Dawkins, April M. "Ex Post Facto Self-Censorship: When School Librarians Choose to Censor." *School Library Connection*, October 2017, schoollibraryconnection.com/Home/Display/2126754.

Dawkins, April M. "Ten Steps to Creating a Selection Policy that Matters." *School Library Connection*, October 2018, schoollibraryconnection.com/Home/Display/2145378.

Dawkins, April M. "Whose History Is It?: Diversity in Historical Fiction for Young Adults." *School Library Connection*, May 2017, schoollibraryconnection.com/Home/Display/2073486.

Dickinson, Gail K. "The Challenges of Challenges: Understanding and Being Prepared (Part 1)." *School Library Media Activities Monthly*, 23, no. 5, January 2007. *School Library Connection*, schoollibraryconnection.com/Home/Display/2226252.

Dickinson, Gail. "The Challenges of Challenges: What to Do? Part Two." *School Library Media Activities Monthly*, 23, no. 6, February 2007. *School Library Connection*, schoollibraryconnection.com/Home/Display/2207751.

Eldred, Christine. "The Choices that Count." *School Library Monthly*, 31, no. 1, September 2014. *School Library Connection*, schoollibraryconnection.com/Home/Display/1967184.

Franklin, Pat, and Claire Gatrell Stephens. "Equitable Access, the Digital Divide, and the Participation Gap!" *School Library Media Activities Monthly*, 25, no. 5, January 2009. *School Library Connection*, schoollibraryconnection.com/Home/Display/2153849.

Gangwish, Kim. "Deaf ≠ Silenced: Serving the Needs of the Deaf/Hard-of-Hearing Students in School Libraries." *School Library Connection*, October 2015, schoollibraryconnection.com/Home/Display/1984746.

Green, Lucy Santos, and Michelle Maniaci Folk. "Research into Practice. Literature as Mirrors, Windows, and Sliding Glass Doors." *School Library Connection*, November 2018, schoollibraryconnection.com/Home/Display/2180392.

Heck, Chad. "All Access. Banned Books and Celebrating Our Freedom to Read." *School Library Connection*, July 2019, schoollibraryconnection.com/Home/Display/2214593.

Heck, Chad. "All Access. Confidentiality and Creating a Safe Information Environment." *School Library Connection*, October 2019, schoollibraryconnection.com/Home/Column/2227751?topicCenterId=1945911&terms=Confidentiality and Creating a Safe Information&tab=2.

Hill, Rebecca. "The Problem of Self-Censorship." *School Library Monthly*, 27, no. 2, November 2010. *School Library Connection*, schoollibraryconnection.com/Home/Display/2010366.

Keuler, Annalisa. "Privacy Solutions for Cloud Computing: What Does It Mean?" *School Library Monthly*, 31, no. 5, March 2015. *School Library Connection*, schoollibraryconnection.com/Home/Display/1967107.

Kurtts, Stephanie, Nicole Dobbins, and Natsuko Takemae. "Using Assistive Technology to Meet Diverse Learner Needs." *Library Media Connection*, 30, no. 4, January 2012. *School Library Connection*, schoollibraryconnection.com/Home/Display/1979566.

Moorefield-Lang, Heather. "Technology Connections. Google Accessibility for Your Library." *School Library Connection*, August 2016, schoollibraryconnection.com/Home/Display/2029166.

Moorefield-Lang, Heather. "Technology Connections: Online Accessibility Tools." *School Library Connection*, February 2018, schoollibraryconnection.com/Home/Display/2137090.

Moreillon, Judi. "Leadership: Filtering and Social Media." *School Library Monthly*, 30, no. 4, January 2014. *School Library Connection*, schoollibraryconnection.com/Home/Display/1966976.

Moreillon, Judi. "Policy Challenge: Closed for Conducting Inventory." *School Library Monthly*, 29, no. 8, May 2013. *School Library Connection*, schoollibraryconnection.com/Home/Display/1967386.

Moreillon, Judi. "Policy Challenge: Consequences that Restrict Borrowing." *School Library Monthly*, 29, no. 4, January 2013. *School Library Connection*, schoollibraryconnection.com/Home/Display/1967472.

Moreillon, Judi. "Policy Challenge: Leveling the Library Collection." *School Library Monthly*, 29, no. 5, February 2013. *School Library Connection*, schoollibraryconnection.com/Home/Display/1967453.

Moreillon, Judi. "Progressive Collection Development = A Foundation for Differentiated Instruction." *School Library Connection*, May 2017, schoollibraryconnection.com/Home/Display/2073489.

Naidoo, Jamie Campbell. "Serving Rainbow Families in School Libraries." *School Library Connection*, May 2017, schoollibraryconnection.com/Home/Display/2073484.

Venuto, Dee Ann. "Managing Challenges to Library Resources." *School Library Monthly*, 31, no. 3, December 2014. *School Library Connection*, schoollibraryconnection.com/Home/Display/1967150.

Wolf, Sara. "Coping with Mandated Restrictions on Intellectual Freedom in K–12 Schools." *Library Media Connection*, 27, no. 3, November 2008. *School Library Connection*, schoollibraryconnection.com/Home/Display/2148398.

Zeluff, Kristin. "Collection Development Policies in Juvenile Detention Center Libraries." *Library Media Connection*, 30, no. 5, March 2012. *School Library Connection*, schoollibraryconnection.com/Home/Display/1948720.

Zilonis, Mary Frances, and Chris Swerling. "On Common Ground. Building School Library Collections with Windows and Mirrors." *School Library Connection*, April 2017, schoollibraryconnection.com/Home/Display/2071416.

Zilonis, Mary Frances, and Chris Swerling. "On Common Ground. Collection Development for Readers: Providing Windows and Mirrors." *School Library Connection*, March 2017, schoollibraryconnection.com/Home/Display/2064085.

Zilonis, Mary Frances, and Chris Swerling. "On Common Ground. Moving Diverse Books from Your Library Shelves and into the Hands of Readers." *School Library Connection*, May 2017, schoollibraryconnection.com/Home/Display/2073504.

About the Editor and Contributors

HELEN R. ADAMS is a retired Wisconsin school librarian and online instructor in intellectual freedom, privacy, and copyright. She has served on the ALA Intellectual Freedom Committee and its Privacy Subcommittee and as trustee of the Freedom to Read Foundation, which named her a Roll of Honor member. Helen also served as an American Association of School Librarians blogger on the topics of intellectual freedom and privacy and is author of numerous articles and several books on these topics.

KATHRYN K. BROWN retired after 16 years as an elementary school library media specialist for Fairfax County Public Schools. She now raises alpacas in Pennsylvania and is the author of *The Alpaca-bet! The ABCs of Alpacas.*

ELIZABETH BURNS, PHD, is an assistant professor in the Library and Information Studies Program at Old Dominion University, Norfolk, VA. Her research and publications focus on school library advocacy and integrating library standards into the curriculum. Previously, she was both a classroom teacher and a school librarian. She has served on several national committees to include the ALA Committee on Library Advocacy and the AASL Advocacy Committee.

MONICA CABARCAS is a librarian at Sutherland Middle School in Charlottesville, VA. She also serves as the Chair of the Diversity and Inclusion Committee for the Virginia Association of School Librarians.

MARIA CAHILL, MLIS, PHD, is an associate professor at the University of Kentucky in both the School of Information Science and the Department of Educational Leadership. She received her master's degree from the University of South Carolina and her doctorate in education from the University of Tennessee. She is author of numerous papers in such journals as *Knowledge Quest, School Libraries Worldwide,* and *School Library Research* and has served in several professional leadership positions, including on the American Association of School Librarians Board of Directors and on the American Library Association's Literacy and Outreach Services Committee.

SABRINA CARNESI has worked as a K–12 educator and school librarian for more than 30 years. She currently teaches young adult literature as Adjunct Instructor for University of Washington's iSchool.

ERNIE COX, MLIS, is the teacher-librarian at Prairie Creek Intermediate in Cedar Rapids, IA. He earned his master's from the University of Iowa. Cox served on the Board of Directors for the Association for Library Service to Children, 2011–2014, and was the chair of the 2016 Newbery Book Award committee.

APRIL M. DAWKINS, PHD, is assistant professor in library and information studies at the University of North Carolina at Greensboro. She earned her doctorate in library and information science from the University of South Carolina. Prior to joining the faculty at UNCG, Dawkins was a high school librarian for 15 years. Her research examines intellectual freedom issues in school libraries with an emphasis on self-censorship, access, and equity.

GAIL K. DICKINSON, PHD, is associate dean of graduate studies and research at Old Dominion University in Norfolk, VA. She earned her master's in library science from the University of North Carolina at Chapel Hill, and her doctorate in educational administration from the University of Virginia. Dickinson is a past-president of AASL, was editor-in-chief of *Library Media Connection,* and is the author of *Achieving National Board Certification for School Library Media Specialists* and coeditor of the seventh edition of Linworth's *School Library Management.*

DR. NICOLE DOBBINS is an Associate Professor in the Department of Teacher Preparation in the College of Education at North Carolina Agricultural & Technical University.

CHRISTINE ELDRED lives in Vermont and worked as a high school librarian for 14 years. Christine served as the Intellectual Freedom Representative for the Vermont School Library Association from 2005 to 2015.

MICHELLE MANIACI FOLK, MLS, is the librarian at Fort Atkinson Middle School in Fort Atkinson, WI. She earned her MLS in 2007 at the University of Wisconsin–Madison and has been a school librarian at both the elementary and middle school level for over 20 years. She was the librarian at Luther Elementary when it was chosen as an outstanding school library on the 2011 AASL Vision Tour and also served as a member of the 2016–2017 AASL Presidential Initiative Task Force. She has authored a chapter in *Collaborative Models for Librarian and Teacher Partnerships* (2014).

PATRICIA FRANKLIN retired after 29 years working as library media specialist most recently at Timber Creek High School in Orlando, FL. Pat is also a National Board Certified Teacher in Library Media and the coauthor of four books for Libraries Unlimited.

DR. KIMBERLY GANGWISH is the IDEAS Room and LiveText Coordinator for the College of Education, University of Nebraska at Omaha. Additionally, she is an instructor in the School Library and Instructional Technology Leadership programs. She writes the Future Forward column for *School Library Connection.* Dr. Gangwish serves on the AASL Council for the Accreditation of Educator Preparation (CAEP) Coordinating Committee and is the AASL liaison for the Nebraska School Librarians

Association. Dr. Gangwish's research interests are focused on school libraries, cultural representation, and educational technology.

LUCY SANTOS GREEN, EDD, is associate professor of Library and Information Science at the University of South Carolina. She earned her MLIS at Texas Woman's University and her doctorate in instructional technology at Texas Tech University. Her article with Dr. Melissa P. Johnston, "Still Polishing the Diamond: School Library Research over the Last Decade," was recently published in *School Library Research*, the scholarly refereed research journal for the American Association of School Librarians. Lucy is the past-chair for the Educators of School Librarians Section of AASL, and most recently served on the AASL Accreditation of Educator Preparation (CAEP) Coordinating Committee.

CHAD HECK, JD, is a school librarian at Pike High School in Indianapolis, IN. He earned a degree in law and a graduate certificate in intellectual property from Indiana University Robert H. McKinney School of Law and his master's in library science from Indiana University. He presently serves on the board of the Indiana Library Federation and is the co-chair of the intellectual freedom committee. Follow Chad on Twitter @4theloveofheck.

REBECCA HILL has written on libraries, literacy, science, technology, science education, and many other issues for a variety of national, online, and local publications. She has a Masters in Information and Library Sciences from Indiana University. Currently, she writes on intellectual freedom issues for the American Library Association Intellectual Freedom Blog. Her work can be found at https://www.rebeccaahill.com/.

ANNALISA KEULER is a school librarian at Mountain Brook High School in Mountain Brook, Alabama. She also is a former committee chair for the AASL Intellectual Freedom Committee and member of the ALA Intellectual Freedom Committee.

STEPHANIE KURTTS is an Associate Professor in the Department of Specialized Education Services at the University of North Carolina at Greensboro.

HEATHER MOOREFIELD-LANG, EDD, is an associate professor for the Department of Library and Information Studies at the University of North Carolina at Greensboro. To see more of Heather's work, visit her website at www.techfifteen.com or follow her on Twitter @actinginthelib.

JUDI MOREILLON, MLS, PHD, is a literacies and libraries consultant. She earned her master's in library science and her doctorate in education at the University of Arizona. Judi is a former school librarian who served at all three instructional levels. She has taught preservice school librarians for 25 years, most recently as an associate professor. Her latest professional book for school librarians and classroom teachers, *Maximizing School Librarian Leadership: Building Connections for Learning and Advocacy*, was published in 2018 by ALA Editions. Judi's homepage is http://storytrail.com and she tweets @CactusWoman.

JAMIE CAMPBELL NAIDOO, PHD, is the Foster-EBSCO Endowed Professor at the University of Alabama School of Library and Information Studies in Tuscaloosa. Jamie has served as an elementary school librarian and head public children's librarian, and was the 2018–2019 President of the Association for Library Service to Children (ALSC). He publishes and presents frequently on topics related to library services to diverse populations, particularly rainbow families and Latinx families. His website is http://jcnaidoo.people.ua.edu.

CLAIRE GATRELL STEPHENS is the District Media Specialist for Orange County Public Schools in Orlando, Florida. Claire has 27 years' experience in Library Media and was a National Board Certified Teacher. Claire has authored six books for Libraries Unlimited including four with Pat Franklin.

CHRIS SWERLING, MS, earned her bachelor's in English literature at Boston College and her master's in library science from Simmons College Graduate School of Library and Information Science. She is the former District Library Coordinator K–12 for the Newton, Massachusetts, Public Schools. In addition, she has taught collection development and instructional strategies courses at the graduate level and presented at state and national school library conferences. She achieved National Board Library Certification and currently supervises library student practicums for Simmons University.

DR. NATSUKO TAKEMAE is an Assistant Professor in the Department of Special Education and Interventions at Central Connecticut State University.

DEE ANN VENUTO is a high school librarian at Rancocas Valley Regional High School District, Mt. Holly, NJ. She has dealt with challenges in her school and served on ALA's Intellectual Freedom Committee.

SARA E. WOLF, PHD, is associate professor of library media and educational technology at Auburn University, Auburn, AL. She earned her doctorate in curriculum and instruction with a concentration in educational media and computers from Arizona State University, Tempe, AZ. She is the coauthor of the 6th edition of *Copyright for Schools* with Carol Simpson, and has a companion title forthcoming about teaching copyright to students in a variety of settings. She holds the Creative Commons Certificate for Educators.

KRISTIN ZELUFF is a Youth Librarian at the Portage District Library in Portage, Michigan.

MARY FRANCES ZILONIS, EDD, is a former Professor of Practice and Director of the School Library Teacher Program at Simmons University and a former Professor and Chair of Secondary Education and Professional Programs, Coordinator of the Graduate Library Media Program, and of the Graduate Instructional Technology Program at Bridgewater State University. She earned her bachelor's and master's degrees from Bridgewater State College and her doctorate from Boston University. She is coauthor of *A Strategic Planning Guide for School Library Media Centers* (2002). She has presented at state and national conferences in administration, school librarianship, and instructional technology. In 2010, she was awarded the Massachusetts School Library Association *Lifetime Achievement Award* and in 2002, she was awarded the Massachusetts Computer Users *Pathfinder Award*.

Index

AASL Standards Framework for Learners, 15, 72, 114

Accelerated Reader, 8, 31, 39–40, 41

Acceptable Use Policies (AUPs), 49–50, 113

access to information, 3, 14, 15, 23, 47, 77; and access to technology, 123–124; creating a safe environment for, 150–151; for deaf/HoH students, 168–170; and the digital divide, 120–122; equitable access, 120–122; online accessibility tools, 164–165; sensitive issues, 150–151

Adichie, Chimamanda Ngozi, 182

administrators. *See* principals

advocacy: calendar as plan for, 30–33; definition/understanding of, 24, 26–28; for effective action, 28–29; and the librarian, 23–25, 27, 109; plans and goals for, 28; resources for, 26; in school libraries, 28; toolkit, 24

ALA Code of Ethics: on censorship, 34, 85, 108; on intellectual freedom, 34, 85, 108; and the librarian, 43, 53, 85, 108, 141, 143, 149; posting, 32; privacy rights, 8, 134, 136, 137, 141, 143, 146, 149; and self-censorship, 7; "sticky" situations, 36, 53

Allie the Ally, 187

American Association of School Librarians (AASL), 15; advocacy resources, 26; definition of advocacy, 24; efforts to combat filtering, 117–118; on inclusion and equity, 168; *Knowledge Quest* blog, 32; on labeling books by reading level, 39; National School Library Standards for Learners, Librarians, and School Libraries, 115; online "advocacy toolkit," 24; *Position Statement on Labeling Books with Reading Levels*, 76; *Position Statement on the School Librarian's Role in Reading*, 69; "Privacy: An Interpretation of the Library Bill of Rights," 146; "School Libraries Count," 118; six shared foundations, 72; Standards Framework for Learners, 15, 72, 114

American Civil Liberties Union (ACLU), 23, 87; "Don't Filter Me" campaign, 114

American Indians in Children's Literature blog, 192

American Library Association (ALA): advocacy resources, 26; Bill of Rights Day, 54; Challenge Support website, 97; Choose Privacy Week (CPW), 32, 137, 140–141; Code of Ethics, 8, 32, 36, 43, 53, 85, 134, 137, 141, 143, 146, 149; efforts to combat filtering, 117–118; "Fencing Out Knowledge," 118–119; "Freedom to Read," 4–5, 54, 59; Frequently Challenged Books, 107;

American Library Association (*cont.*)
  on intellectual freedom, 3, 20, 47;
  Intellectual Freedom Committee Privacy
  Subcommittee, 140; "Intellectual
  Freedom News," 141; "Internet Filter-
  ing," 118; "Libraries and the Internet
  Tool Kit," 118; *Library Bill of Rights*
  (LBOR), 32, 36, 37, 43, 48, 59, 66, 86,
  95, 149, 150; "Library Privacy Check-
  list for Students in K–12 Schools," 140;
  "Library Privacy Guidelines for Stu-
  dents in K–12 Schools," 139; "Library
  Services to the Poor," 174; list of
  challenged books, 34; "Minors and
  Internet Activity," 118; "Minors and
  Internet Interactivity," 118; Office for
  Intellectual Freedom (OIF), 3, 21, 87,
  88, 92, 95, 118, 140–141, 145; online
  resources, 11; Privacy Toolkit, 140–
  141; Selection & Reconsideration Policy
  Toolkit, 95; "State Privacy Laws," 134;
  strategies for promoting intellectual
  freedom, 23–24; suggestions for
  Banned Book Week, 31; Workbook for
  Selection Policy Writing, 56
American Sign Language, 170
Anti-Defamation League, 184
Asheim, Lester, 93, 106
assistive technology (AT), 160–162
Association for Library Services to
  Children (ALSC), 31
Association of American Publishers, 4;
  "Freedom to Read," 4–5, 54, 59
Association of Specialized and Coopera-
  tive Library Agencies (ASCLA), 62–63;
  *Library Standards for Juvenile Correc-
  tional Facilities*, 65
at-risk students, 8–9

Banned Books Week, 10, 31, 34–35
Banned Websites Awareness Day, 114,
  118
Batchelder Award, 192
Berman, Erin, 140
Bertin, Joan E., 88–89
Best Books for Young Adults (BBYA),
  192
Bill of Rights Day, 31–32
Bishop, Rudine Sims, 177, 179,
  195–196
Blackboard, 126, 127, 128
*Board of Education, Island Trees Union
  Free School District v. Pico*, 6, 104

Boguszewski, Kathy, 175
book challenges. *See* challenges to library
  resources
book clubs, 185
book covers, 137
book levels, 8
books: access to, 71–72; banned, 34–35,
  103–104, 106; challenged, 34–35; for
  deaf/HoH students, 169; emotional
  level, 101; global literature, 196–197;
  graphic novels, 11, 106, 196; intellectual level, 101; interest level, 15, 20,
  101; labeling, 94; leveling of, 76–78; on
  LGBTQ topics, 21, 178, 185, 188–190,
  196; lost/damaged, 4, 66–67, 146, 176;
  as mirrors and windows, 177–182;
  multicultural titles, 181–182; multicultural titles to avoid, 182; overdue,
  66–68, 146; on poverty and homelessness, 176; redacting, 94; restricting,
  94; transferring, 94; weeding, 94. *See
  also* borrowing; censorship; challenges
  to library resources; library materials;
  reading levels
borrowing: encouraging responsible
  habits, 74–75; policies that restrict,
  73–75; unrestricted, 69–72
Brisco, Shonda, 13
bullying, 190, 196
BYOD (Bring Your Own Device), 123–124

Caldwell-Stone, Deborah, 134
Case v. Unified S.D., 104
censorship, 7, 23; and the ALA *Code of
  Ethics,* 34, 85, 108; in juvenile detention centers, 63–64; and materials
  selection policy, 53—54. *See also*
  self-censorship
Center for the Study of Multicultural
  Children's Literature, 184
"Challenge-Proofing Your School Library
  Checklist," 108–109
challenges to library resources: avoiding,
  107–110; based on mature content, 94;
  and censorship, 90–92; challenged
  books, 34–35; defense against, 7,
  53–54, 91–92; defining "appropriate,"
  101; documenting, 104–105; handling,
  10–11, 86–87, 97–98, 103–106; in a
  juvenile detention facility, 63–64;
  LGBTQ titles, 21; long-term cost of, 90;
  managing, 85–87; negative effects of,
  89; by parents, 36–37; preventive

measures, 97; and the problem of self-censorship, 88–92; reconsideration policies and procedures, 58–60; response to, 103–106; and the selection policy, 85–86; understanding and being prepared for, 99–102

checkout. *See* circulation

Cheney, Amy, 62

child abuse, 148–149, 150

Children's Internet Protection Act (CIPA), 7, 51, 113–114, 116, 117, 149

Choose Privacy Week (CPW), 32, 137, 140–141

circulation: checkout history, 142–143; checkout limits, 157–158; policies, 50; records, 142–143

closed captioning, 164–165, 166, 169–170

cloud computing, 152–153

Code of Ethics. *See* ALA Code of Ethics

cognitive disabilities, 14

Collection Analysis Tool, 181

¡Colorín Colorado!, 184

Comic Book Legal Defense Fund, 11, 23

Common Core State Standards Initiative (CCSS), 76, 191

Communicating through Literature program, 91

confidentiality, 8, 15, 20, 31, 78, 141; creating a safe information environment, 150–151; and troubled students, 148. *See also* privacy issues

Cooperative Children's Book Center, 178, 179, 192

Counts v. Cedarville School District, 3

court decisions: *Board of Education, Island Trees Union Free School District v. Pico*, 6, 104; *Case v. Unified S.D.*, 104; *Counts v. Cedarville School District*, 3; *Tinker v. Des Moines Independent Community School District*, 104, 133

Crutcher, Chris, 90, 92

curriculum development, 128, 185

cyberbullying, 113, 117

cyber-safety lessons, 126

data governance policies, 153

data mining, 153

data security policies, 153

data storage, 152–153

deaf/hard-of-hearing students (HoH): books for, 169; equitable access for, 168–169; instructional strategies, 170; technology for, 169

Defending Intellectual Freedom: LGBTQ+ Materials in School Libraries toolkit, 190

Dewey, John, 99

Dias, Marley, 180

differentiated instruction (DI), 195–197

digital citizenship education, 113–114

digital divide, 120–122

digital literacy, 120–121

Dillon, Ken, 93

district policies, 10

diversity: in children's literature, 177–178; and collection development, 179–182; cultural, 196–197; deaf/hard-of-hearing students (HoH), 168–170; and differentiated instruction (DI), 195–197; ethnic and racial, 179–182; in historical fiction, 191–194; homelessness, 172–176; rainbow families, 186–190; resources for expanding, 184–185; special needs students, 160–162, 164–167; strategies for promoting multicultural titles, 185

"Don't Filter Me" campaign, 114

Doyle, Robert P., 34

economic barriers, 4, 15, 66–67

Education of Homeless Children and Youth (EHCY) programs, 172

educational disabilities, 160–162

emotional level, 101

English language learners (ELL), 8–9, 15, 67–68, 195

equitable access. *See* access to information

Ewbank, Ann Dutton, 15

faculty. *See* teachers

Family Educational Rights and Privacy Act (FERPA), 8, 20, 133–134, 146, 152

Family Policy Compliance Office, 133–134

family values, 36

Federal Communications Commission (FCC), 51

federal laws and acts, 50–51; Children's Internet protection Act (CIPA), 7, 51, 113, 113–114, 116, 117, 149; Family Educational Rights and Privacy Act

federal laws and acts (*cont.*)
(FERPA), 8, 20, 133–134, 146, 152;
Protecting Children in the 21st Century
Act, 117
filtering, 6, 7–8, 12, 14, 51, 116–119; and
CIPA, 113–114; efforts to combat, 114,
117–118; overly restrictive, 31; and
social media, 113–115. *See also*
Internet access
fines, 4, 15, 66
First Amendment rights/liberties, 3–4, 5,
6, 9, 14, 23, 24, 31–32, 33, 44, 54, 66,
86, 118–119, 149, 176
flexible scheduling, 157
Flipgrid, 164
flipped content, 128
Floyd, Scott, 124
Forbeck, Ann, 174
Forst, Karen, 175
free speech rights, 3, 6. *See also* First
Amendment rights/liberties
free voluntary reading (FVR), 70
"Freedom to Read," 4–5, 54, 59
Future of Privacy Forum, 153

genre categories, 159
gifted and talented students, 8–9
GLSEN (Gay, Lesbian & Straight Educa-
tion Network), 190
Google Accessibility, 165, 166–167
Google Docs, 167
Google Hangouts, 166–167
Google Search, 167
graphic novels, 11, 106, 196
guidance counselors, 148

Harris, Shannon, 196
Harry Potter series, 3, 71, 90, 99, 106
high-tech tools, 162. *See also* technology
historical fiction: award-winning, 191–
192; collaborating with history teachers, 193–194; diversity in, 191–194;
evaluating quality in, 193; sources for
diverse, 192
homeless students, 8–9, 15, 67–68, 74,
123; defined, 172–173; education for,
172–173; and the experience of
homelessness, 173–174; practical
strategies for librarians, 175–176;
responsibilities of librarians for, 174;
school district efforts, 175; school
policies, 174–175
Hudson, Cheryl, 184

Hudson, Wade, 184
Hughes-Hassell, Sandra, 196

iMovie, 170
Independent Reading Level Assessment
(IRLA), 20. *See also* reading levels
Individuals with Disabilities Education
Act (IDEA), 160
instruction design, 127
intellectual freedom: and acceptable use
policies, 49–50; advocating for with
principals and teachers, 23–25; ALA
position on, 3, 20, 34, 47, 85, 108;
calendar, 30–33; and circulation
policies, 50; defined, 3; electronic lists,
23; federal laws and acts, 50–51;
fundamental principles, 6–9; levels of
engagement, 10–12; mandated restrictions on, 47–52; principle of, 85;
promotion of, 23–24; role of the
librarian, 4, 9, 11, 12, 14–15; and
school-based policies, 51–52; and
selection policies, 48–49; spirit of, 4; as
students' right, 19–22, 23; teaching
students about, 109
intellectual freedom network, 44
"Intellectual Freedom News," 141
intellectual level, 101
interest level, 15, 20, 101
interlibrary loan, 4, 14, 21, 24, 63, 74,
108, 134, 144
International Day Against Homophobia
and Transphobia, 187
International Family Equality Day, 187
Internet access, 4; and acceptable use
policies, 49–50; and social media,
113–115. *See also* filtering
inventory: anytime, 79; keeping track of
stuff, 79–80; timing, 80–81
Irwin, Marilyn, 196

Jenkins, Henry, 120
Johnson, Doug, 121
Journal for Intellectual Freedom & Privacy
(JIFP), 141
Just Us Books, 184
juvenile detention centers (JDCs), 62–65

Kachel, Deb, 14
Krashen, Stephen D., 69

labeling: of LGBTQ titles, 189; privacy
issues, 42, 77; by reading level, 8,

39–40, 41, 42, 76–78; recommendations for, 86; as self-censorship, 90, 94;
unintended consequences of, 42; as
"YA," 94
Lance, Keith Curry, 14
Lankes, R. David, 80–81
Laurent Clerc National Deaf Education
Center, 169
leadership: and fear, 19–20; filtering and
social media, 113–115; in intellectual
freedom, 21–22; opportunities for, 115;
and risk, 21; supporting deaf/HoH
students, 170
learning disabilities, 14, 195
Lee and Low publishers, 184
leveling, 42; school-based policies, 76–78.
See also labeling
Lexile levels, 76
LGBTQ topics, 21, 178, 185, 186–190,
196; recommended resources, 189
librarians: as advocates, 23–25; and the
ALA *Code of Ethics*, 43, 53, 85, 108,
141, 143, 149; collaboration with
teachers, 127; and homeless students,
174–176; impact on student learning,
28–29; as indispensable resources,
29; and juvenile detention centers, 65;
and one-to-one programs, 128–129;
protecting students' rights, 43–44;
in public libraries, 44; reasons for
violating student's privacy, 148–149;
reduction in numbers, 13–15;
response to filtering, 118–119; role of,
4, 9, 11, 12, 14–15, 60, 100–101;
support for, 12
libraries: access to, 13, 157–159; closed
for conducting inventory, 79–81; and
the digital divide, 121–122; in juvenile
detention centers, 62–65; mission of,
56; participatory space in, 159; poor/
homeless patrons, 174; privacy tools
for, 139–140; as safe havens, 175;
self-service, 158
Library Bill of Rights (LBOR), 32, 36, 37,
43, 48, 59, 66, 86, 95, 149, 150
library buddies, 175
library materials: banning, 34–35,
103–104, 106; collection development,
179–180; diversity in, 21, 177–185;
multimedia, 11; online resources, 80;
and personal choice, 8; positive impact
of, 197; questioning, 103; reconsideration of, 86–87, 94; selection of, 4, 6–7,

11, 14, 15, 53–54, 91. *See also* books;
challenges to library resources;
materials selection policy
Library Media Specialists (LMS), 126–128
library open house, 31
library records: records requests, 145;
retention of, 144–145
Library Services and Technology Act
(LSTA), 113
*Library Standards for Juvenile Correc-
tional Facilities*, 65
lip reading, 170
literacy skills, 32
literacy tools, 32
lost/damaged books, 4, 66–67, 146, 176

Maronek, Mary, 173, 175
materials selection policy, 11, 48–49,
108; and controversial materials, 57;
creation of, 55–57; as defense against
censorship, 53–54; for gifts and
donation, 55, 57, 63; for juvenile
detention centers, 63–65; nonbook
materials, 63; removing worn and
outdated items, 57; revision of, 57
McKinney-Vento Homeless Education
Act, 172
Michael J. Printz Award for Excellence in
Young Adult Literature, 192
missing books. *See* lost/damaged books
Moeller, Robin, 196
Multiculturalism Rocks, 184
multimedia resources, 48
Mysimpleshow, 164

National Coalition Against Censorship,
11, 23, 87, 88–89, 91
National Council of Teachers of English
(NCTE), 11, 23, 98
National School Board Association, 92
National Standards for School Librarians,
55

one-to-one device programs: adjusting to
the trend, 128–129; grade-level pilot,
125–126; implications for the school
library, 126–127; implications in the
classroom, 127–128
online accessibility tools, 164–165
online databases, 48
online literacy tools, 32
online resources, 127
online safety, 117

Overberg, Elizabeth, 196
overdue books, 66–68, 146; policies for addressing, 66–67; strategies for dealing with, 67–68

parents: book club for, 32; and BYOD approaches, 124; communication with, 31, 36–38; complaints from, 58–59; education about diverse literature, 185; education about materials selection, 109; perceptions of restricted borrowing, 74; perceptions of the labeled library, 77; reading group for, 37; reasons for challenging materials, 99–100; role of, 37–38
parent/teacher conferences, 31
participatory space, 159
Pekoll, Kristin, 21
physical disabilities, 14, 195
Pico v. Island Trees, 6, 104
Positive Behavior Interventions and Support (PBIS), 157
principals: communication with, 30, 32, 43–44; education about materials selection, 108; education about student privacy rights, 140; and intellectual freedom, 24; perceptions of restricted borrowing, 74; perceptions of the labeled library, 77; and the troubled student, 148
privacy issues: and the age of the patron, 146–147; and the ALA Code of Ethics, 8, 134, 136, 137, 141, 143, 146, 149; checkout history, 142–143; and child abuse, 148–149; and cloud computing, 152–153; impact of circulation systems on, 142–143; and intellectual freedom, 15, 20, 23; and the labeled library, 77; legal protections, 133–134; in library use, 3; OIF staff assistance, 141; online information sources, 140–141; pertinent state laws, 11; practical ideas, 136–137; previous borrower records, 142; and rainbow families, 187; and reading level labels, 42; resources and tools, 139–141; role of the librarian, 15, 20, 32, 33; state laws, 8, 11; and the troubled student, 148–149. See also confidentiality; privacy policies
privacy policies, 8, 137, 140, 143, 152, 153; "Confidentiality of School Library Records Policy," 145; library records retention, 144–145; posting, 12; "School Library Privacy Policy," 145
professional development: about diverse literature, 185; for library staff, 20; for teachers, 12, 27, 125–126
professional learning communities (PLCs), 127
Protecting Children in the 21st Century Act, 117
push technologies, 121

rainbow families, 186–190; resources for welcoming, 187–188
reader's advisory, 159
reading levels, 8, 14, 15, 20, 39–40, 101; arranging shelves according to, 76–78
reading management programs, 8, 14, 31, 41–42
reconsideration committee, 60
reconsideration policy, 57, 58–61, 95
Reese, Debbie, 192
relationship building, 28
restricted access, 8
right to read, 6
Robinson, Michael, 140
Ruefle, Anne E., 70–71

Scales, Pat, 90–91
school culture, 10
School Library Month, 32
school-based policies; on intellectual freedom, 51–52; leveling the library collection, 76–78; regarding homeless students, 174–175; restrictions on borrowing, 73–75
selection policies, 48–49, 95, 98, 100–102; and challenges to library resources, 85–86
self-censorship, 7, 11–12, 88–92, 107; ex post facto, 93–95; variations of, 90–91. See also censorship
self-check, 158
self-service libraries, 158
social media, 114–115
software, for assistive technology, 162
Software and Information Industry Association, 153
software services, 153
special education services, 161; for homeless students, 173
special needs students, 8–9, 14, 43
staff book clubs, 185
Stone, Deborah Caldwell, 141

student book clubs, 185
students: access to books, 71–72; at-risk, 8–9; and banned/challenged books, 34–35; deaf/hard-of-hearing (HoH), 168–170; de-identifying data about, 152; with disabilities, 14, 160–162, 195, 196; disadvantaged, 123–124; encouraging exploration by, 77–78; English language learners (ELL), 8–9, 15, 67–68, 195; gifted and talented, 8–9; as part of intellectual freedom network, 44; perception of restricted borrowing, 73–74; perceptions of the labeled library, 77; protecting the privacy of, 136–137; protecting the rights of, 43–44; from rainbow families, 186–190; reading for different pur-poses, 77–78; records of, 133–134; right to read, 78; special needs, 8–9, 14, 43; teaching about intellectual freedom, 109; troubled, 148–149. *See also* homeless students; privacy issues
Substitution-Augmentation-Modification-Redefinition progression (SAMR model), 128
suicide, 148, 150, 190
Symbaloo, 126–127

teachers: collaboration with, 121, 127; communication with, 30, 44; education about materials selection, 108; educa-tion about student privacy rights, 140; and intellectual freedom, 24; as part of intellectual freedom network, 44; perceptions of restricted borrowing, 74; perceptions of the labeled library, 77
Teaching for Change, 184
technology: assistive, 160–162; BYOD (Bring Your Own Device) approaches, 123–124; for deaf/HoH students, 169–170; equitable access to, 123–124; one-to-one device programs, 125–129
technology committee, 128–129
TED-Ed, 165
Tinker v. Des Moines Independent Community School District, 104, 133
troubled students, 148–149
tutorials, 128

United Nations Children's Fund (UNICEF), 186
Universal Design for Learning (UDL), 161–162
Universal Service Fund E-Rate Program, 113
unrestricted checkout, 69–72; AASL's position, 69–70; addressing concerns, 71; and the power of choice, 70

Venuto, Dee Ann, 89, 90
Virtual Learning Commons (VLC), 126–127
virtual learning space, 128

We Need Diverse Books (WNDB) Campaign, 178, 180
websites: banned, 114, 118; process for unblocking, 116–117
Welcoming Schools website, 187
Williams, Claire Louise, 93
Williamson, Donna, 153
Woodson, Jacqueline, 177, 178

"YA" designation, 94
Young, Tyrone, 194
Young Adult Library Services Association (YALSA), 169
YouTube closed captioning, 164–165, 166